DONOR-LINKED FAMILIES IN THE DIGITAL AGE

How are siblings who were conceived using the same sperm or egg donor making connections in the absence of legal support? What is it like to discover you are part of a fifty plus donor sibling group? How are donor-conceived adults using new technologies to connect with their genetic family and explore their identity? This edited collection considers the donor-linking experiences of donor-conceived adults and children, recipient parents, and donors in a global context. It includes contributions from legal academics, social workers, sociologists, psychologists, and policy makers who work in the assisted conception field. As a result, it will be of particular interest to scholars of reproductive law, sociology, and digital media and reproductive technologies. It will also engage those following the debate around donor linking and the use of do-it-yourself technologies, including direct-to-consumer genetic testing and social media.

FIONA KELLY is Dean of La Trobe University Law School, Victoria, Australia. Her research explores the intersection between family law and health law, focusing on the legal regulation of assisted reproduction. Her research has contributed to Australian and Canadian law reform in the areas of assisted reproduction and family diversity.

DEBORAH DEMPSEY is a sociologist and Adjunct Associate Professor in the Department of Social Sciences at Swinburne University of Technology, Victoria, Australia. Her broad research interests encompass fertility, technology, and family change. She has published extensively on queer parenthood and families created through donor conception in Australia, and her work has been influential in law reform processes.

ADRIENNE BYRT is a postdoctoral research fellow at Swinburne University of Technology, Victoria, Australia. As a design sociologist, her research draws together feminist theory and design methods to highlight systemic gendered inequity. Her interdisciplinary research spans the sociology of families, mothering and motherhood, women's financial safety, and service design.

DONOR-LINKED FAMILIES IN THE DIGITAL AGE

Relatedness and Regulation

EDITED BY

FIONA KELLY

La Trobe University

DEBORAH DEMPSEY

Swinburne University of Technology

ADRIENNE BYRT

Swinburne University of Technology

CAMBRIDGE
UNIVERSITY PRESS

Shaftesbury Road, Cambridge CB2 8EA, United Kingdom

One Liberty Plaza, 20th Floor, New York, NY 10006, USA

477 Williamstown Road, Port Melbourne, VIC 3207, Australia

314–321, 3rd Floor, Plot 3, Splendor Forum, Jasola District Centre, New Delhi – 110025, India

103 Penang Road, #05–06/07, Visioncrest Commercial, Singapore 238467

Cambridge University Press is part of Cambridge University Press & Assessment,
a department of the University of Cambridge.

We share the University's mission to contribute to society through the pursuit of
education, learning and research at the highest international levels of excellence.

www.cambridge.org
Information on this title: www.cambridge.org/9781316518519

DOI: 10.1017/9781009008129

First published 2023

A catalogue record for this publication is available from the British Library.

Library of Congress Cataloging-in-Publication Data
NAMES: Kelly, Fiona J., 1975– editor. | Dempsey, Deborah, editor. |
Byrt, Adrienne, 1983– editor.
TITLE: Donor-linked families in the digital age : relatedness and regulation /
edited by Fiona Kelly, La Trobe University, Victoria, Deborah Dempsey,
Swinburne University of Technology, Victoria, Adrienne Byrt,
Swinburne University of Technology, Victoria.
DESCRIPTION: Cambridge, United Kingdom ; New York, NY :
Cambridge University Press, 2023. | Includes bibliographical references and index.
IDENTIFIERS: LCCN 2023005680 | ISBN 9781316518519 (hardback) |
ISBN 9781009008129 (ebook)
SUBJECTS: LCSH: Artificial insemination, Human – Social aspects. | Artificial insemination,
Human – Law and legislation. | Children of assisted reproductive technology –
Family relationships. | Children of egg donors – Family relationships. |
Children of sperm donors – Family relationships.
CLASSIFICATION: LCC HQ761 .D66 2023 |
DDC 304.6/32–dc23/eng/20230221
LC record available at https://lccn.loc.gov/2023005680

ISBN 978-1-316-51851-9 Hardback

*To families, in all their complexity, however
they might define themselves.*

Fiona Kelly

To Rusty, Jack, and Juno.

Adrienne Byrt

*To my partner Letizia, in recognition of her ongoing love and support,
and in memory of my father Edward Noel Dempsey (1928–2021).*

Deborah Dempsey

Contents

Tables

Contributors

DAMIAN ADAMS Flinders University, Australia

ADRIENNE BYRT Swinburne University of Technology, Australia

NAOMI CAHN University of Virginia, USA

ISABEL CÔTÉ University of Quebec in Outaouais, Canada

MARILYN CRAWSHAW University of York, UK

DEBORAH DEMPSEY Swinburne University of Technology, Australia

LUCY FRITH University of Liverpool, UK

LEAH GILMAN The University of Manchester, UK

ROSANNA HERTZ Wellesley College, USA

SALLY HINES University of Sheffield, UK

ASTRID INDEKEU KU Leuven, The Netherlands

FIONA KELLY La Trobe University, Australia

A. JANNEKE B. M. MAAS Fiom, The Netherlands

GISELLE NEWTON University of New South Wales, Australia

PETRA NORDQVIST The University of Manchester, UK

RUTH PEARCE University of Glasgow, UK

CARLA A. PFEFFER Michigan State University, USA

DAMIEN W. RIGGS Flinders University, Australia

YUKARI SEMBA Ochanomizu University, Japan

RHONDA M. SHAW Victoria University of Wellington, New Zealand

RENÉE-PIERRE TROTTIER CYR University of Quebec in Outaouais, Canada

FRANCIS RAY WHITE University of Westminster, UK

MARIE-CHRISTINE WILLIAMS-PLOUFFE University of Quebec in Outaouais, Canada

CAL VOLKS La Trobe University, Australia

SABRINA ZEGHICHE University of Quebec in Outaouais, Canada

Acknowledgements

A project of this magnitude, especially one that was completed during the Covid-19 pandemic, succeeds at least in part because of the support provided by others. We would like to thank our families and colleagues for their ongoing encouragement of our work, as well as each of the contributors for persevering through some very difficult times. Across the studies included in this collection, we would also like to extend our gratitude to the participants who shared their experiences as donor-conceived people, donors, and recipient parents. We are proud of the outcome and believe it will make an important contribution to what is a rapidly evolving debate.

This book was made possible by funding from the Australian Research Council Discovery Grant scheme for the project 'Families of Strangers? The Socio-Legal Implications of Donor Linking' (DP180100188).

Donor-Conceived Families
Relatedness and Regulation in the Digital Age
Fiona Kelly and Deborah Dempsey

Hundreds of thousands of people globally have been conceived through use of donated eggs, sperm or embryos (i.e. 'third-party assisted reproduction' or 'reproductive donation'), most at a time when donations were anonymous (Harper et al., 2016). In many countries that have reproductive donation programmes, anonymity for sperm, egg and embryo donors prevails, and research indicates that a significant number of parents continue not to tell their children that they are donor conceived (Readings, Blake, Casey, Jadva, & Golombok, 2011; Nordqvist & Smart, 2014). However, over the past two decades, there has been growing international debate about the potentially harmful effects of secrecy in donor-conception families. It is increasingly asserted that knowledge of one's genetic origins is constitutive of identity and emotionally important to people born of donated gametes (Turner, 2000; Blyth, 2012). In response to this cultural shift, a number of countries have ended donor anonymity by providing donor-conceived people with access to their donor's identity when they reach a certain age. Others have gone one step further and created mechanisms by which donor-conceived people and their donors can meet. This practice is known as 'donor linking'.

Donor-linking laws have emerged as a controversial policy response to the desire for information about 'donor relatives', that is, the term commonly used for the people to whom one has a biogenetic connection as a result of the use of donated eggs or sperm. Some jurisdictions, including Australia, Sweden, the Netherlands and the UK, have introduced laws mandating that identifying information about donors be registered and available to donor offspring, in the event that they want information about, or contact with, donors or, in some cases, donor siblings (offspring who share a donor). Each jurisdiction has taken a slightly different approach, with the key differences relating to who can access information, who can be the subject of a request for information, at what age a donor-conceived person might have access, and the nature and extent of support services available to donor-conceived people, recipient parents and donors who request information. For example, some jurisdictions such as Austria and Finland, limit information access to donor-conceived people who wish to know the identity of their donor, where conception occurred after the date the legislation commenced. In Finland this is possible at age 14, while Australia permits access at 18, unless there is a medical reason supporting earlier access. In other jurisdictions, such as the Netherlands, donor-conceived people can access information about their donors and their donor siblings. The latter is facilitated by a government-funded organisation. In 2015, the state of Victoria, Australia became the first jurisdiction in the world to provide retrospective access to donor records (but not donor-sibling records), which meant that the identities of previously anonymous donors can be released to donor-conceived people (Kelly & Dempsey, 2016). The delicate process of releasing this information and facilitating contact between the parties is undertaken by a statutory body and includes extensive counselling services. In this collection, a number of these systems are explored in detail.

Alongside legislative responses, non-statutory 'do-it-yourself' (DIY) linking options – where individuals use web-based donor registers, social media and direct-to-consumer genetic testing (DTCGT) to locate donor relatives – have become increasingly common globally, even in jurisdictions where statutory donor registers are available (Dempsey & Kelly, 2017; Crawshaw et al., 2015). DIY linking typically allows for connections between a much broader range of donor relatives than statutory systems, which tend to limit linking rights to donor-conceived people and their donor. In the DIY context, connections can be made between families who share the same sperm or egg donor, between the donor's children and his or her donor offspring, and donor siblings. Connections can also be made at any age, with a growing number of parents connecting with donor siblings and even their child's donor, while the child is still a minor. Many of these connections are enabled through new technologies that were not anticipated when anonymity laws were passed or even when more recent 'open' donor frameworks were introduced.

In this collection, we are particularly interested in the possibilities for donor linking in the digital age, defined here as the period during which Internet-facilitated online communications have enabled people to meet and connect, sometimes across vast geographic distances. We argue that these new technologies have created opportunities for relationships between donor relatives that were barely imaginable in the past. They also extend a new degree of agency to donor-conceived people, recipient parents and donors, creating emotional complexities and ethical dilemmas that were previously unforeseen. The impact of the digital age is now felt at every stage of the donor conception journey. Web-based introduction sites such as UK-based Pride Angel and Sperm Donors Australia have normalised the relatively new phenomenon of 'online sperm donation', where potential donors and recipients meet each other online, just as dating sites such as Tinder have made it commonplace to find sex or love online. The emergence of these digital means by which to find a donor and/or maintain a connection after a child is conceived, has resulted in a democratisation of the process of donor conception and some relocation of power from fertility clinics to consumers. When prospective parents recruit their donors online, the boundaries around information sharing or contact between donors and their offspring are no longer dictated by fertility clinics or sperm banks. In the world of online sperm donation, the parties negotiate their own arrangements. While there have always been known donors, particularly within the lesbian and gay communities (McNair & Dempsey, 2002; Dempsey, 2010, 2012a, 2012b), the scale and geographic reach of online donation is new. In the past, known donor agreements were typically between friends or acquaintances. In the digital age, it is common for all interactions – with the exception of the insemination itself – to occur online.

Once children are conceived, various digital and medical technologies have enabled the formation of global online communities of donor-linked families (Hertz & Nelson, 2018), making it difficult for sperm banks and fertility clinics to control contact between families who used the same donor. Even in jurisdictions where anonymous donors are available, or where anonymity is imposed for the first 18 years of a child's life, recipient parents and donor-conceived children and adults are unwilling to passively accept their fate. As communications and genetic technologies become more sophisticated, parents and offspring demonstrate ingenuity and creativity in subverting the law and clinical policies. Armed with donor numbers and non-identifying information such as hair and eye colour, parents and donor-conceived people can use the Internet to find donor siblings. Alternatively, direct-to-consumer DNA tests can be used to identify donor siblings, or even the donor or his relatives. While some sperm banks now counsel prospective donors about the possibility of their identity being revealed via DNA testing, others have doubled down on the promise of anonymity. For instance, a sperm bank in the United States recently took legal action against a mother who identified her daughter's donor using a DNA test, in violation of the contract she signed which stated she would not attempt to locate or identify him.

The affordances of genetic and online technologies, coupled with the resourcefulness of those who use them, have changed the parameters of the long-standing debate about whether secrecy or openness is the best way for the state or the fertility industry to manage families created through third-party assisted reproduction. To a large degree the debate is moot, as the ability to maintain anonymity is no longer guaranteed. Some commentators have even proclaimed the 'end of anonymity' (e.g. Harper & Kennett, 2016) due to the relative ease with which a direct-to-consumer DNA kit, sometimes in tandem with online detective work, can reveal genetic relatives with a great degree of accuracy. While these assertions may be true in a practical sense, their relational and legal consequences demand further scrutiny (see Zadeh, 2016). For instance, does ending anonymity via digital means inevitably lead to openness, or at the very least, the end of secrecy? How is that openness experienced by those who choose it or have it forced upon them? Is there still a role for the law or the state in legislating for, and facilitating, openness in the digital age?

Overview of the Collection

Global in scope, this collection explores the practice, implications and challenges of donor linking. Through an exploration of the experiences of those who have engaged in donor linking across a variety of jurisdictions, it interrogates how cultural setting and family-type influence how openness and secrecy are understood and experienced.

The editorial position of the collection is that there is urgent need for a more nuanced approach to the somewhat polarised 'secrecy' versus 'openness' debate that has dominated public narratives and global policy discussions about donor-conception families, particularly in light of the technological advancements that have arguably led to a relocation of power over information from sperm banks and medical professionals to consumers and donor offspring themselves. It is often presumed that abolishing anonymity is an endpoint in the donor-conception debate. However, by exploring experiences of donor linking across a variety of jurisdictions, the collection provides new insights into what the 'end of anonymity' actually means for donor-conceived people, donors and parents and, perhaps most importantly, what happens after identities are revealed. At times, we question whether the 'secrecy versus openness' dichotomy is as straightforward as often presumed in the public narrative, particularly in light of research on the new Victorian legislation, which suggests that openness laws can create new secrets for some families

(Cosson, Dempsey & Kelly, 2022). In keeping with this approach, the collection interrogates the claim that we have in fact reached the 'end of anonymity' in third-party assisted conception, with reference to contemporary international evidence about how people conceive relatedness in donor conception and how they are using new technologies such as DNA testing and social media, as well as statutory systems for donor linking, to access information.

Part I: 'DIY' Donor Linking: Issues and Implications

Part I of the volume explores the increasing role of DIY technologies, sometimes used in tandem with legislative frameworks, to enable members of donor-linked families to discover and/or meet donor relatives, or to recruit donors that will be known to children from birth. This new dimension to donor linking demonstrates the ways in which decisions about secrecy and openness are no longer solely in the hands of fertility clinics and law makers. Rather, donor-conceived people, donors and parents have a new technology-enabled agency that allows them to connect with donor relatives outside of legal frameworks and according to their own timeline. The chapters in Part I highlight the vast array of DIY technologies available to the donor-conception community, from direct-to-consumer DNA testing, discussed in the Adams et al. chapter, to social media 'creeping' and other online sleuthing, discussed by Byrt and Dempsey, and also by Kelly. In their chapter about 'online sperm donors' – men who advertise their services via online platforms – Volks and Kelly highlight how new technologies are being used to bring prospective parents and donors together prior to conception, bypassing formal donation via a fertility clinic or sperm bank, and enabling contact between donor-conceived children and their online sperm donors from birth. All the chapters in Part I reveal the gap between what is permitted by law and what is happening online, raising the question of whether donor-linking laws continue to be relevant in the digital age.

Part I begins with the bold assertion by Adams et al. that 'donor anonymity is dead'. Through an exploration of the use by British donor-conceived people (DCPs) of both formal registers and DTCGT they argue that we have entered a new era where the prevalence of DTCGT has enabled the circumvention of existing policies and practices regarding donor conception, resulting in a dramatic expansion of opportunities to find genetic relatives. Consequently, control over information has moved from clinics, parents and legislators to DCPs themselves.

In her chapter on parents who use DIY methods to make contact with their child's donor siblings and/or donor while their child is still a minor, Kelly also argues that the widespread availability of new technologies, coupled with the ingenuity of those who use them, has resulted in the relocation of control over information from clinics and the government, to parents, DCPs and even donors. The parents in Kelly's sample, most of whom were single mothers by choice, believed that it was in the best interests of their children to have the opportunity to integrate their donor relatives into their lives from an early age. Their commitment to 'early contact' made them comfortable pursuing donor and donor-sibling connections via new technologies such as DTCGT and online sleuthing, even in circumstances where no legal right to information existed. Kelly speculates that this new trend, which is likely to increase with time as new technologies emerge, may undermine or even supplant the law, which currently puts relatively tight controls on contact between donor relatives. Perhaps surprisingly, however, Kelly found that while parents had fully embraced the opportunities provided by new technologies to engage in donor linking, the majority still favoured a formal system for early contact linking, regulated by law.

Byrt and Dempsey also explore the ways in which new technologies, particularly Facebook, are used to identify donor relatives. However, they do so through the prism of surveillance, exploring how DCPs, without the knowledge or consent of their donor relatives, engage in what has been referred to as 'creeping': an 'intense form of background checking that involves silently following an individual on one or more social media outlets without posting or commenting and doing expanded research on the person by following their social media friends and family members online' (Standlee, 2019). Byrt and Dempsey argue that the normalising of Internet 'creeping' raises questions about how the concept of contact should be understood in the digital age, and whether the law is capable of adequately responding to the non-consensual forms of contact enabled by new technologies.

The chapter by Volks and Kelly also explores the democratising power of the Internet, but through an analysis of the early contact experiences of 'online sperm donors', defined as men who donate their sperm via the growing number of online meeting groups for prospective parents and donors. For the men profiled by Volks and Kelly, one of the benefits of being an online sperm donor was the opportunity to negotiate ongoing contact with their donor offspring, an option that is not available when donating to a fertility clinic. While the nature and extent of contact sometimes became a source of conflict between donors and their recipients, most were able to maintain a relationship with their donor offspring. These findings once again highlight the gap between what is permitted under the formal legal system and the opportunities afforded by new technologies.

In the final chapter in Part I, Zeghiche et al. draw on qualitative interviews with recipient parents and DCPs to explore the role DTCGT testing has played in revealing fertility fraud in Canada. In each case, genetic testing exposed the sperm substitution activities of fertility doctors that had occurred decades earlier. Zeghiche et al. argue that while sperm substitution has historically been treated as a marginal issue by both the public and the fertility industry, the availability of DNA testing means that this type of discovery could become more widespread, and that potential victims have the power to reveal the truth. As case numbers rise, it will be increasingly important to document the consequences for the affected families and the impact the information has on their understandings of family.

Part II: Children's and Adults' Lived Experiences in Diverse Donor-Linked Families

Part II of the collection explores the myriad experiences of DCPs, recipient parents and donors who attempt to connect with donor relatives, and the social and cultural significance given to these relationships. Each chapter addresses new forms of relatedness from the perspective of a particular group within the donor-conception community, highlighting the shifting nature of the role each plays in an era where anonymity is no longer the norm. As new types of kinship emerge, parties struggle with the limitations of language and existing familial categories, the shadow of anonymity that persists even when information is revealed and the challenges of integrating new members into established groups of donor relatives.

It begins with the exploration by Rosanna Hertz of the importance of donor-sibling networks to teens and young adults. Hertz draws on a qualitative study of donor-conceived young people who have connected through online registers and social media to explore how they situate their donor siblings within their existing kinship structures, and how they actively construct these new relationships. Traditional notions of kinship are challenged by these donor-sibling networks, which do not follow the usual rules of family. For many of the young people in these sibling networks, the genetic link created an expectation of emotional closeness between donor siblings, but actual closeness was the result of 'activating' the genetic relationship via practices of intimacy.

Similar themes emerged from the chapter by Indekeu and Maas, which explores the experiences of DCPs who make contact with 'same-donor offspring' via the Dutch organisation Fiom, which runs a voluntary DNA database (Fiom KID-DNA Database) for those conceived via gamete donation. Using the database, Fiom identifies 'same-donor offspring' groups and facilitates a group meeting for them. The chapter explores, from the perspective of the regulator, how to support same-donor offspring integrate these new relations into their lives, how to manage group dynamics, and the challenges of negotiating a continuously growing, often global network, of offspring, as new members join the register. While Hertz identifies largely positive experiences, Indekeu and Maas touch on the negative emotions experienced by some offspring, such as offspring of 'prolific donors' who struggled with the 'yuk factor' of being 'one of so many'.

The challenges posed by new forms of kinship are explored further by Gilman and Nordqvist, this time from the perspective of egg and sperm donors who have been located by their donor offspring or recipient parents. As anonymity is replaced with different forms of 'identity release', a growing number of donors are having to fashion new familial identities. While donors are cautioned to respect the parental boundaries of the families to which they have donated, they are also expected to be 'available' to their donor offspring. Unable to always reconcile the two, donors nonetheless commit to 'following the lead' of the families and donor-conceived people.

In Newton's chapter, which draws on the concept of 'familial haunting' to explore donor-conceived people's experiences of living with anonymity and absence, we witness the complex impact of anonymity on donor-conceived people. While many scholars in this field have asserted that anonymity is over, Newton explores the experiences of the many donor-conceived people for whom anonymity, and its effects, continue. Newton is particularly interested in the 'terrain of non-relationships and their links to (unbe)longing'. Her participants grapple with the ways in which unknown donor relatives are experienced as a 'ghostly presence', making themselves felt in the daily lives of DCPs, and often across generations.

Rhonda Shaw explores the cultural significance of kinship affinities among the Māori of Aotearoa and the implications for the social identity of people conceived using assisted reproduction. Shaw argues that the transfer of reproductive materials between known and unknown donors and recipients may have identity implications for Māori that may not be as significant for Pākehā. The chapter explores the experiences of recipients of gametes, both Māori and non-Māori, and the ways in which they attempt to honour their children's whakapapa (their ancestral line), often through making arrangements that would give their children information about where they came from.

In the last contribution of Part II, Damien Riggs and colleagues consider how men, trans/masculine and non-binary people are bearing children through the use of known donor sperm and the relational complexities involved in explaining and navigating these relationships, both in the lead up to conception and throughout the children's lives. Riggs et al. argue there is a greater need to assist this diverse group of parents to navigate the complexities of disclosure and storytelling to children about donor conception, and to challenge prevailing cis-genderism in the way assumptions about the role of sperm donors may be made.

Part III: Institutionalised Resistance to Openness

The final part of the collection explores resistance to openness at the level of policy and law. In the digital age, institutionalised donor anonymity persists. Just as there are strong cultural impulses in play supporting legislative openness, there may be very strong cultural barriers to ending anonymity at the level of policy and law, as the case studies of the United States and Japan exemplify.

In the context of the United States, Naomi Cahn observes the extent to which the donor gamete industry is lightly regulated by both the federal government and individual states, linking this to the broader issue of why calls for legislative openness have been less successful in US jurisdictions. For Cahn, several factors are implicated in the reluctance to bolster regulation. These include concerns about the sperm supply, and the notion that ending anonymity would lead to a decrease in donor numbers, although this claim has been challenged in other jurisdictions. There is also the issue of reproductive politics in the United States more broadly, notably whether anti-abortion legislation could be deemed to apply to assisted reproductive technology.

Finally, Yukari Semba explores why donor anonymity prevails in Japan despite increasingly strong lobbying on the part of donor-conceived adults for information about their genetic origins. Semba traces the history of sperm donor anonymity in Japan, reviewing the position of various governmental committees since the late 1990s, which have reinstated anonymity for gamete donors despite increasing activism among donor-conceived individuals. She observes that donor conception remains a marginal issue for Japanese politicians because it is perceived to affect a very small proportion of the electorate. Sperm donor records, as medical records, are routinely destroyed after five years and there is a great deal of reluctance to challenge the status quo.

References

Blyth, E. (2012). Discovering the 'facts of life' following anonymous donor insemination. *International Journal of Law, Policy and the Family*, *26*(2), 143–161. https://doi.org/10.1093/lawfam/ebs006

Cosson, B., Dempsey, D., & Kelly, F. (2022). Secret shame – male infertility and donor conception in the wake of retrospective legislative change. *Men and Masculinities*, *25*(3), 497–515. https://doi.org/10.1177/1097184x211038329

Crawshaw, M., Daniels, K., Adams, D., Bourne, K., van Hooff, J. A. P., Kramer, W., … & Thorn, P. (2015). Emerging models for facilitating contact between people genetically related through donor conception: a preliminary analysis and discussion. *Reproductive Biomedicine & Society Online*, *1*(2), 71–80. https://doi.org/10.1016/j.rbms.2015.10.001

Dempsey, D. (2010). Conceiving and negotiating reproductive relationships: lesbians and gay men forming families with children. *Sociology*, *44*(6), 1145–1162. https://doi.org/10.1177%2F0038038510381607

Dempsey, D. (2012a). More like a donor or more like a father? Gay men's concepts of relatedness to children. *Sexualities*, *15*(2), 156–174. https://doi.org/10.1177%2F1363460711433735

Dempsey, D. (2012b). Gay male couples' paternal involvement in lesbian-parented families. *Journal of Family Studies*, *18*(2–3), 155–164. https://doi.org/10.5172/jfs.2012.18.2-3.155

Dempsey, D., & Kelly, F. (2017). Transnational third-party assisted conception: pursuing the desire for 'origins' information in the internet era. *Babies for Sale? Transnational Surrogacy, Human Rights and the Politics of Reproduction*, 204–217. https://doi.org/10.5040/9781350218567.ch-011

Harper, J. C., Kennett, D., & Reisel, D. (2016). The end of donor anonymity: how genetic testing is likely to drive anonymous gamete donation out of business. *Human Reproduction*, *31*(6), 1135–1140. https://doi.org/10.1093/humrep/dew065

Hertz, R., & Nelson, M. K. (2018). *Random Families: Genetic Strangers, Sperm Donor Siblings, and the Creation of New Kin*. Oxford University Press.

Kelly, F. J., & Dempsey, D. J. (2016). Experiences and motives of Australian single mothers by choice who make early contact with their child's donor relatives. *Medical Law Review*, *24*(4), 571–590. https://doi.org/10.1093/medlaw/fww038

Kelly, F., & Dempsey, D. (2016). The family law implications of early contact between sperm donors and their donor offspring. *Family Matters*, (98), 56–63. https://doi.org/10.1093/lawfam/ebz011

McNair, R., & Dempsey, D. (2002). Exploring diversity in lesbian-parented families Paper 1: Family formation and women's roles. *Family Matters*, (63), 40–49.

Nordqvist, P., & Smart, C. (2014). *Relative Strangers: Family Life, Genes and Donor Conception*. Springer. https://doi.org/10.1057/9781137297648

Readings, J., Blake, L., Casey, P., Jadva, V., & Golombok, S. (2011). Secrecy, disclosure and everything in-between: decisions of parents of children conceived by donor insemination, egg donation and surrogacy. *Reproductive Biomedicine Online*, *22*(5), 485–495. https://doi.org/10.1016/j.rbmo.2011.01.014

Standlee, A. (2019). Friendship and online filtering: The use of social media to construct offline social networks. *New Media & Society*, *21*(3), 770–785. https://doi.org/10.1177/1461444818806844

Turner, A. J., & Coyle, A. (2000). What does it mean to be a donor offspring? The identity experiences of adults conceived by donor insemination and the implications for counselling and therapy. *Human Reproduction*, *15*(9), 2041–2051. https://doi.org/10.1093/humrep/15.9.2041

Zadeh, S. (2016). Disclosure of donor conception in the era of non-anonymity: safeguarding and promoting the interests of donor-conceived individuals? *Human Reproduction*, *31*(11), 2416–2420. https://doi.org/10.1093/humrep/dew240

PART I

'DIY' Donor Linking:
Issues and Implications

CHAPTER I

Accessing Origins Information
The Implications of Direct-to-Consumer Genetic Testing for Donor-Conceived People and Formal Regulation in the United Kingdom

Damian Adams, Marilyn Crawshaw, Leah Gilman, and Lucy Frith

I.I Introduction

Recent years have seen a growing number of jurisdictions move to prospectively mandate the release of identifying donor information, usually at the age of majority (Allan, 2016; Blyth and Frith, 2015). The only jurisdiction that has currently legislated for this retrospectively is the State of Victoria, Australia (in 2016) though South Australia may follow with the proposed Assisted Reproductive Treatment (Donor Conception Register) Amendment Bill 2021.

Crucially, donor-conceived people (DCP) can only request identifying information through officially regulated systems such as the UK's Human Fertilisation and Embryology Authority (HFEA) Register if they are aware of their donor-conceived origins. The decision about whether to inform a DCP of their origins typically rests with parents, as most governments have been reluctant to mandate disclosure (Ishii and de Miguel Beriain, 2022; Adams, 2021). The HFEA Register is required by law to record, among other information, details of all donor-conception treatments that have taken place in UK licensed treatment centres since 1991 and information about donors and recipients.

There are two parallel developments that have resulted in a growing role for information systems outside of the formal regulation of donor conception. First, more people – including DCP – are using direct-to-consumer genetic testing (DTCGT) to find out about, and connect with, relatives or are being found by such relatives. Second, the use of 'informal' donation is increasing. People can find sperm donors on the Internet and make their own arrangements for insemination rather than using fertility clinics or gamete banks. Such donors are consequently known to the parent(s).

However, it is not yet clear how far this translates into DCP being aware of their donor-conceived origins, or able to access information about their parent's donor.

These expanded possibilities for finding genetic relatives and extended family regardless of legislative measures are producing new landscapes where different systems of information provision collide and interact. In turn these create new spaces of sociality, new possibilities for interacting with donor relatives, and consequently new ways for self-determination and identity construction.

In this chapter, our focus is on the impact of DTCGT on DCP, the group arguably most affected by existing donor conception policy and regulatory frameworks but whose influence has, until recently, been limited. We will discuss the implications for DCP of information about their genetic relations being located predominantly within two very different systems: publicly funded information-release systems (using examples from the UK, the HFEA Register and UK Donor Conceived Register, as case studies); and digital online systems, such as DTCGT, ancestry sites and internet groups. We will consider how pre-existing informal and formal power structures, relationships and cultural norms are being affected by DTCGT, focusing on DCP's rights to access information about their conception. We will argue that the prevalence of DTCGT is enabling the circumvention of existing policies and practices regarding donor conception. Consequently, the control of information by parents, legislators and fertility treatment providers has not only been eroded but is increasingly shifting to DCP themselves.

1.2   The Official Route to Accessing Information: Publicly Funded Donor Conception Registers

There are donor conception registers in a number of jurisdictions, including Ireland, Finland, the Netherlands, New Zealand, Norway, Croatia and the Australian states of Victoria, New South Wales and Western Australia.

1.2.1   The Human Fertilisation and Embryology Authority (HFEA) Register

In the UK, the HFEA regulates all licensed fertility treatments and is responsible for any associated information release systems. Anyone conceived with donated gametes in a licensed clinic after 1 August 1991 has a legal right to approach the HFEA for non-identifying information about their donor from the age of sixteen, or to ask if anyone to whom they are married, or with whom they have a civil partnership, or an actual or intended intimate relationship was conceived with the same donor. Those conceived after 1 April 2005 have the right to identifying information from the age of eighteen. They can also receive identifying information about donor-related siblings but only if both parties have registered their agreement. Donors who donated prior to the law change lifting donor anonymity in 2005[1] have the right to re-register as an identifiable donor. There is no charge for these services and a limited amount of free counselling is available to DCP aged sixteen and over and donors approaching the HFEA.

DCP conceived between 1991 and 2005 whose donor has not re-registered can only access non-identifying information as the law change was not retrospective. Recipient parents can request non-identifying information about their donor and their child(ren)'s donor-related siblings until their child's eighteenth birthday. Donors can request information at any stage about the number, gender and year of birth of anyone born as a result of their donation. In the UK, for surrogacy arrangements through licensed centres the rules relating to any gamete donor (where one is used) remain as above.

It is a criminal offence for the HFEA or a licensed clinic to release identifiable information unless it falls within the parameters described above. This means that any such information provided by the donor must be redacted by the clinic or the HFEA until the DCP reaches the age of eighteen, regardless of the donor's wishes. There are concerns that this requirement can inhibit donors in what they write for their pen portraits. These pen portraits are meant to provide non-identifying information about the donor, such as their interests, hobbies and so on. However, if the clinic staff advising them on the drafting of these are driven more by fear of reprisals than by understanding the potential later significance of such information for DCP, these pen portraits may provide little information or the space on the form left blank. There have also been reports of inconsistencies in the amounts and types of information collected, linked to limited understanding of its significance for DCP and/or varied views about the responsibilities of clinics to collect it (Crawshaw and Dally, 2012). Although UK donors can update their information at any time, it is not known how many donors are made aware of this at the time of donation nor how many actually do so. Further, the Register is not open

---

[1] Human Fertilisation and Embryology Authority (Disclosure of Donor Information) Regulations 2004.

to non-DC offspring of donors, nor to descendants of the donor or of the DCP. The threat of criminal sanction has also meant the use of strict restrictions on what information, for example on heritable conditions, can be passed between the parties.

1.2.2   UK Donor Conceived Register (DCR)

Anyone conceived prior to August 1991 (i.e. prior to UK legislation) can join the voluntary Donor Conceived Register (DCR) (previously the government-funded UK DonorLink Register and now funded by the HFEA) for DCP, donors and their non-DC offspring. The register uses a DNA database of its registrants as its main source of 'matching' DCP, donors and donor-related siblings. There is no registration charge, and a limited amount of free counselling is available, but the DNA tests incur a charge. While the type of paternity and maternity testing using this DNA database can produce definitive results, it is less reliable than DTCGT companies for determining sibling-ship and can produce false positives and false negatives (Adams and Lorbach, 2012). The authors are aware of growing numbers of DCR registrants who are also using DTCGT to search for donor relatives.

1.3   The Unofficial Route to Accessing Information: Direct-to-Consumer Genetic Testing (DTCGT)

DTCGT companies are marketed as ways for people to find information about their ancestors or their health. In 2017, they were among the fastest growing businesses in the world and more people tested that year than in all preceding years combined. Extensive advertising and a drop in costs make them easily accessible. The prevalence of DTCGT, in addition to other resources such as social media, means that DCP may discover the identity of the donor or donor relatives and could also unexpectedly learn of their origins as a result of them or genetic relatives previously unknown to them undertaking DTCGT (Ishii and de Miguel Beriain, 2022; Crawshaw 2018). This can happen even if the donor has not had their DNA tested themselves, as if one of the donor's genetic relatives is on the database this can produce a match. This will likely become more prevalent as greater numbers continue to join these databases. While numbers stood at 3 million in total in 2016, by 2021 the international databases of 23andMe had over 12 million; Ancestry had over 20 million; FamilyTreeDNA had over 1.7 million; and MyHeritage had over 5 million (O'Brien, 2021). Subsequently, this led to McGovern and Schlaff (2018) concluding that a donor's anonymity and privacy can no longer be guaranteed, a conclusion with which we agree (Darroch & Smith, 2021).

The growth of commercial DNA testing has been accompanied by an increased use of internet-based forums to help interpret results, undertake genealogy tracing and/or come to terms with unexpected results (Moore, 2016). The International Society of Genetic Genealogists has set up dedicated webpages (see ISOGG, 2021) with guides for DCP and donors (developed with their input) on what to consider ahead of searching and/or making contact. Groups have also been set up to help with tracing relatives and one of the largest, DNA Detectives (Facebook), has a membership of over 178,000 and its offshoot, DNA for the Donor-Conceived (DNA Detectives), has over 2,800 members.

In response to the increased use of DTCGT, in 2018 the HFEA alerted all UK licensed treatment clinics to the need to provide information routinely to actual and prospective donors and parents about the likelihood of being traced. In 2019, it incorporated this into its Code of Practice and reported some progress in their attempts to ensure DTCGT companies make potential customers aware of possible unintended consequences of testing and where to seek support (HFEA, 2019).

1.4 The Right to Know and the Right to Choose

In this section, we will examine the cultural norms and arguments which underpin the shifting policy landscape in donor conception, particularly the move to identity-release donation in the UK and internationally. We will discuss rights-based arguments, which have been influential, concerning DCP's 'right to know' the identity of their genetic parents (the donor/s) and DCP' agency over accessing (or not) this information.

Whilst in previous decades, debates about the ethics of donor-conception practices often centred on questions of harm or welfare, more recent debates on information sharing in donor conception have increasingly used a rights-based logic (Frith, 2001; Johns, 2013; Tobin, 2012). Although some bioethicists have invoked the 'right to privacy' (of both recipient parents and donors) to argue against policies of openness (Ravelingien and Pennings, 2013), the rights of the DCP to know about their conception or the identity of the donor have been argued to be paramount (Ravitsky, 2017; Frith, 2001a). Rights-based approaches to openness typically cite human rights conventions, especially Article Eight of the European Convention on Human Rights, the right to respect for family life and Article Seven of the United Nations Convention on the Rights of the Child (UNCRC), which describes the right to know one's parents (Blyth and Farrand, 2004; Council of Europe, 2019). This, in turn, is part of the wider cultural shift to give more prominence to children's rights and voices and the UNCRC thus has significant rhetorical value.

Klotz's (2014) work discusses how a recognition of DCP's rights are enacted in the UK, through the policies of the HFEA. Her analysis demonstrates how the HFEA manages the potentially profound implications that knowledge about genetic relatives may have for DCP through a principle of assigning agency to DCP in choosing whether and when to access this information. The HFEA emphasises the importance of supporting informed decision-making for any DCP approaching its Register. They describe it as a 'big decision' with potentially profound emotional consequences, which should be thought about carefully, and ideally with the support of a counsellor (Gilman and Nordqvist, 2018). Such statements convey both the perceived implications of donor information for identity and relationships but also the principle that the choice to access this information should belong to DCP themselves. The attempt to manage the implications of donor information through the model of individual informed choice is also reflected in the UK debates which preceded the introduction of identity-release donation. Melanie Johnson, then Public Health Minister, explained it thus:

> The regulations do not force access to information on donor-conceived people. Instead, they give them the option of choosing to obtain access to information about their origins. Some may choose not to use the option at all; others may want only the non-identifying information. For others, however, the identifying information will be very important.[2]

However, what both rights-based arguments against donor anonymity and the HFEA's emphasis on informed choice fail to address is that DCP have not been given the right to be told that they are donor conceived, a necessary precursor to being able to exercise choice about accessing information (Frith, 2001). Even with improved campaigns to inform parents of the benefits of disclosing to their children such as 'Time to Tell' in the state of Victoria, Australia, only 11 per cent of adult DCP in a small sample from that state were informed of their origins (Bourne et al., 2018). In a recent international online survey, the majority of those conceived prior to the 2000s and 40 per cent of those conceived in the 2000s, had not been told (WADC, 2020). Such findings are reflected in the meta-analysis of

---

[2] Human Fertilisation and Embryology Authority (Disclosure of Donor Information) Regulations 2004 Deb 18 May 2004 c.5.

parental intent to tell by Tallandini et al. (2016). Hence, even though there has been an increasing trend to openness and disclosure, there is still a significant proportion of DCP that are not being informed of their origins.

A number of DCP have pointed to the importance of an 'ethic of openness' between recipient parents and DCP. The reasons given by parents for withholding information can be manifold and complex (Crawshaw and Daniels, 2019). Regardless of the reasons, it can be argued that secrecy conflicts with being a virtuous parent (Adams, 2013), defined as a parent who sees the child's welfare as paramount and in this context truthfulness about donor conception from a young age is important for the child's welfare, to prevent or reduce possible trauma and facilitate the flourishing of the child. A participant in a UK study, on registrants of the UK DonorLink, which is now the DCR, whose mother withheld information from her in order to 'protect' her (infertile) husband stated:

> When I probed my mum as to why she didn't tell me as a child, she has always been hazy. She claims that if I had known as a child, I may have been mean to my father about it and not respected him. The most painful thing is this … to think that she wanted to protect him more than me. Had I been in her position I would have put my child first. (Frith et al., 2018, p. 9)

While the earlier decision in the UK to leave the disclosure decision with parents was not unusual across other jurisdictions, it remained in place even after legislative changes in 2008 stating that clinics must provide recipient parents with information about the importance of informing children of their origins at an early age (HFEA, 2019). This is perhaps reflective of wider family policy that views parents as the ones who should decide the best interests of their children except where there are safeguarding concerns. Recently, the UK Birth Registration Reform Group (BRRG) concluded that the approach to disclosure following the lifting of donor anonymity has failed to realise Parliament's intention to enable all DCP to grow up being aware of their origins. David Gollancz, a BRRG member and DCP, argued that there is an urgent need for changes to the birth registration system to provide an 'official' route to enable DCP to be made aware they are donor conceived (Gollancz, 2020).

1.5 Donor-Conceived People's Voices – The Role of DTCGT

As the Internet and DTCGT break down the potential barriers of formal, regulated access to information about donor relatives and enable the development of virtual communities of DCP, debates about 'geneticisation' and 'choice' are increasingly informed by the views and experiences of DCP themselves. This includes international activist and support groups such as We are Donor Conceived, Worldwide Donor Conceived People Network, US Donor Conceived Council and Anonymous Us. Although DCP have been written about – and positioned – as the 'subjects' of research, they have recently found a more direct platform for their voices through the 'grey' literature, online and in media outlets. Activism among DCP, parents and advocates has been growing since the 1990s. In the UK it made donor anonymity a matter for public debate and discussion, culminating in the lifting of donor anonymity (Wincott and Crawshaw, 2006). This included a legal challenge to donor anonymity under the Human Rights Act 1998 (Frith, 2015).[3] All such actions are in keeping with the principles of Participation, Accountability, Non-discrimination, Empowerment and Legality (PANEL) used in human rights approaches more generally (www.scottishhumanrights.com/media/1409/shrc_hrba_leaflet.pdf).

Academic literature was initially geared heavily towards reporting the views and experiences of recipient parents and professionals. As recently as 2012, a review of research directly with donor-conceived children and/or adults, found only thirteen studies, with more than half published since 2008 (Blyth et al., 2012). Interestingly, a common finding was that some DCP considered it their right to have access to information, regardless of whether it carried significance for them at the time. There was also evidence of the frustration and distress of those unable to access the information they wanted and the negative impact on their well-being when disclosure of their origins occurred after childhood and/or in an unplanned way (Frith et al., 2018). DTCGT offers an alternative route to accessing information.

The right to choose and exercise choice based on adequate information have become increasingly important to DCP. Reports from online DCP communities suggest that growing numbers are exercising a 'choice' to use DTCGT to connect with donor relatives, including those for whom this would not be possible through formal routes. The yearly 'We Are Donor Conceived' survey, provides some indication of the extent of the use of DTCGT. Participation in the survey grew from 82 responses in 2017, to 481 responses in 2020, with the percentage of respondents reporting that they had undertaken DTCGT

---

[3] *Rose and Another* v. *Secretary of State for Health and Human Fertilisation and Embryology Authority*, 2002.

growing from 76 per cent to 95 per cent (WADC, 2017, 2020). In the 2020 survey, 34 per cent had learnt that they were DCP as a result of taking a DTCGT test; 78 per cent had identified their genetic parent through DTCGT and only 4 per cent had done so through an official registry. That said, it is important to acknowledge that some respondents had failed – yet – to identify their donor (22 per cent) or donor siblings (30 per cent). In addition, the findings highlighted that 5 per cent of respondents had identified more than fifty siblings and 79 per cent had between one and ten siblings (WADC, 2020). We return to this below. Perhaps the key feature of DTCGT for DCP is that it provides an avenue of investigation that they can choose themselves and hence control.

1.6   Some Challenges Raised by DTCGT for DCP

Using DTCGT offers new possibilities for finding donor relatives but also throws up complex challenges. Through the use of DTCGT growing numbers of DCP are finding out that they are donor conceived for the first time. These DCP are sometimes described as 'late discoverees' and learning of one's origins in this way has been found to be traumatic for some (Adams, 2013; Dingle 2021). A report in 2019 recounts one woman's story of receiving an Ancestry testing kit for Christmas. It revealed that her father was not her genetic father. When she talked about this to her parents, they had no idea that a sperm donor had been used during their fertility treatment (Cooke, 2019). In the same year, the story broke of a man and woman dating each other who learnt that they were donor-related siblings after receiving 23andMe kits as Christmas presents (Ojomu, 2019). Such discoveries are not unique to DCP: one recent survey with people using DTCGT reported that 61 per cent found something new about themselves or their relatives, including finding that one parent was not their biological parent or that they had unknown siblings (Guerrini et al., 2022).

In other situations, some DCP have found out that the donor was in fact the treating doctor (Huffman and Smith, 2021). Increasing accounts of doctors using their own sperm to treat their patients has led to the introduction of legislation prohibiting and penalising such practices in the states of Indiana and Texas, for example (Fox et al., 2019).

DTCGT is also increasing the likelihood of connecting to larger numbers of donor-related siblings than has been reported through formal registers and this may be psychologically challenging (Indekeu et al., 2021).

US photographer Eli Baden-Lasar describes the complexity of being part of a large sibling group in a *New York Times* article:

> Looking through the camera, I had a feeling I couldn't shake: that these people were all versions of me, just formed in different parts of the country – but were also strangers who might as well have been picked out of a hat. (Peterson, 2019)

Crawshaw (2018) described the experiences of three DCP in their fifties and sixties, all connected as a result of their adult children undertaking DTCGT for health-related reasons. All three learnt the donor's identity and that they had fifteen other donor-related siblings (a number that has now risen to more than fifty). Instead of parents considering whether to be open with their DCP children, DTCGT has turned the question on its head. It is now adult children who can be left with the decision about whether to inform their parents what they have uncovered, decisions that can expose family secrets with all the ensuing emotional and relationship repercussions.

In certain circumstances, DTCGT appears to increase the agency of DCP by giving them the option to choose whether and when to search and/or connect with donor relatives. Research with DCP confirms that using DTCGT can be experienced as empowering, particularly in the context of late or shock discoveries of being donor-conceived. This empowerment is in a context where seeking information in other ways is often unavailable, or limited (i.e. by age restrictions), or dependent on the person's date and place of conception, or involves going through slow and bureaucratic 'official' channels or gatekeepers such as clinics (Klotz, 2016). However, not all DCP who use DTCGT to search will find donor relatives, as reported earlier. Even if they find donor-related siblings, they may well not know if they have identified all their siblings, especially if they have no access to official or clinical records, if the clinic has kept inaccurate records, if the donor's samples were transported to other clinics, if the donor donated at other clinics or if they have offspring through other routes. Of those notified of a potential 'match' through DTCGT some may find that person uncontactable, unwilling to communicate further or even disbelieving of the genetic connection between them. As 'relationship pioneers', DCP are having to investigate and manage connections to relatives they previously did not know existed and navigate what may be very emotionally and psychologically sensitive issues with these new connections (Hertz and Nelson, 2018).

1.7 Donor-Conceived People's Voices – Taking Control

Both recipient parents and fertility health professionals have been found at times to display complex and/or contradictory attitudes towards the significance of genetic relationships and whether genetic knowledge is 'constitutive' of kinship and identity regardless of legislative intent about promoting early disclosure (Crawshaw and Daniels, 2019). These can be enacted within power relations between service providers and recipients in the formative treatment stages, for example with the service provider offering 'reassurance' that the donor's genes will carry little influence on the resulting child while attempting to match donors with the intended parents. Recipient parents may opt for donor conception rather than adoption in order for at least one parent to have a genetic link with the child (Daniels, 2004) and can later highlight perceived physical and trait resemblances to themselves or extended family members rather than acknowledging the possibility of such resemblances to their donor (Isakkson et al., 2019), suggesting the enduring social value of a genetic link. This may also help explain the finding that some recipient parents employ cognitive dissonance, the suspension of prior beliefs about the significance of genetics or views about the nature–nurture debate, as part of entering donor-conception treatment and later when not respond-ing to their child's interest in knowing more about the donor or donor-related siblings (Van den Akker, 2010). Some parents 'choose' to present their family as genetically 'intact' to the outside world, sometimes going to great lengths to do so, seeing genetics as important in one context, yet minimising its importance when seeking to keep donor conception secret from their child (Frith et al., 2018).

Better understanding is needed about how DCP themselves perceive the significance of genetics, including the extent to which they see genetic knowledge as 'constitutive' (Strathern, 1999) of kinship and identity and how much this drives their desire for information/contact with the donor and donor-related siblings. DCP have identified the importance of the donor's biography, including their interests, lifestyle, education history and reasons for donating, rather than physical and medical information alone (Blyth et al., 2012). Some wish to know the identity of, and meet, donor-related siblings as well as the donor (Jadva et al., 2010). The donor and donor-related siblings are seen as carrying potentially different genetic significance for the DCP's identity given that donor-related siblings are affected by their non-donor parent and upbringing as well as by their shar-ing of genes with the donor (Indekeu and Hens, 2019). Some DCP report feeling an immediate connection on meeting donor-related siblings, but others do not. Some find it difficult to adjust to the realisation that they are genetically disconnected from people whom they thought were genetic relatives (i.e. the non-genetic parent and their extended family), following late or accidental disclosure (for narrative accounts see Shapiro, 2019 and Dingle, 2021). That said, although many DCP embrace the ethic of openness and their right to information, DCP may also be wary of seeking out their donor or donor-related siblings due to concerns that this might disrupt existing kinship relationships (Adams and Lorbach, 2012).

DCP's growing public voices make it clear that they are deciding for themselves the significance of their origins and its repercussions rather than having it ascribed to them by others. In November 2019, DCP and surrogate-born people presented at a United Nations event to mark the 30th anniversary of the UN Convention on the Rights of the Child. They concluded: 'We are the products of this industry, and we have not been heard … We are now grown, and our voices are stronger. We know what is in our best interests and what is not, and we hope you are listening.' Their recommendations for national and international measures, based on consultation with a broad representation of DC and surrogacy-born persons, stressed the importance of access to information about their donor-conceived relatives (www.donorkinderen.com/united-nations-2019; https://youtu.be/GEP3ZGPFdeQ).

1.8   Conclusion

Increasing use and accessibility of DTCGT is undermining existing policies and practices in donor conception, thereby removing the ability of parents, legislators and fertility treatment providers to dictate what information DCP are able to access about their genetic donor relatives and when and how they are able to access this information. DCP are using DTCGT to take control over accessing information about donor relatives, deciding for themselves if, and when, such knowledge is important to them. Thus, there is a need for more research into the needs and experiences of DCP and their networks on the impact of DTCGT.[4] However, while the regulatory frameworks may be increasingly unfit for purpose as they currently stand, they are not completely redundant as central registers, such as the HFEA Register provide – for some DCP if born in the right place at the

---

[4] Frith and Gilman are undertaking research in this area; see: https://sites.manchester.ac.uk/connecte-d-n-a/

right time – a way of having guaranteed access to certain types of information. Such registers may also provide services such as specialist counselling or other support, although this is not always guaranteed.

While DTCGT potentially offers DCP a route to realising 'the right to know' and 'the right to choose' in relation to locating information about and/or contact with finding donor relatives when 'official' options are limited or non-existent, choice needs to be seen in its socially constituted context. In the context of wider policies and practices around donor conception, the concept of 'informed choice' in relation to DTCGT as well as to any 'official' options rings hollow. DCP's choices are limited by gatekeeping by parents and/or fertility providers, national laws, family and social obligations and perceptions of how this will affect existing relationships. Choices can also be affected by available levels of support be that from peers, family or professional counselling. Neither fertility clinics, commercial DNA companies nor state bodies see this as their ethical or social responsibility to provide funding for professional support to help DCP navigate the potentially challenging and complex process of searching and connecting. DCP and donors have made it clear that they should not have to foot the bill, and funded professional support, such as counselling, should be more generally available (Crawshaw et al., 2016).

Reform of present-day practices in the fertility industry, regulatory bodies and legislative structures to ensure meaningful choice for DCPs could include: requiring central record-keeping; collecting good quality biographical donor information and having robust updating processes; greater flexibility about age limits on information access – a measure that has been mentioned by Peter Thompson, the chief executive of the HFEA, in a newspaper article (*The Guardian*, 2022); and the provision of ongoing professional support to families and to DCP; and the provision of educational campaigns and support services to assist recipient parents in being open with their children about their origins. Options such as birth registration reform have also been proposed by the BRRG, which could go some way to operationalising the original intent of the UK's Parliament to enable all DCP to grow up aware of their donor-conceived origins.

If parents are not made aware of the power of DTCGT to unravel their secrets, their ability to control the manner in which this information is made available to their child is removed (Kirkham-Brown et al., 2022). In sum, DTCGT testing can be both a benefit and burden to DCP and their families and it is important that all parties are well informed about these new technologies and the implications they can have for all involved in donor conception both directly (i.e. donors, DCP, recipient parents) and indirectly (i.e. their extended families and networks and subsequent generations).

References

Adams, D. (2021). *Child Welfare Paramountcy: The Donor Conception Paradox.* Bedford Park, South Australia: Flinders University.

Adams, D. H. (2013). Conceptualising a child-centric paradigm. *Journal of Bioethical Inquiry, 10*(3), 369–381. https://doi.org/10.1007/s11673-013-9454-7

Adams, D., & Allan, S. (2013). Building a family tree: donor-conceived people, DNA tracing and donor 'anonymity'. *Australian Journal of Adoption, 7*(2), 1–16.

Adams, D., & Lorbach, C. (2012). Accessing donor conception information in Australia: a call for retrospective access. *Journal of Law and Medicine, 19*(4), 707–721. PMID: 22908615.

Allan, S. (2011). Psycho-social, ethical and legal arguments for and against the retrospective release of information about donors to donor-conceived individuals in Australia. *Journal of Law and Medicine, 19*(2), 354–376.

Allan, S. (2016). *Donor Conception and the Search for Information: From Secrecy and Anonymity to Openness.* Abingdon: Routledge. https://doi.org/10.4324/9781315568171

Blyth, E., Crawshaw, M., Frith, L., & Jones, C. (2012). Donor-conceived people's views and experiences of their genetic origins: a critical analysis of the research evidence. *Journal of Law and Medicine, 19*(4), 769.

Blyth, E., & Farrand, A. (2004). Anonymity in donor-assisted conception and the UN Convention on the Rights of the Child. *The International Journal of Children's Rights, 12*, 89.

Blyth, E., & Frith, L. (2015). Access to genetic and biographical history in donor conception: an analysis of recent trends and future possibilities. In K. Horsey (Ed.), *Revisiting the Regulation of Human Fertilisation and Embryology* (pp. 136–152). Abingdon: Routledge.

Bourne, K., Johnson, L., Anderson, C., & Hunter, E. (2018). Donor applications to the Victorian central register. In *The ART of Caring Book of Abstracts* (p. 63). Australia: Fertility Society of Australia.

Chicoine, S. (2020). The birth of fertility fraud: how to protect Washingtonians. *Washington Law Review Online, 95*, 168.

Cooke, M. (2019) *Ohio family devastated by IVF terror.* BioEdge (accessed 6 October 2021) www.bioedge.org/bioethics/ohio-family-devastated-by-ivf-error/13166.

Council of Europe (2019) *Anonymous Donation of Sperm and Oocytes: Balancing the Rights of Parents, Donors and Children.* Strasbourg: Parliamentary Assembly. http://assembly.coe.int/nw/xml/XRef/Xref-XML2HTML-EN.asp?fileid=27680

Crawshaw, M., & Dally, J. (2012). Producing sperm, egg and embryo donors' pen portraits and other personal information for later use by donor offspring: an exploratory study of professional practices. *Human Fertility*, 15(2), 82–88. https://doi.org/10.3109/14647273.2012.68712

Crawshaw, M., & Daniels, K. (2019). Revisiting the use of 'counselling' as a means of preparing prospective parents to meet the emerging psychosocial needs of families that have used gamete donation. *Families, Relationships and Societies*, 8(3), 395–409. https://doi.org/10.1332/204674318X15313158773308

Crawshaw, M., Daniels, K., Adams, D., Bourne, K., van Hooff, J. A. P., Kramer, W., ... & Thorn, P. (2015). Emerging models for facilitating contact between people genetically related through donor conception: a preliminary analysis and discussion. *Reproductive Biomedicine & Society Online*, 1(2), 71–80. https://doi.org/10.1016/j.rbms.2015.10.001

Crawshaw, M., Frith, L., van den Akker, O., & Blyth, E. (2016). Voluntary DNA-based information exchange and contact services following donor conception: an analysis of service users' needs. *New Genetics and Society*, 35(4), 372–392. https://doi.org/10.1080/14636778.2016.1253462.

Crawshaw, M. (2018). Direct-to-consumer DNA testing: the fallout for individuals and their families unexpectedly learning of their donor conception origins. *Human Fertility*, 21(4), 225–228. https://doi.org/10.1080/14647273.2017.1339127

Daniels, K. R. (2004). *Building a Family with the Assistance of Donor Insemination*. Palmerston North, NZ: Dunmore Press.

Darroch, F. and Smith, I. (2021) Establishing identity: how direct-to-consumer genetic testing challenges the assumption of donor anonymity. *Family Court Review*, 59(1), 103–120.

Dingle, C. (2021). *Brave New Humans – The Dirty Reality of Donor Conception*. London: Hardie Grant Books.

Donovan, C. (2006). Genetics, fathers, and families: exploring the implications of changing the law in favour of identifying sperm donors. *Social & Legal Studies*, 15(4), 494–510. https://doi.org/10.1177%2F0964663906069543

Finkler, K. (2000). *The New Genetics: Family and Kinship on the Medical Frontier*. Philadelphia: University of Pennsylvania Press.

Fox, D., Cohen, I. G., & Adashi, E. Y. (2019). Fertility fraud, legal firsts, and medical ethics. *Obstetrics & Gynecology*, 134(5), 918–920. https://doi.org/10.1097/AOG.0000000000003516

Frith, L. (2001). Beneath the rhetoric: the role of rights in the practice of non-anonymous gamete donation. *Bioethics*, 15(5–6), 473–484. https://doi.org/10.1111/1467-8519.00255.

Frith, L. (2001a). Gamete donation and anonymity: the ethical and legal debate. *Human Reproduction*, 16(5), 818–824. https://doi.org/10.1093/humrep/16.5.818

Frith, L. (2015). The limits of evidence: evidence-based policy and the removal of gamete donor anonymity in the UK. *Monash Bioethics Review*, 33(1), 29–44. https://doi.org/10.1007/s40592-015-0017-z

Frith, L., Blyth, E., Crawshaw, M., & van den Akker, O. (2018). Secrets and disclosure in donor conception. *Sociology of Health & Illness*, 40(1), 188–203.

Gilman, L., & Nordqvist, P. (2018). Organizing openness: how UK policy defines the significance of information and information sharing about gamete donation. *International Journal of Law, Policy and the Family*, *32*(3), 316–333. https://doi.org/10.1093/lawfam/eby014.

Gollancz, D. (2020, 17 December) *The right to establish identity: donor-offspring.* UK Human Rights Blog. https://ukhumanrightsblog.com/2020/12/17/the-right-to-establish-identity-donor-offspring-david-gollancz/

Guardian, The. (2022, 20 May), UK fertility watchdog could recommend scrapping donor anonymity law. www.theguardian.com/society/2022/may/20/uk-fertility-watchdog-could-recommend-scrapping-donor-anonymity-law

Guerrini, C. J., Robinson, J. O., Bloss, C. C., Brooks, W. B., Fullerton, S. M., Kirkpatrick, B., ... & McGuire, A. L. (2022). Family secrets: experiences and outcomes of participating in direct-to-consumer genetic relative-finder services. *The American Journal of Human Genetics*, *109*(3), 486–497.

Harper, J. C., Kennett, D., & Reisel, D. (2016). The end of donor anonymity: how genetic testing is likely to drive anonymous gamete donation out of business. *Human Reproduction*, *31*(6), 1135–1140. https://doi.org/10.1093/humrep/dew06

Hertz, R., & Nelson, M. K. (2018). *Random Families: Genetic Strangers, Sperm Donor Siblings, and the Creation of New Kin.* New York: Oxford University Press.

Huffman, C. S., & Smith, M. (2021, May 14). *Dallas woman advocates expanding fertility fraud law.* WFAA. www.wfaa.com/article/news/local/investigates/dallas-woman-eve-wiley-advocates-expanding-fertility-fraud-law/287-5ad8424f-ed1f-4b48-9f5c-b3dfied6cbc4.)

Human Fertilisation and Embryology Authority. (2019). Code of Practice. https://portal.hfea.gov.uk/media/1605/2019-12-03-code-of-practice-december-2019.pdf

Indekeu, A., Bolt, S. H., & Maas, A. J. B. (2021). Meeting multiple same-donor offspring: psychosocial challenges. *Human Fertility*, 1–16. https://doi.org/10.1080/14647273.2021.1872804

Indekeu, A., & Hens, K. (2019). Part of my story: the meaning and experiences of genes and genetics for sperm donor-conceived offspring. *New Genetics and Society*, *38*(1), 18–37.

Isaksson, S., Sydsjö, G., Svanberg, A. S., & Lampic, C. (2019). Managing absence and presence of child–parent resemblance: a challenge for heterosexual couples following sperm donation. *Reproductive Biomedicine & Society Online*, *8*, 38–46. https://doi.org/10.10.org/j.rbms.2019.07.001

Ishii, T., & de Miguel Beriain, I. (2022). Shifting to a model of donor conception that entails a communication agreement among the parents, donor, and offspring. *BMC Medical Ethics*, *23*(1), 18.

ISOGG (2021, 28 September) *DNA testing for the donor conceived.* International Society for Genetic Genealogists Wiki. https://isogg.org/wiki/DNA_testing_for_the_donor_conceived

Jadva, V., Freeman, T., Kramer, W., & Golombok, S. (2010). Experiences of offspring searching for and contacting their donor siblings and donor. *Reproductive Biomedicine Online*, *20*(4), 523–532. https://doi.org/10.1016/j.rbmo.2010.01.001

Johns, R. (2013). Abolishing anonymity: a rights-based approach to evaluating anonymous sperm donation. *UCLA Women's Law Journal, 20,* 111.

Kirkman-Brown, J, Calhaz-Jorge, C, Dancet, E, Lundin, K, Martins, M, … Frith, L. (2022). Good practice recommendations for information provision for those involved in reproductive donation. *Human Reproduction Open,* (1), https://doi.org/doi:10.1093/hropen/hoac001

Klotz, M. (2014). *(K) Information: Gamete Donation and Kinship Knowledge in Germany and Britain* (Vol. 32). Frankfurt: Campus Verlag.

Klotz, M. (2016). Wayward relations: novel searches of the donor-conceived for genetic kinship. *Medical Anthropology, 35*(1), 45–57. https://doi.org/10.1080/01459740.2015.1012615

Lippman, A. (1991). Prenatal genetic testing and screening: constructing needs and reinforcing inequities. *American Journal of Law & Medicine, 17*(1–2), 15–50. https://doi.org/10.1017/S0098858800007917

Londini V. (2019). *The open future of donor conception.* BioNews. www.bionews.org.uk/page_143093

McGovern, P. G., & Schlaff, W. D. (2018). Sperm donor anonymity: a concept rendered obsolete by modern technology. *Fertility and Sterility, 109*(2), 230–231. https://doi.org/10.1016/j.fertnstert.2017.12.011

Moore, C. (2016). The history of genetic genealogy and unknown parentage research: An insider's view. *Journal of Genetic Genealogy, 8*(1), 35–37.

O'Brien M. (2021, 17 July) *Who has the largest DNA database?* Data Mining DNA. www.dataminingdna.com/who-has-the-largest-dna-database/

Odze, L. (2018) Surrogacy and risks of family secrets. In R. Cabeza, V. Flowers, E. Pierrot, A. Rao, B. O'Leary and L Odze (Eds.), *Surrogacy: Law, Practice and Policy in England and Wales* (pp. 133–160). Bristol: LexisNexis.

Ojomu, N. (2019, 13 January) *Man's horror as DNA test reveals he's dating his half-sister.* Yahoo!Lifestyle. https://au.lifestyle.yahoo.com/mans-horror-dna-test-reveals-hes-dating-half-sister-044310902.html

Pennings, G. (2019). Genetic databases and the future of donor anonymity. *Human Reproduction, 34*(5), 786–790.

Peterson, P. (2019, 26 June). He found out he had 32 siblings. For The Times magazine, he took their pictures. *The New York Times.* www.nytimes.com/interactive/2019/06/26/magazine/sperm-donor-siblings.html

Ravelingien, A., & Pennings, G. (2013). The right to know your genetic parents: from open-identity gamete donation to routine paternity testing. *The American Journal of Bioethics, 13*(5), 33–41. https://doi.org/10.1080/15265161.2013.776128.

Ravitsky, V. (2017). The right to know one's genetic origins and cross-border medically assisted reproduction. *Israel Journal of Health Policy Research, 6*(1), 1–6. https://doi.org/10.1186/s13584-016-0125-0

Sforza, T. (2007). Fertility fraud settlements cost millions. *The Orange County Register,* 26 June.

Shapiro, D. (2019). *Inheritance: A Memoir of Genealogy, Paternity, and Love.* New York: Alfred A. Knopf.

Sharak, S. (2020). Richards v. Kiken and the legal implications of fertility fraud. *American Journal of Law & Medicine, 46*(4), 528–535.

Smart, C. (2011). Families, secrets and memories. *Sociology, 45*(4), 539–553. https://doi.org/10.1177%2F0038038511406585

Strathern, M. (1999). Refusing information. In M. Strathern (Ed.), *Property, Substance, and Effect: Anthropological Essays on Persons and Things* (pp. 64–86). London: Athlone Press.

Tobin, J. W. (2012). Donor conceived individuals and access to information about their genetic origins: the relevance and role of rights. *Journal of Law and Medicine, 19*(4), 742–757.

Tallandini, M. A., Zanchettin, L., Gronchi, G., & Morsan, V. (2016). Parental disclosure of assisted reproductive technology (ART) conception to their children: a systematic and meta-analytic review. *Human Reproduction, 31*(6), 1275–1287.

van den Akker, O. (2010). Nature and nurture: what do theory and research tell us. In M. Crawshaw and R. Balen (Eds.), *Adopting after Infertility: Messages from Practice, Research, and Personal Experience* (pp. 164–179). London: Kingsley Publishers.

WADC. (2017) *We are donor conceived 2017 survey results.* We Are Donor Conceived. www.wearedonorconceived.com/uncategorized/survey-results/

WADC. (2020) *We are donor conceived survey report.* We Are Donor Conceived. www.wearedonorconceived.com/2020-survey-top/2020-we-are-donor-conceived-survey/

Weiner, K., Martin, P., Richards, M., & Tutton, R. (2017). Have we seen the geneticisation of society? Expectations and evidence. *Sociology of Health & Illness, 39*(7), 989–1004. https://doi.org/10.1111/1467-9566.12551.

Wincott, E., & Crawshaw, M. (2006). From a social issue to policy: social work's advocacy for the rights of donor conceived people to genetic origins information in the United Kingdom. *Social Work in Health Care, 43*(2–3), 53–72. DOI: 10.1300/J010v43n02_05

CHAPTER 2

Recipient Parents Using Do-It-Yourself Methods to Make Early Contact with Donor Relatives
Is There Still a Place for Law?

Fiona Kelly

2.1 Introduction

For decades, parents of donor-conceived children were counselled by doctors and fertility clinics to keep their child's conception story a secret. This approach was facilitated, at least in part, through the use of anonymous donors whose identities were known only to the fertility clinic staff. Donor-conceived children and their parents were prohibited from accessing this information. Over the past 20 years, however, attitudes towards information release in many jurisdictions have begun to shift (Allan, 2016; Golombok et al., 2016). Recipient parents are now encouraged to tell children their conception story and donor-conceived adults increasingly demand access to information about their donors and donor siblings.

In response to changes to the norms around donor conception, state-based laws in Australia put an end to anonymous donation, commencing with Victoria in 1998. A nationwide ban followed in 2005.[1] Anonymous donation was replaced with "open identity" donation, which requires that the donor consent to their identifying information being released to donor offspring when the donor-conceived person (DCP) turns 18. While these changes have challenged the norms of secrecy and shame that have dominated donor conception in Australia (Cosson et al., 2021), control over the information, the timing of when it can be released, and what information is available to whom, still largely resides with clinics and state governments. Adult DCPs have questioned these limitations, advocating for easy and early access to information about their donors and donor siblings. Increasingly, adult DCPs argue that children have a right to "grow up"

---

[1] National Health and Medical Research Council, *Ethical Guidelines on the Use of Assisted Reproductive Technology in Clinical Practice and Research* (2017).

with their donor relatives (We are Donor Conceived, 2020). In Australia, a growing number of recipient parents (RPs) are responding to the concerns of adult DCPs by creating opportunities for their children to have "early contact" with donor relatives, defined as contact between a child and their donor relatives prior to the age of 18 (Kelly & Dempsey, 2016). Except for the state of Victoria, however, there are no legal avenues in Australia for making early contact.

In the absence of legislative mechanisms for achieving early contact, some RPs have taken donor linking into their own hands, using a variety of "do-it-yourself" (DIY) techniques to successfully identify donor relatives, including DNA testing, informal online donor registers, other forms of online sleuthing, and negotiations with clinics (Kelly & Dempsey, 2016; Crawshaw et al., 2015; Hertz & Nelson, 2018). The widespread availability of new technologies has resulted in a democratisation of access to information that was not anticipated when most legal frameworks were introduced. As the use of DIY donor linking increases among RPs, there is the possibility that it may undermine or even supplant the law.

Through interviews with RPs residing in Australia, this chapter explores motivations for, and the methods used by, RPs to make early contact with their child's donor relatives, including both donors and donor siblings. It reflects on the ways in which the availability of new technologies has resulted in a relocation of power from the state and fertility clinics to consumers, providing RPs and their children with access to information to which they are not (yet) legally entitled. The chapter concludes by considering whether the democratisation of access to information has diminished the importance of law reform in this area or whether RPs still believe law has a role to play.

2.2 Background: The Law

In Australia, where assisted reproduction is regulated at both a federal and state level, the law plays a central role in determining who has access to information about donor relatives and when it can be obtained. To be granted a licence by the Reproductive Technology Accreditation Committee (RTAC) to provide assisted reproduction services, fertility clinics must meet industry Standards of Practice. In addition, clinics must adhere to the federal Ethical Guidelines on the Use of Assisted Reproductive Technology in Clinical Practice and Research (NHMRC Guidelines, 2017), which require clinics to encourage parents to disclose to their children their genetic origins and only accept donations from donors who consent to having their identifying information released to offspring. In the four states and territories with legislation regulating assisted reproduction, fertility clinics must also comply with state and territory law.

The five Australian states and territories that regulate assisted reproduction –Victoria (VIC), New South Wales (NSW), South Australia (SA), Western Australia (WA) and Northern Territory (NT) – provide some of the most expansive donor-linking laws in the world. Victoria, NSW and WA each have a framework for facilitating donor linking between DCPs and their donor relatives. The law applies prospectively in WA and NSW, meaning that donor information is available to DCPs conceived after the law was passed. In Victoria, the law applies retrospectively, enabling all DCPs, whenever they were conceived, to access their donor's identity.[2] A bill that is currently before the South Australian Parliament is similar in its effect to the Victorian law, including retrospective application.[3]

In Victoria, WA and NSW (and likely SA), the process of information disclosure is also regulated by the law. Each of these states require clinics to provide donor information to a statutory authority or state health department who, in turn, maintain donor registers and facilitate donor linking when DCPs become eligible. In the remaining states and territories, clinics manage donor information and are obliged to facilitate the transfer of information when DCPs become eligible.

Only Victoria and WA law currently provides for early contact with donors.[4] In WA, information disclosure and contact with the donor can occur at 16 upon the request of the DCP. In Victoria, however, contact with donors can occur at any age if the RP applies to the Central Register and the donor consents. The information disclosure and contact are facilitated by counsellors at the Victorian Assisted Reproductive Treatment Authority (VARTA). RPs in Victoria can also join the Voluntary Register and, if other families who used the same donor or donor siblings also register, a match is made and information can be exchanged with the consent of both parties. Victoria's Voluntary Register remains the only mechanism in Australia for making contact with donor siblings. Applications for early contact with donors are common in Victoria, particularly among single mothers. In 2018/19, early contact applications by

---

[2] Assisted Reproductive Treatment Act 2008 (Vic).
[3] Assisted Reproductive Treatment (Donor Conception Register) Amendment Bill 2021.
[4] The SA Bill includes provisions for early contact between DCPs and donors, as well as between donor siblings, if all parties consent.

RPs represented 43 per cent (n = 43) of total applications to VARTA's Central Register (VARTA, 2018/19). An additional 30 RPs lodged their information with the Voluntary Register. Research examining applications to VARTA's registers found that single mothers of young children used the registers more than any other RP group (Kelly et al., 2019; Dempsey & Kelly, 2019).

Despite the extensive legal framework regulating assisted reproduction in Australia, much of which is designed to protect the interests of DCPs, options for making early contact between DCPs and their donor relatives are limited. If RPs approach clinics, they are often told that the law prevents them from providing information. Therefore, if a parent wishes to pursue early contact for their child, they must explore informal methods.

2.3 Methodology

The data reported on in the article, which focuses on RPs who have participated in donor linking, is part of a larger study on donor linking in Australia that includes interviews with donor-conceived adults, donors and recipient parents. Recruitment took place over a 6-month period between June 2019 and December 2019. Three separate advertisements were tailored to target three groups: donor-conceived adults, donors and recipient parents. The advertisements designed to recruit RPs were posted on several Facebook groups, including Australian Solo Mums by Choice, Donor Parents Australia, Solo Mums by Choice, and several DCP groups. Advertisements were also posted in 90 regional newspapers, both print and online. Finally, a snowball strategy with participants was used to see if their donor relatives might be willing to participate.

Thirty-two RPs were interviewed for the study. All RPs interviewed were female. Twenty-eight were the recipients of donor sperm, while the remaining four were the recipients of both egg and sperm donation. Most of the children were under the age of 10. The majority of RP participants (25) were single mothers by choice (SMCs). Five RPs were in a same-sex relationship, and two parented in a heterosexual couple.

Seven RPs were in contact with their child's sperm donor only, while four were in contact with both the sperm donor and donor-siblings. The majority of RPs (18) were in contact with donor siblings only. Two RPs were linked to their child's egg donor, and one RP was linked to their egg donor, sperm donor and donor siblings. The majority of RPs used more than one method to identify, and make contact with, donor relatives. The most common identification method was online registers and/or social media where donor numbers were shared by RPs. Legislative mechanisms for locating donor relatives were used by only six families.

RPs were evenly spread across the east coast of Australia, with nine in NSW, nine in VIC and seven in Queensland (QLD). The remainder were from SA and Tasmania. Two had conceived overseas, one in South Africa and the other in the United States.

There were some response gaps in the RP participant group, including male RPs, heterosexually coupled RPs, and gay and lesbian RPs. Boosted and targeted posts were placed to attract more participants in these populations, but they remained less responsive than other groups. As noted above, previous research, including research on applications to VARTA's donor registers, suggest that heterosexual couples and gay or lesbian RPs are less likely to seek early contact with their child donor's relatives than SMCs (Dempsey et al., 2019; Goldberg & Scheib, 2015). It therefore may be that the distribution of participants in the study reflects who is most likely to participate in early contact.

There are several possible reasons for the disproportionate desire of SMCs to pursue donor linking. First, the donor is a potentially less threatening presence in the life of the child of a single mother because they do not threaten the position of a genetically unrelated parent as they might for lesbian or heterosexual couples (Freeman et al., 2016, Goldberg & Scheib, 2015, Hertz et al., 2013). The social pressure to 'find a father' could also be fuelling single mothers' desire to contact their child's sperm donor when the child is young. Finally, single mothers who seek contact with donor siblings may be hoping to provide their children with an 'expanded family' or 'future support system', particularly if they have an only child (Goldberg & Scheib, 2015).

Data were collected through phone and face-to-face, semi-structured interviews of 25–90 minutes duration. Interview schedules were designed to elicit the RPs' experience of donor linking and to capture their personal story of searching for their child's donor relatives. Interview questions covered: the decision to engage in donor linking; how the donor-linking process unfolded; the impact of donor linking on self and existing family; and views on support services, current legislation and law reform. Interviews were audio-recorded and transcribed by an external provider and then de-identified.

2.4   Motivations for Seeking Early Contact

While RPs expressed a variety of reasons for seeking early contact, the most frequently cited and strongly felt motivation was a belief that it was in the best interests of their children to have the opportunity to integrate their donor relatives into their lives from an early age. When exploring with RPs *why* they thought having early contact was important for their children, most explained that they had been influenced by adult DCPs whose stories they had read in online support groups or the media. The common narrative in these accounts, which permeate the donor-conception landscape in Australia via the media, online support groups and law reform debates, is that donor-conceived children need early access to their donor relatives so they can integrate them into their personal identity during childhood. Some adult DCPs argue that this can be achieved by using a known donor or by making contact with a child's unknown donor and donor siblings while the child was still a minor (Dingle, 2021). This narrative resonated particularly strongly with SMCs, who made up the bulk of the sample. As a result, many of the RPs pursued donor linking before their child was old enough to express an opinion. It was not uncommon to make contact when the children were babies.

Tasha, an SMC with a two-year-old son who had made contact with donor siblings and was actively pursuing the donor's identity, typified the views of the RPs, particularly the SMCs. Tasha felt strongly that it was important for her son to know his donor relatives while he was young so he could integrate them into his life and identity. As she explained:

> For me I think it's really important for these people to be part of [my son's life] from day dot. Living 18 years of your life with this expectation of what your donor father might be like and that expectation of "does he want to meet, doesn't he want to meet, what's he like?" and then having to wait 18 years to find that out. I think that's really cruel … So if you can sort of say "yes we know who your donor father is, we know who your donor siblings are" … then that's something you could raise your child knowing, as opposed to the unknown.

Tasha's comments and actions suggest an urgency about her search, as if the longer she waited, the more damage would be done to her son. She began her search when her son was only a few months old.

For Genevieve, also an SMC, it was the impact of reading DCP's account in various Facebook groups that convinced her that pursuing early contact was in her son's best interests. Genevieve had located several of her child's donor siblings and connected with their families in person. She explained her motivations:

> I have been involved in … a couple of Facebook group including one that had donor conceived adults on it … The feeling there, the sentiment there, seemed to be fairly strong that donor conceived children should not be kept from their families, their biological family.

Genevieve accepted the premise that, though they were strangers, her son's donor relatives were his "family" and that it was important she do everything she could to (re)unite them. She first pursued contact when her son was only six months old. Like many of the RPs interviewed, Genevieve treated face-to-face contact as the goal of her investigations. As she noted, "Information's good, but contact is better." Sheryl, an SMC who was also heavily involved in DCP-run Facebook groups and had met many of her child's 60-plus siblings, expressed a similar sentiment, stating "I understand now how painful it can be for people to have that missing parent and a photo and some information is not enough" (RP 37). After several years of reading DCP accounts, Sheryl became an advocate for early contact in Australia, using SMC Facebook groups to "encourage people to connect". She felt that waiting until the child was old enough to express their views and make their own connections was too late. As she explained:

> I see so many [RPs] saying, "I don't want my kids to catch up [with donor relatives], maybe later." And then I hear DCPs [saying], "Why do the parents make us wait? We catch up with cousins, uncles, grandparents, why do they keep us apart from our [donor] siblings? ... [For] a lot of them there was grief and anger around the fact that they lost 20, 25 years of their lives [not] knowing their siblings.

Some RPs of older children believed so strongly in the importance of early contact that they pursued it despite their children's lack of interest. Verena, for example, who was an SMC to four donor-conceived teenagers, had frequently raised with them the possibility of connecting with donor relatives. As she explained:

> I've got four high school children – they're just really not interested. I said, "I'm just putting it out there so that you've got that in the back of your mind, if that's something that you're interested in" and they were like "Why? Why? Just no ... We've got teenage lives to live with actual people we know and that's just not even something we're going to take five minutes to think about.

Despite her children's lack of concern about the matter, Verena joined an online donor register, arguing that "I may as well, because you never know". Through the register she made contact with a number of families who had used the same donor and arranged for her children to meet one of their donor siblings who lived nearby. While her children participated, they told Verena afterwards they were not interested in spending any more time with the donor sibling. Several years later when Verena raised the possibility with her 14-year-old twins of doing DNA testing so they could locate additional siblings and possibly the donor, they had flatly refused.

The impact of DCPs narratives, as well as discussions in RP social media groups, around the importance of early contact had had a significant impact on the RPs interviewed. Most unquestioningly adopted the view that it was their responsibility to make early contact with their child's donor relatives, often before their child was old enough to express their views and even in circumstances where their children showed no interest. However, because only two states in Australia enable early contact via legislation, RPs were required to take matters into their own hands to identify donor relatives. In doing so, they found the most effective ways in which to undertake DIY linking were discussed in online groups for the donor-conception community and were often recommended by DCPs themselves.

2.5   How Did RPs Locate Donor Relatives?

Most RPs used multiple methods to locate their child's donor relatives. This reflects the complicated nature of DIY approaches to donor linking, where it is often necessary to gather information from multiple sources. The majority of RPs had contact with more than one relative, particularly where their searches had focused on donor siblings. Once they found a relative, others often followed as each new link came with their own connections.

All of the RPs used a mix of four methods to locate donor relatives: online searches, including online donor-conception forums and registers; direct requests to sperm banks or clinics; DNA testing; and an application to VARTA (Victorian RPs only). Three RPs also met at least one donor relative by chance while attending social events for RPs.

The most common method for locating donor relatives, and particularly donor siblings, was online forums and registers. These included Facebook groups for RPs, free registers that RPs had set up online to serve families who had used a certain clinic or lived in a particular country, and the not-for-profit online Donor Sibling Registry (DSR), which charges a membership fee for registration but has more than 75,000 members worldwide. These online forums were often used alongside social media to track down donor relatives.

Many of the RPs posted their details on several online forums, casting their net as wide as possible. Angela, whose sperm donor had been recruited by a Queensland fertility clinic from the United States, started searching for her son's donor relatives when he was a year old. After watching an episode of the Oprah Winfrey show featuring the founder of the DSR, Angela joined the US-based registry. She paid a membership fee of US$70 (now US$99) and within minutes had located one donor sibling in Canada and a second an hour away from her home. She immediately got in touch with the local family and they had a face-to-face meeting the following week. Shortly after, an American family with the same donor joined the DSR and also got in touch. Angela then stumbled across another online RP-operated donor register, which she described as "free and ... lower tech" than the DSR, where she connected with the parents of a fourth donor sibling who lived in the United States. Thus, in less than a month of online searching, Angela had identified and made contact with the parents of four of her child's donor siblings across three different countries. Since that initial meeting, she had had ongoing online and face-to-face contact with them and had also connected them with each other.

Not every RP had such quick success with online searching. For example, Alannah (RP 21) joined the DSR when her son was two, but it took more than decade for a sibling to surface. When a match was finally made, it was with a family of five donor-conceived children who lived just 15 minutes from Alannah and her son in Queensland. After initial online contact, the families now meet regularly and have even holidayed together. Alannah refers jokingly to her and the other mother, Shaye, as "sperm sisters". Both consider the other to be family members. Through connecting with Shaye and her children, Alannah has now also identified her son's donor. Shaye had her eldest son do a direct-to-consumer DNA test which identified the donor's great uncle. Alannah explained what happened next:

> And so, we had a name. So, then we went stalking. [W]e had a surname and we knew certain things like when the donor had finished school and all that sort of stuff. So, we were kind of thinking okay, let's try. We Facebooked the [great] uncle, there's nothing much on that. And then this is while we're at work and we're both texting each other, trying to figure all this out. And then I remembered, "oh my God he used to play rugby." So, I put his surname in and rugby and boom there he was. And there was a name and that he finished school in 1997. It's like, "Yeah, that's him. Holy shit."

> So, between the two of us we found his Facebook page and found his work page. He's a tradesman. So Shaye rang him up just to hear his voice ... [she pretended to be a customer]. And then she thought, "I can't do that, that's awful," so she rang him back. And at first, he denied that he had donated and then he went, "Yeah, okay." She could tell by his reaction that it was

him. And she said he was really nice. Obviously, he didn't hang up on her and tell her to bugger off or anything like that. He listened to what she had to say. She said, "I'm not after anything, I'm just telling you that this is my family and we're so grateful and thank you," and all that kind of stuff. So, she doesn't seem to think she'll ever hear from him. And even though I didn't speak to him, I'm fine with that as well. I think just knowing, it's got rid of that curiosity factor of, "Okay, who is this person and what does he look like and why did he donate?"

Alannah and Shaye have since found additional photos of the donor online and they monitor his activities on Facebook. However, despite all the detective work undertaken by their mothers, none of the children have shown any interest in him. Alannah has speculated that because they have connected with their siblings, the donor may feel less significant.

Alannah's story demonstrates how much technology has democratised the field of assisted reproduction, removing the layers of secrecy that have been the bedrock of the industry for decades. Promises of donor anonymity and legislative barriers to identifying donor siblings are often easily overcome through a combination of online donor-linking forums, Internet sleuthing, and DNA testing. While laws that permit donor linking and early contact would streamline the process, it is clear that law reform is no longer a necessary precondition to connecting with donor relatives.

2.6   Donor Linking via Fertility Clinics

In recent years, some Australian fertility clinics have been willing to facilitate early contact between RPs and their child's donor relatives (Kelly et al., 2019). Clinics are not required by law to provide early contact opportunities to RPs and their children. Thus, any support provided is entirely at the discretion of the individual clinic and responses to a request vary from clinic to clinic.

Early contact via a clinic often flows from an inquiry by an RP who is seeking information about donor relatives. The initial inquiry may be about how many offspring the donor has or a request that the clinic pass on a thank-you letter to the donor. Sandy, who conceived in South Australia, found that while some clinics refuse to support donor-linking activity, others were willing to act as a conduit between donor relatives. Sandy contacted her clinic after her daughter was born to ask if they would be willing to send the donor updates on her behalf. In her letters, which she has now sent for several years, she has told the donor about her daughter and "registered [her] interest" in meeting. Sandy wanted her daughter to know her donor from a young age so they "had something more concrete" to talk about when they discussed her origins. After several letters back and forth between Sandy and the donor, he agreed to meet her. A single meeting between the donor and Sandy took place at the clinic, facilitated by the donor coordinator. While Sandy would like more contact, she feels that asking for more risks her positive relationship with the clinic. As she explained:

> I hope there's more, but at the same time I live in constant fear that [the clinic] is going to say "you're expecting too much, or you want too much, or when you signed up you knew that there was not supposed to be contact or anything like that", so I get too afraid to ask for anything more.

It was the clinic, however, who approached Sandy about contact with donor siblings. Sandy's daughter was only a few months old when the clinic reached out to her, indicating that another RP had expressed interest in sharing contact information. Sandy accepted a letter from the other RP before they made contact via email. The second RP had already met two other families who had used the same donor, providing instant donor siblings for Sandy's daughter. A fifth family was then located via a Facebook group for RPs, where donor numbers are shared.

What was most striking about the stories of DIY early contact was the resourcefulness of the RP community. They had created an entire infrastructure, mostly online, for searching, monitoring, and registering their various connections. Many of those who had identified a donor sibling pooled their knowledge with other RP(s) to find other siblings or even the donor, sharing information they obtained via their online networks. Skye, an SMC who had used VARTA's service to identify her donor, but online forums to find donor siblings, summarised the different resources she and other SMC friends had utilised:

> [T]here's a donor sibling registry in the US … there's an Australian Facebook group here. I put my [donor] code up there very early. There's another forum I'm aware of where they do the same thing. So that's already happening, so these people are finding out that they have, it's mainly sibling connections rather than donor connections. But they're literally finding them in the blink of an eye, you know, they've both obviously gone with the intention of making a connection … Some people are now using DNA. My girlfriend, she's gone through the VARTA process now, but her donor profile had enough information [to find the donor]. She'd figure it out. She Google stalked him. Because he gave away so much information … she was able to do that.

In their accounts of DIY linking, RPs rarely reflected on the privacy of the donor or donor sibling families. As can be seen in Skye's quote above, when referring to their donor searches, several of the RPs even used the word "stalking" to describe their behaviour. While most connections made with donor siblings were enabled through online forums where both parties had registered their details, connections with donors rarely began consensually (Byrt & Dempsey, Chapter 3 in this volume). This did not deter RPs, however, most of whom argued they were acting in their children's best interests by searching for their child's donor. The fact that donors had not agreed to early contact when they donated, and that the law did not give RPs the right to seek early contact, took less precedence than the child's interest in knowing their donor.

2.7   Is There Still a Place for Law?

With the emergence of new technologies that enable identification of donor relatives, one might assume that the law no longer has a place in early contact linking. RPs can now identify and make contact with donor siblings and even donors without the imprimatur of the law. However, RPs consistently argued that while DIY methods for identifying donor relatives have provided opportunities for donor linking that were not available in the past, significant gaps remained. Most believed that the state should not withdraw from its responsibility to provide fair and equal access to donor-linking services. This finding is important in an era where many DCPs have argued that, with the advent of DIY linking, "anonymity is dead" (Harper et al., 2016; Australian Broadcasting Company, 2015). However, RPs argued that while the emergence of informal means by which to identify donor relatives may have gone some way towards democratising donor linking, a formal system of early contact donor linking, regulated by law, was preferable.

The most consistently expressed reason for supporting the introduction of early contact donor-linking laws was that they would provide equal access to information, something which could not be guaranteed with informal linking mechanisms. Success with DIY linking often turned on luck: a responsive clinic, other RPs being members of an online forum, or the donor or the donor's family having done DNA testing. RPs argued that access to information and the opportunity for contact should be available to everyone and that this required state legislation and government-managed registers. For example, Skye, who was able to use the Victorian legislation and VARTA's counselling services to make early contact, argued that while RPs may be able to successfully locate donor relatives using informal methods, a legal pathway ensures everyone has the same access and support services.

> I just feel like legislation, it gives people more ... there's more support around it, to make sure that it's done in a controlled way, and people understand the consequences of what they're doing. But I think it's also there are some states where people have no option to do that, so they're forced into [informal pathways], rather than having the option to go through it in a more controlled environment.

Not surprisingly, the strongest support for donor-linking laws came from RPs who conceived in states without legislation. Even though they had successfully contacted at least some of their children's donor relatives, the unequal access to information across Australian jurisdictions was evident to them when they participated in online RP discussion groups. For example, Danielle, an SMC from Queensland where there is no legislation regulating assisted reproduction, stated that she gets "a little bit cranky about the inconsistencies between states and between the clinics and stuff like that". In the absence of a state register, Danielle worried that the clinic, which was not bound by any rules regarding maintaining donor records, may lose track of her son's donor. As she explained:

> [I]n Queensland it's really up to the clinics to chase up the donor every two years and he could easily fall off – what's the word – disappear, yeah. So that's my main concern for Rowan, if he's interested, turns 18 and then they can't locate the donor.

Many of the RPs also favoured the introduction of donor-linking laws because they anticipated they would be accompanied by support services. They were most interested in counselling that would assist them in negotiating a relationship with their child's donor(s). Skye was an SMC who used VARTA's services to connect with her daughter's donor. When comparing her experience of early contact via VARTA with the experiences of SMCs who had relied on informal methods, Skye was struck by how much she relied on VARTA counsellors to guide her through the process. As she observed, there are now "lots of informal ways of going about donor linking", but there is "no support around it". RPs who connected via the sharing of donor numbers online or DNA testing were required to navigate the process alone.

When asked who should facilitate donor linking under any new law, RPs almost uniformly favoured a third-party agency – for example, a statutory authority like VARTA – which would operate at arm's lengths from clinics, which were perceived as having a conflict of interest. As Meredith put it, "If New South Wales had a VARTA I'd be thrilled". Angela, an SMC who had identified her son's donor through her American sperm bank's online register, also favoured a statutory authority, noting in particular the importance of the process being separated from fertility clinics:

> [We] definitely [need] a separate agency. The fertility clinics in my experience really don't know what they're doing. And their primary thing is to make money out of people getting pregnant. But the long-term connection isn't their role, and it shouldn't be expected of them and they wouldn't do it well.

Janice, a Victorian SMC, also believed early contact linking should be managed by a third-party agency. However, she came to this position, in part, after reflecting on what it would be like to be the *subject* of an application. She noted that, "I'd be comfortable with being contacted through a third party. I wouldn't be comfortable with someone contacting me directly." For Janice, the arm's-length nature of a government agency felt less invasive than a call or email from a stranger, whether that stranger had obtained her details informally or via a legal process. She believed that a trained counsellor would be better at imparting the information than the donor relatives themselves and could also offer impartial support.

Thus, while most of the RPs interviewed had successfully utilised DIY mechanisms to identify their child's donor relatives, they did not believe that the law should retreat from the field. Donor-linking laws guaranteed equality of opportunity and were likely to be accompanied by support services that would help guide families through the process of making early contact. In contrast, informal mechanisms relied on luck and left RPs to navigate what were often complex situations alone.

2.8   Conclusion

The ingenuity applied in using various new technologies, combined with a growing culture of openness, means that making early contact with a child's donor relatives is not only possible, but often presumed to be in the child's best interests. It is now common for RPs, particularly SMCs who now make up the majority of users of donor sperm in Australia, to contact their child's donor relatives at an ever earlier age, with some RPs providing early contact opportunities for their children before they are old enough to express an opinion. However, although RPs acknowledge that DIY methods for donor linking have, to some extent, democratised the process of donor linking, they still believed the law had an important role to play. Most notably, they supported the introduction of state-based laws that facilitated early contact because they would provide equality of opportunity, relocate responsibility for linking from the clinics to the state, and were presumed to include the provision of counselling expertise and other support services like those that exist in Victoria. This last finding is particularly important for those who favour greater openness in donor conception, as it suggests RPs feel most comfortable making early contact if they are supported by a comprehensive regulatory framework. In the absence of such a framework, they may be less likely to make early contact or have fewer positive experiences.

RP initiated early contact via DIY methods is likely to continue, if not increase, in Australia, independent of any legal change. The law, however, has a role to play in ensuring that early contact is available equally across jurisdictions and safely managed. Victoria's model for early contact provides an example of how such a system might operate. When an RP makes an application for early contact under the Victorian legislation, the donor is contacted by a member of the VARTA counselling team and, where they give their consent, contact is facilitated. VARTA's counsellors are available to both parties to negotiate the process.

The only element missing from the Victorian model is a mechanism for seeking early contact with donor siblings. At present, Victorian law only offers a passive process for sibling linking, where the RP lodges an application with the Voluntary Register and waits for an RP who used the same donor to do the same. Given the strong interest among RPs in connecting with their child's donor siblings, any law-reform process should consider the inclusion of early contact sibling applications, perhaps modelled on Victoria's existing system for applying for early contact with donors. However, given that each donor can donate to 5 or 10 families (depending on the state), the resources needed to support RP-initiated sibling applications would be significant.

References

Allan, S. (2016). *Donor Conception and the Search for Information: From Secrecy and Anonymity to Openness.* Routledge.

Australian Broadcasting Company. (2015). *The Donor Detectives*, Background Briefing (available at: www.abc.net.au/radionational/programs/backgroundbriefing/the-donor-detectives/6996896).

Cosson, B., Dempsey, D., & Kelly, F. (2021). *Secret* shame – male infertility and donor conception in the wake of retrospective legislative change. *Men and Masculinities, 25*(2), 497–515.

Crawshaw, M., Daniels, K., Adams, D., Bourne, K., van Hooff, J. A. P., Kramer, W., ... & Thorn, P. (2015). Emerging models for facilitating contact between people genetically related through donor conception: a preliminary analysis and discussion. *Reproductive Biomedicine & Society Online, 1*(2), 71–80.

Dempsey, D., Kelly, F., Horsfall, B., Hammarberg, K., Bourne, K., & Johnson, L. (2019). Applications to statutory donor registers in Victoria, Australia: information sought and expectations of contact. *Reproductive Biomedicine & Society Online, 9*, 28–36.

Dingle, S. (2021). *Brave New Humans: The Dirty Truth behind the Fertility Industry.* Hardie Grant Books.

Freeman, T., Zadeh, S., Smith, V., & Golombok, S. (2016). Disclosure of sperm donation: a comparison between solo mother and two-parent families with identifiable donors. *Reproductive BioMedicine Online, 33*(5), 592–600.

Goldberg, A. E., & Scheib, J. E. (2015). Female-partnered and single women's contact motivations and experiences with donor-linked families. *Human Reproduction, 30*(6), 1375–1385.

Golombok, S., & Wilkinson, S. (Eds.), (2016). *Regulating Reproductive Donation.* Cambridge University Press.

Harper, J. C., Kennett, D., & Reisel, D. (2016). The end of donor anonymity: how genetic testing is likely to drive anonymous gamete donation out of business. *Human Reproduction, 31*(6), 1135–1140.

Hertz, R., & Nelson, M. K. (2018). *Random Families: Genetic Strangers, Sperm Donor Siblings, and the Creation of New Kin.* Oxford University Press.

Hertz, R., Nelson, M. K., & Kramer, W. (2013). Donor conceived offspring conceive of the donor: the relevance of age, awareness, and family form. *Social Science & Medicine, 86*, 52–65.

Kelly, F. J., & Dempsey, D. J. (2016). Experiences and motives of Australian single mothers by choice who make early contact with their child's donor relatives. *Medical Law Review, 24*(4), 571–590.

Kelly, F., Dempsey, D., Power, J., Bourne, K., Hammarberg, K., & Johnson, L. (2019). From stranger to family or something in between: donor linking in an era of retrospective access to anonymous sperm donor records in Victoria, Australia. *International Journal of Law, Policy and the Family, 33*(3), 277–297.

Kelly, F., Dempsey, D., & Frew, C. (2019). The donor-linking practices of Australian fertility clinics. *Journal of Law and Medicine, 27*(2), 355–368.

National Health and Medical Research Council. (2017). Ethical Guidelines on the Use of Assisted Reproductive Technology in Clinical Practice and Research.

Victorian Assisted Reproductive Treatment Authority. (2018/19). Annual Report.

We Are Donor Conceived. (2020). 2020 Survey Report (available at: www.wearedonorconceived.com/2020-survey-top/2020-we-are-donor-conceived-survey/).

CHAPTER 3

Donor-Linked Families Connecting through Social Media
Creeping and Contact on Facebook

Adrienne Byrt and Deborah Dempsey

3.1 Introduction

Curiosity and a desire for medical history often motivate donor-conceived people (DCP) to search for their donor and/or other donor relatives (Bolt et al., 2019; Jadva et al., 2010; Dempsey, Nordqvist and Kelly, 2021; Kelly et al., 2019; Van den Akker et al., 2015). According to Dempsey and Kelly (2017) there are at least three ways in which the Internet greatly facilitates this search. First, it is critical to the marketing and uptake of direct-to-consumer genetic testing, which is commonly used by donor-conceived adults as a means to finding their sperm donor or donor siblings (see Chapter 1). Second, it provides a platform to host donor sibling registers and other communities of support for donor-conceived adults, recipient parents and donors. Thirdly, it facilitates other kinds of information seeking, or 'detective work' whereby adults and young people, armed with partial information (e.g. a name, a donor number or a photograph), can discover publicly available identifying information or locate someone through a search engine such as Google and social media platforms such as Facebook.

Facebook's popularity with young people has waned in recent years with the rise of alternative video- and image-based platforms such as Instagram and TikTok, yet it remains a critical tool in the search for and connection between donor relatives (Newton and Southerton, 2021). It is used by over 16 million Australians, including 10 million aged between 25 and 44 and 4 million over the age of 55, the age groups in our experience most likely to be the instigators or subjects of a search related to donor conception. Facebook is known to be highly searchable, key to which is its foundational convention that those who sign up use their real names and a personal photograph attached to their profile. These photographs along with their friend list and personal profile information (birthdays, work history, relationships status, education) are publicly available by default. If users keep this information public, intentionally or not, fellow users can quite easily use it to identify, locate them and potentially monitor them with or without their knowledge.

In this chapter, we take an in-depth look at how Facebook was used as a search and surveillance tool by the Australian participants in our national study of donor-conceived adults, recipient parents and donors, including their views about acceptable and more controversial uses of the platform. A critical backdrop to our analysis is the 'contact preference' legislation in the State of Victoria, which prohibits donor-conceived adults who discover the identity of their donor from 'making contact' if the donor does not give consent. We argue that the affordances of Facebook and the developing cultures of use by members of the donor-conception communities considerably normalise online surveillance of donor relatives and our research demonstrates just how easy it is to find and watch genetically connected others without knowledge or explicit consent. Furthermore, our research raises questions about how the concept of contact should be understood in the digital age, and whether or not additional legislative safeguards are needed or even possible to protect the privacy of parties who refuse or withdraw contact.

3.2   The Normalisation of Social Surveillance Online

On social media, there is a potential blurring or loss of boundaries between social contexts in a spatial or temporal sense (Duguay, 2016). Facebook and other social media platforms have been much discussed for the capacity they afford to gather information about or observe others without their consent or knowledge. Context collapse is the notion that once disparate groups or individuals in a person's social network (such as parents, employers, lovers) can become (inadvertently or purposefully) merged or revealed to each other (Marwick and Boyd, 2011), and this also applies to strangers.

Facebook privacy settings, which are both fixed by the platform and to some extent controlled by the user, facilitate context collapse. There are some aspects of one's information that will be made public if one chooses to use certain functionalities of the platform, such as cover and feature photographs. Cover photos cannot be made private, nor the six feature photos available to all users. One can make a choice not to upload them, but not to alter the privacy settings once they are uploaded. Profile information such as work history, birthday and year, education and relationship status is public by default, and the user must leave this information out or take additional steps should they wish to keep it private. The list of friends or people who comprise your social network on the platform is also public by default. Adding to this complexity are the varying degrees of knowledge about privacy settings and basic competence in altering the default settings that many users lack. Duffy and Chan (2019) discussed and questioned the perceived effectiveness of privacy settings on social media platforms. People may assume they are unfindable or their behaviour untraceable because they have set their privacy to high, but this is not always the case, and can also be altered without much warning if the platform itself changes its terms of use.

Often, social media users take for granted this capacity to observe others without their knowledge or consent (Gangneux, 2021). Increasingly, it can be seen as a responsible or common-sense way of 'doing homework' or carrying out 'background checks' on people (Standlee, 2019), for instance, those one is thinking of dating, employing or incorporating into friendship circles. Colloquially termed 'facebook stalking', such acts of surveillance have become increasingly normalised (Gangneux, 2021). Gershon (2018) defines 'facebook stalking' as an act that 'entails collecting information about others without indicating online (and especially to the other person) that one is collecting this information' (p. 112). Gershon (2018) also makes the point that to use the term 'stalking' to describe the unseen profile checking undertaken by Facebook users is a misused term. To 'stalk' someone has historically implied the stalker's intention to make the stalked feel watched, whereas the intention of Facebook stalking is guided by the stalker's desire to remain invisible (Gershon, 2018).

Standlee (2019) proposes instead the term 'creeping' and describes it as follows:

> Creeping is a more intense form of background checking that involves silently following an individual on one or more social media outlets without posting or commenting and doing expanded research on the person by following their social media friends and family members online. (2019, p. 778)

People who enact 'creeping' consider it a useful way to determine whether someone is worth pursuing as a potential friend (Standlee, 2019). However, Duguay (2016, p. 900) found that some social media users recognised that 'close examination of profiles does constitute a violation of privacy norms' and is potentially regarded as a controversial practice.

There is little doubt that pathways to finding genetic relatives can be more easily navigated through use of Facebook when fertility clinic records are either missing, partial or non-existent, or in tandem with using official search strategies such as government-funded registers. Participants in our Australian national study used Facebook extensively to unearth information about donor relatives that they could not access via statutory means or clinic records, while they were waiting for information from the statutory authorities or to add to information they had obtained from official sources. In the pages that follow, we document their various practices including their views about acceptable and unacceptable uses of the platform.

3.3   About the Families of Strangers? Study

Data for this chapter were collected through phone and face-to-face semi-structured interviews during 2017–2019 as part of an Australian Research Council funded study exploring the socio-legal implications of donor linking in Australia. We defined 'donor linking' as DCPs, donors or recipient parents having sought or made contact with a donor relative via a statutory body/government-funded register (e.g. the Victorian Assisted Reproductive Treatment Authority (VARTA) in our home state of Victoria), or non-statutory methods (e.g. social media, direct-to-consumer DNA testing site). Linking could include contact sought or made by letter, phone, email or direct messaging, or through an in-person approach. The study research questions were as follows:

1.   How are statutory donor-linking frameworks implemented, who is making applications and what are their motivations for doing so?
2.   How are assisted reproductive technology (ART) professionals engaged in the management and disclosure of identifying and non-identifying information in clinical settings (a form of non-statutory linking)?
3.   How and why do individuals engage in statutory and non-statutory donor linking and how do they perceive its impact on family relationships and identities?

The final participant cohort consisted of 39 DCP, 28 donors and 32 recipient parents from all states and territories of Australia with the exception of the Northern Territory. For the purposes of this chapter, we have focused on the experiences of the DCP and sperm donor participants only.

All DCPs in the study were conceived using donor sperm. Thirty-six DCPs were raised in heterosexual families, while one was raised in a same-sex parented family, one by a single parent, and one was born into a heterosexual family and post-separation was raised in a same-sex parented family. Nineteen DCPs were linked with the donor only, while 14 DCPs were linked with both the donor and some donor-siblings. Two DCPs had attempted to contact their sperm donor via Victoria's statutory authority, VARTA, but were informed that the donor had put a contact preference in place. In the state of Victoria, donors can specify through a legally binding contact preference that they do not want to have contact with their donor offspring, even though they cannot prevent their identity being released (see Kelly and Dempsey, 2016). Three DCPs were in contact with donor-siblings only. One DCP was unable to connect with their donor, as he had died. Sperm donors made up most of the donor participant cohort, totalling 25 male donors. All sperm donors in the study had either been contacted by, or made contact with, some of their donor offspring.

Ethical clearance for the study was obtained through La Trobe and Swinburne Universities. All identifying details including names have been changed to protect the privacy of the participants.

3.4 Results

3.4.1 Obtaining a Name or Number: Sparking the Social Media Search

Our analysis revealed that almost all participants were active on social media platforms, notably Facebook, in the pursuit of information about donor relatives. There was a high degree of consensus that searching on the Internet and social media was always an option, whether to enhance or confirm information discovered from a statutory authority or where there was no official information source to turn to. Many of the DCPs in our study were active in or had made contact with the Facebook group RUDC? after finding out they were donor conceived, and their subsequent social media search activity was often sparked from connections made in that group.

Participants in Victoria would often use a social media search once they had obtained the name or other information about their donor through an application to VARTA. For instance, Chelsea, who had applied for information about her donor under Victorian law, had had a donor-linking counselling session with VARTA. Through this process, she received her donor's donor number, allocated to him by the clinic where he donated. Her application had been made before the laws in Victoria changed to make the donor's name available to all DCPs. A few weeks later, the counsellor at VARTA called with the additional information that she had 11 donor siblings living in her region. Shocked, Chelsea put her information on the voluntary register, a Victorian mutual consent register for donors, donor-conceived people and parents that is managed by VARTA, in the hope that a connection could be made with one of these donor siblings. Nothing happened, so she took an Ancestry DNA test, and found the names of six close matches. Using Facebook, Chelsea looked up one of her matches, and discovered that one match was in the same donor-conception support group.

Bella obtained her donor's name through VARTA and, after making her application to have contact with him, was informed that he had lodged a no-contact preference, which prevented her from having contact. Bella subsequently turned to Facebook. She found her donor's social media presence was 'super private' but was ultimately able to locate him on the platform anyway through the ingenuity of a younger work colleague, a public Facebook group, and the publicly available profiles of his children:

> I had mentioned something about this process at work, and she [colleague] had said, 'Ugh, let's find him. Let's find a picture. He can't disappear from the whole of the Internet.' And I said, 'Well, good luck, because I have not been able to find anything at all.' And then I told her about the sheet of paper [information about the donor supplied by VARTA], and she goes, 'Okay, so we've got some information here. He's Canadian.' And one of the interests was archery. So, she looked up some local archery places on Facebook, and one of them happens to talk about him with his first and last name. And the information all matched, and he looked like me. So yeah, we found him that way. And then through that, we got his children's names, we were able to find their profiles on Facebook, which were more open than his. So, being younger and probably not knowing why they're having to put their profile on private … (Bella, DCP)

In Bella's situation, despite the donor's own high privacy settings, using his name in tandem with the other information in his donor profile had enabled her to find out more about him on social media, and subsequently monitor his children's profiles.

Gabrielle was also in the position of being able to make an application to the VARTA for her donor's identifying information. But before the results of this official search came through, she had already found out his name through a direct-to-consumer (DTC) genetic test. With the assistance of a 'DNA detective' or person skilled at interpreting and using DTC ancestry results to find genetic relatives, Gabrielle was able to locate distant cousins, and learn her genetic father's name through her contact with them and a process of deduction. She turned to Google with that information in hand.

> Gabrielle: ... So I started googling ... with Facebook, I found his kids, I found his wife on LinkedIn ... So, it's amazing how easy it is to find all this out.

Blair, by contrast, discovered her donor's identity through use of a DNA test and social media. After finding out names of several genetic matches on the DNA test site she found a marital familial connection to one of these people that led to the discovery of her donor's identity. She explains the complicated chain of social connections pieced together through use of Facebook:

> I knew who her [DNA site match] daughter was through Facebook, and so I was googling her daughter, and I realised her daughter knew a friend of mine who I am related to through marriage, who's my brother-in-law's brother. And they knew each other because they were both architects. So, I rang my friend, and I said, 'do you know Isobel?' He goes, 'yeah, I know Isobel', and I explained our connection. And so, he rang her and she's really nice and she said, 'well, get Blair to come and meet me,' which I did, and in the meantime, she had asked her mother, Millie, the one who had done the DNA test, 'which of your brothers do you think it is, Blake or Owen?' And immediately she [Millie] went, 'it's got to be Owen ... Blake is way too conservative. He would never have done that.' So, by that point I was like, oh, my god, it's this guy, Owen. (Blair, DCP)

Other participants had discovered their donor's or donor relatives' names inadvertently, due to a failure in clinical record keeping and gained access to private information they were subsequently able to use in a social media search. For instance, Liz discovered her DC status around the age of 10 during an argument between her (subsequently divorced) parents and was given a redacted letter from the fertility clinic by her mother. The letter contained details about the donor's life, including his children's names, and his concealed surname. However, Liz was able to see the surname by holding the letter up to the light. With these identifying details in hand, Liz searched Facebook many years later and found his children.

Facebook searches were not always effective and for other participants it had turned up nothing at all. Monique had tried everything she could think of to find her donor by name on Facebook and other social media platforms but had had to accept he was undiscoverable. Although there

was a view among some of our participants that if you cannot find someone on Facebook you are not looking hard enough, Monique's experience
demonstrates that a social media presence is not universal.

3.4.2   Family Resemblances and Facebook Photos

Some participants reported that striking family resemblances had been
found in photographs posted to Facebook by donor relatives. These could
serve to confirm the identity of the person they were searching for, and
photos could also further motivate their interest in donor relatives. DCPs
and sperm donors alike were struck by the emotional resonance of finding
photographs in which they detected a physical resemblance.

For Paige, a DCP, photos posted to Facebook confirmed her belief in
the information obtained from VARTA. Once she located a Facebook
profile with her donor's name, it was pictures she found that confirmed for
her he was indeed her biological father. She explains:

> I had seen a picture. And it was a very pixelated picture. It wasn't great ...
> I didn't feel it was super striking, but I believed it ... He has a niece on
> his Facebook friends list who I think looks like she could be my sister. We
> look – I showed my parents this picture of his niece and they were – their
> jaws hit the floor. It's just quite incredible ... There's a connection. So,
> I was quite comfortable and confident that that was almost certainly – all
> the dots were lining up, all the connections with all the extended family
> were all lining up that it would make sense that I'd be biologically his
> daughter.

Donors also recalled the power of physical resemblances discovered in
publicly available Facebook photographs. Adam, a donor, had found
photos of his donor-conceived offspring on Facebook after inadvertently
finding out their names through a letter sent to him from the clinic by
mistake. Although Adam had promised the very concerned social worker
who was responsible for the privacy breach that he would not make any
contact with the family, he kept their names and many years later turned
to social media to try and find them 'out of curiosity'. By typing in the
mother's name, Adam was able to find all members of the family. For
Adam, finding their Facebook profiles and discovering a strong physical
resemblance between himself and one of the children further activated his
curiosity. He explained:

> Well, I found them all. I found the parents and the children ... And one of
> them looks just like me. Yes, and I thought, 'Hmm.' And then I was quite
> interested in them after that. I didn't think I would be, but I was.

Once Adam had found his donor offspring on Facebook, the resemblance he discerned between himself and his genetic daughter fuelled an interest in monitoring the family over time. He was able to, in his words, 'watch them', and 'keep track of them' over a number of years during their childhood unbeknown to the children themselves or their parents.

3.4.3   *The Perceived Ethics of Online Surveillance*

Despite the fact that our participants generally felt entitled to use any publicly available social media information to search for and monitor donor relatives, they did have some reservations. They expressed some unease about monitoring others without their consent, along with some commentary about the perceived line between acceptable and unacceptable behaviour. DCPs who monitored donors had some reservations about the effects of this monitoring, and on the other hand, surveillance of DCPs was acknowledged by the donors as quite problematic.

After engaging a 'DNA detective' (as defined earlier, a person skilled at interpreting and using DTC ancestry results to find genetic relatives) to help them build out their family tree on Ancestry DNA, Chelsea and the donor sibling she had found in the online group discovered another connection on Ancestry DNA, this time, a 'first cousin' or 'uncle' match. Although Chelsea had expressed no reservations about connecting with siblings on Facebook, she suggested that looking up this new match 'is probably a little bit invasive, but we did it'. The new match was in fact her biological uncle, and from this connection, she was able to find photos of her biological grandmother, who had a striking resemblance to one of her donor siblings. She and her siblings Facebook messaged the 'first cousin' or 'uncle' and provided him with all the information they had, and he confirmed that his brother had been a sperm donor. Chelsea and her siblings were still waiting to hear from the donor through their VARTA application at the time of the interview. Chelsea's statement that it was 'invasive' to look up this uncle DNA match contrasted with her lack of caution in reaching out to the donor siblings she found. This is potentially because the behaviour seems more acceptable within the same generation, or it could have more to do with the knowledge that her donor siblings were already engaged in their own search and were not guaranteed anonymity in the same way as donors.

Paige revealed some embarrassment and shame about having located her donor on Facebook, and then having worked her way through his publicly available friend list to find out more about his children, all without his knowledge. She recalled: 'This is embarrassing. Facebook stalking him. And fortunately, I've told him all of this now, so I don't feel anxious telling you.' It was apparent in Paige's story that she only felt comfortable discussing her social media behaviour with the research team because she had told her donor about it. It was as if she believed this information could undermine trust or damage their relationship in some way, had the donor found out from another source about the extent of her 'Facebook stalking'.

Adam, on the other hand, who at the time of the interview had had several meetings with his donor offspring and their parents, has never told them that he had their names and monitored them on Facebook over a number of years prior to meeting. Adam recalled that his wife advised him, '… "nothing good will come from it, so just leave it," so I did'. In the context of Adam's story, it was not entirely clear whether his wife's comment applied to his disclosure of the social worker's mistake in releasing the names or of the monitoring, or both, but there was a sense in his story that it was better for all parties' future relationships if he kept this to himself. It was clear that Adam's wife believed disclosure of the information would only cause harm, and in his case, the clinic would also have been implicated in a privacy breach.

3.4.4   *From Observation to Contact: Messaging, Friending and 'Likes' on Facebook*

Observing donor relatives online is not the same as contacting them, and in general there were far more reservations expressed about taking this next step. Making contact with donor siblings who were already engaged in their own search also appeared more straightforward for our participants than the prospect of a DCP making contact through social media with a donor, or the other way around.

It was apparent that finding donor relatives on Facebook sometimes led to almost immediate contact, as in Chelsea's story of finding a donor sibling through the online DCP support group. Chelsea, who we met earlier in the chapter, had immediately sent a Facebook message to the woman she suspected was her donor sibling, and once they confirmed they were donor siblings, comparing their shared donor number, they began communicating. Chelsea subsequently linked with four other siblings through this initial connection. Together, they formed a group chat and strong friendships. Though it is not supported by law, connecting with siblings through a process of DNA testing and Facebook linking was perceived to be acceptable by all siblings involved.

Among DCPs, it was much more controversial to 'friend' or in any other way contact the donor you were monitoring in order to make your presence felt. Liz was one participant who did take the step of contacting her donor online after locating him on social media. Many years after discovering his name by accident, Liz searched Facebook and found his children. And at that point, she also discovered through close inspection of their friend lists that she had mutual friends with some of the donor's children:

> And so there was one [mutual friend] that I had seen the week before. I went to her birthday party. And I thought, 'Oh my goodness, it's just meant to be.' … So, then I messaged that girl and I said, 'Oh, I can see that you're friends with so-and-so on Facebook. My dad was actually friends with her dad,' and I made up a big lie. And 'so can you give me his email address?' So, she did, and so I got his email address. (Liz, DCP)

For Liz, the discovery of the connection felt fated and she was motivated to contact her donor via email:

> And then I emailed him, and I basically told him who I was. And he said to me – I don't even remember what the initial email was, but it was a very kind email. He just said, 'Yes, it does sound like this could possibly be the case. But if you want to contact me you have to go through [VARTA]'. And so, I think at that time my pride took a little bit of a hit, because I was like, 'Oh, now I've made contact and now I've embarrassed myself.' So, I didn't contact him for a couple of years. (Liz)

Liz's story shows that with identifying information, donor relatives can be found, and in her case, were contacted impulsively. It appears that the discovery of mutual friends had had a disinhibiting effect. The existence of the mutual acquaintance was common ground that had made her less fearful that her approach would be rebuffed.

Gabrielle, by contrast, hesitated about contacting her donor despite the extensive dossier of information she had been able to put together about him through social media. Instead, she chose to wait for the results of her search through VARTA. She commented:

> I thought it's a bit weird me knowing this much, so I waited … him not knowing that I know exactly who he is and where he lives and where his parents lived and when they died.

Gabrielle's comments revealed a sense in which it was unseemly or inappropriate to know so much about a person without their consent or knowledge, even if this information was publicly available. The potential for creeping to undermine trust or damage any relationship she might form in the future with the donor was implicit in her sense of discomfort.

Adam, the donor we met earlier in the chapter who had monitored his recipient family on Facebook over time, made it clear it would have been inappropriate to go further and friend them or in any way make his presence felt. He understood that either behaviour would be a breach of an ethical boundary.

INTERVIEWER: So you didn't try and friend them or anything? You just –?
ADAM: Oh God, no. God, no.

In the above quote, Adam is appalled at the thought of reaching out on social media to the recipient family, and clearly sees it as not his place to do so. In Adam's case, the taboo in making contact with the recipient family appeared linked to the fact that he had obtained information he was not entitled to (albeit through no fault of his own) and used it. Also, it potentially took on a more sinister tone due to the fact that he was an adult and the people he was observing were children.

3.4.5   *The Uses and Abuses of 'Likes'*

Liking a person's page, posts or photographs is another way to move from the role of undetected observer to someone whose presence is felt. Use of the 'like' function on Facebook emerged as another way in which those monitoring donor relatives could reveal their presence, sometimes intentionally and sometimes inadvertently.

Patricia's story revealed that where there is monitoring, there is always the risk of revealing oneself unintentionally. Patricia's father informed her that she was donor conceived at 23, when she needed to access medical information to determine if there was a genetic cause of some health issues affecting her children. Patricia 'hassled' the clinic where she was conceived for over a year for medical information about her donor, but in the meantime, she also did an Ancestry DNA test. With the help of another DC person, Patricia tracked down her donor's name through Ancestry research. From there, Patricia turned to Facebook, and found his daughter's public profile. Patricia described how she had made herself known to this daughter after inadvertently liking her Facebook page:

> When you're Facebook stalking somebody ... I accidentally liked her page and, of course, at that point he'd provided his kids with my name as well, so she knew, 'This person is my [biological] sister and she's liking my page'. So, then she sent me a message and said, 'I just noticed that you've liked my ... page, you're my sister and dad is going to be in contact with you soon'. And then, I don't know, the next day I think, he sent me a message and it basically went from there. (Patricia, DCP)

For Patricia, the accidental 'liking' of her genetic sibling's page turned out quite well. It seems that the openness in her donor's family and their knowledge of her existence fostered an openness to her making contact at some point in their lives. Unlike Liz, Patricia did not have the experience of her approach being rebuffed as inappropriate.

In cases where families have kept donor conception secret, and the revelation of identifying information is problematic, unsolicited social media contact from donor relatives can be jarring. Aidan's parents had not told him he was conceived with donor sperm. Unexpectedly, he was contacted by VARTA and informed that his donor wanted to link with him. Although he gave consent to the donor knowing his identity, the experience was deeply distressing for him and his parents, and was exacerbated by his donor's behaviour on social media. Soon after Aidan's donor learned of his identity, Aidan was perturbed to find his donor had liked several of his publicly available feature and profile photos on Facebook. Aidan reacted strongly to the donor's unsolicited contact with him on Facebook, which felt very intrusive:

> It was very, it was very awkward because the first thing he did when he got my name was he went on my Facebook and liked all my photos. And then there was a spelling mistake and then he commented on the spelling mistake. And I was, 'Who is this arsehole'?

The donor's entitlement to make his presence known was keenly felt by Aidan, and the actions of the donor, elucidate how Facebook enables a degree of unanticipated visibility. Although Aidan had his privacy settings on high, the design of Facebook's systems made some aspects of his profile visible to his donor, who had no qualms about making his presence felt.

3.4.6   *Creeping in the Absence of Contact*

There are often strong beliefs that as much knowledge as possible about donor relatives is a good thing, and that having this is supportive of the mental health of the donor conceived. However, there was some evidence in our study that prolonged creeping on Facebook could be emotionally detrimental for DCPs who subsequently found out there was no chance of in-person contact. In effect, Facebook creeping enables the creeper to develop a one-sided connection to the person or people of interest, which can be devastating if it is not reciprocated or where in-person contact is ultimately denied.

Gabrielle, who we met earlier in the chapter, had been monitoring her donor and other members of his family online while she waited for her application to VARTA to be processed. Unfortunately for Gabrielle, when her donor was informed of her application, he filed a contact preference in response and refused to have any contact whatsoever. The donor's refusal caused her immense, yet unexpected, emotional distress:

> My expectations weren't that high. I knew this could happen and I didn't really care because, you know, usual quotes, I guess. I'm not looking for a dad; I've already got my dad, and I'm not looking for money, I'm not looking for anything, I'm just curious. So, I thought I was pretty relaxed about it and then it hit me like a tonne of bricks and I just couldn't stop crying. Like, I was a mess. (Gabrielle, DCP)

Gabrielle has continued to respect the limitations of the contact veto her donor put in place. However, through her Facebook investigations, Gabrielle had already discovered they lived nearby and could have easily crossed paths throughout her life. Once it became apparent that the donor did not want to meet her, she began to dwell on the extensive profile of him that she had developed through her creeping activities on Facebook, which became her only means of constructing a narrative about his life and relationships:

> ... his kids all live interstate or overseas and so even I can tell – on their Facebook page, I've seen some of their pictures, and he's not in a single picture but their mum is, and I'm like he must have just a broken relationship with a lot of people. Like, he just mustn't bond with people. And he was an only child, and you start sort of reading into it. (Gabrielle, DCP)

Based on the evidence of his children's Facebook photographs, Gabrielle has developed the narrative that her donor is someone who does not enjoy close relationships with his children. Perhaps this narrative might have eased the distress she felt due to his rejection. However, her story equally raises the prospect that Facebook creeping has intensified her feelings of loss because the gathering of this information was akin to the first step in forming a relationship. When that relationship is subsequently denied, the distress and anger is potentially more acute than if it were denied by someone about whom you had no knowledge.

3.5   Concluding Thoughts

Australian policy and law surrounding donor conception is informed by a strong discourse that the donor conceived have a right to know their biogenetic origins. Following on from this, our research has demonstrated there is a strong sense of entitlement among DCPs to find donors and donor siblings online and observe them, often for long periods of time without their knowledge or consent. These attitudes are no doubt shaped more broadly by more laissez-faire notions of privacy on social media where 'doing homework', 'creeping', and 'Facebook stalking' are now more or less acceptable ways to find out more about relative strangers (Gangneux, 2021; Gershon, 2018; Standlee, 2019). With or without the assistance of the law, and in the era of DTC genetic testing, it is indeed difficult for anyone to disappear from the whole of the Internet, as one of our participants so aptly pointed out.

Information seeking on Facebook exploits the flexible boundary between public and private and reveals that control over one's own information is only as good as that of the privacy settings of friends, and one's knowledge of complex Facebook settings (see also Duffy and Chan, 2019). Photographs, friend lists and donors' family members' profiles were particularly illuminating and a usually freely available source of information. Although most of our participants were looking for a sperm donor when they took to social media, it was through their donor's children's social media pages that a lot of information was gleaned. This highlights the gap between younger adults and older adults' notions of privacy and how this plays out on social media sites. It may not occur to gamete donors that they can be monitored through the social media profiles of their family members and friends, emphasising just how fraught and contested privacy can be in the social media age.

In this chapter, we showed that people think carefully about the potentially negative consequences of making themselves known, and often choose to wait for an intermediary in the form of VARTA or confine themselves to observation. We note fewer reservations about making contact with siblings, as opposed to making contact with donors, or donors making contact with DCPs online. Potentially, this tells us something about the strong desire for, and entitlement to make contact with, genetic relatives of the same generation. For donor siblings who are active social media users, particularly in donor-conceived groups, searching and contact appeared to be desired despite the absence of entitlement in Australian legislation to have access to information about donor siblings. Elsewhere in our interviews with DCPs, there was a great deal of awareness about the possibility that donor siblings had not been told they were donor conceived, and it is apparent that there are emerging protocols and processes for making contact with a sibling online that are widely shared within donor-conception support groups.

We were struck by the number of mutual friends and shared social networks revealed by our participants. This adds weight to the argument that people are entitled to know the identity of their genetic relatives precisely because there is a good chance they may come across them in their daily lives. Close encounters and connections with genetic relatives in neighbourhoods, schools, and social networks were discovered through monitoring Facebook profiles. Similarly, neighbourly proximity and school connections were also discovered. This is concrete evidence of the strong possibility of inadvertently meeting a donor relative. The discovery of shared social networks could also make participants more courageous when reaching out to a donor relative, but this certainly warrants more investigation.

'Creeping' on donor relatives appeared to be normalised for DCPs, and this 'expanded research' confirmed the identity of donor relatives when statutory entitlements failed to provide the information DCPs wanted to know about their donor relatives (Standlee, 2019, p. 778). However, it was apparent that the knowledge gleaned from creeping did not always bring with it good emotional outcomes for donor-conceived adults. It could take on a very distressing cast for the creeper when contact with the donor is ultimately denied. Potentially it heightened feelings of loss and rejection when a much-desired relationship could not be achieved.

Finally, our research has raised some interesting questions about what constitutes contact in the age of social media and how legislation can or should protect donor relatives who do not desire any contact with each other. Does a Facebook 'like' on a donor's daughter's business profile constitute contact, for instance? Would our participant Liz be in breach of a contact preference had her donor taken one out? While DCPs can also lodge contact preferences to restrict contact from a donor, the Act does not define what constitutes contact. For example, a contact preference might include such requests as 'do not contact me via social media', so if a donor relative was found to be 'creeping', it could be a breach of the contact preference. However, given the normalisation of social surveillance on social media platforms (Duffy and Chan, 2019; Duguay, 2016; Gangneux, 2021; Gershon, 2018; Standlee, 2019), how this would be enforced remains unanswered. The lack of a definition of contact in the legislation is an interesting oversight, given the subtle ways in which one can make one's presence felt on social media. Our participants themselves were all too aware of the potential for the behaviours they were engaged in to incite discomfort or unease, or to breach trust, should they become known. For donor-linked families, navigating the virtual boundary between creeping and contact becomes a complex negotiation between curiosity and the 'right to know' one's genetic relatives in the digital age.

References

Bolt, S., Postema, D., van der Heij, A., & Maas, A. J. B. (2019). *Anonymous Dutch Sperm Donors Releasing Their Identity.* Human Fertility.

Costa, E. (2018). Affordances-in-practice: An ethnographic critique of social media logic and context collapse. *New Media & Society, 20*(10), 3641–3656. https://doi.org/10.1177/1461444818756290

Dempsey, D., & Kelly, F. (2017). Transnational third-party assisted conception: pursuing the desire for 'origins' information in the internet era. In M. Davies (ed.) *Babies for Sale? Transnational Surrogacy, Human Rights and the Politics of Reproduction,* 204–217. https://doi.org/10.5040/9781350218567.ch-011

Dempsey, D., Nordqvist, P., & Kelly, F. (2021). Beyond secrecy and openness: Telling a relational story about children's best interests in donor-conceived families. *BioSocieties,* 17(3). https://doi.org/10.1057/s41292-021-00225-9

Duffy, B. E., & Chan, N. K. (2019). 'You never really know who's looking': Imagined surveillance across social media platforms. *New Media & Society, 21*(1), 119–138. https://doi.org/10.1177/1461444818791318

Duguay, S. (2016). 'He has a way gayer Facebook than I do': Investigating sexual identity disclosure and context collapse on a social networking site. *New Media & Society, 18*(6), 891–907. https://doi.org/10.1177/1461444814549930

Gangneux, J. (2021). 'It is an attitude': The normalisation of social screening via profile checking on social media. *Information, Communication & Society, 24*(7), 994–1008. https://doi.org/10.1080/1369118X.2019.1668460

Gershon, I. (2018). Every click you make, I'll be watching you: Facebook stalking and neoliberal information. In *A Networked Self and Birth, Life, Death,* edited by Zizi Papacharissi (pp. 104–120). Routledge.

Jadva, V., Freeman, T., Kramer, W., & Golombok, S. (2010). Experiences of offspring searching for and contacting their donor siblings and donor. *Reproductive Biomedicine Online, 20*(4), 523–532. https://doi.org/10.1016/j.rbmo.2010.01.001

Kelly, F., & Dempsey, D. (2016). The family law implications of early contact between sperm donors and their donor offspring. *Family Matters,* 98, 54–63.

Kelly, F., Dempsey, D., Power, J., Bourne, K., Hammarberg, K., & Johnson, L. (2019). From stranger to family or something in between: Donor linking in an era of retrospective access to anonymous sperm donor records in Victoria, Australia. *International Journal of Law, Policy and the Family, 33*(3), 277–297. https://doi.org/10.1093/lawfam/ebz011

Marwick, A. E., & Boyd, D. (2011). I tweet honestly, I tweet passionately: Twitter users, context collapse, and the imagined audience. *New Media & Society, 13*(1), 114–133.' https://doi.org/10.1177/1461444810365313

Newton, G., & Southerton, C. (2021). Situated talk: A method for a reflexive encounter with# donorconceived on TikTok. *Media International Australia, 186*(1), 66–80.

Standlee, A. (2019). Friendship and online filtering: The use of social media to construct offline social networks. *New Media & Society, 21*(3), 770–785. https://doi.org/10.1177/1461444818806844

Van den Akker, O. B. A., Crawshaw, M. A., Blyth, E. D., & Frith, L. J. (2015). Expectations and experiences of gamete donors and donor-conceived adults searching for genetic relatives using DNA linking through a voluntary register. *Human Reproduction, 30*(1), 111–121. https://doi.org/10.1093/humrep/deu289

CHAPTER 4

The Contact Expectations of Australian Sperm Donors Who Connect with Recipients via Online Platforms

Cal Volks and Fiona Kelly

4.1 Introduction

While it is difficult to know exactly how common the practice of Australian women meeting their sperm donor online is, the growth in online groups connecting sperm donors and women looking to get pregnant suggest that the phenomenon is increasing (Cook & Tomazin, 2021). One reason cited for growth in the practice is that it gives donors the opportunity to develop a relationship with their donor offspring when the children are young. If a donor donates through the formal fertility sector, "early contact" (contact before the age of 18) is not always possible. In Victoria, where early contact between clinic donors and recipient parents (RPs) can be applied for, facilitated through the donor-linking service of the Victorian Assisted Reproduction Treatment Authority (VARTA) applications for early contact between donors and RPs have increased in recent years (VARTA Annual Report, 2018, 2020). RPs and donors are also increasingly making early contact through informal mechanisms such as social media, online registries and forums (Kelly & Dempsey 2016, p. 57).

While there are a handful of survey-based studies exploring the motives of sperm donors who connect with RPs online in Holland and the UK (Graham et al., 2019; Whyte, 2019; Freeman et al., 2016; Woestenburg et al., 2016), very little is known about the post-birth relationships that develop between these donors and their RPs and/or the donor-conceived children (DCC) (Bergen & Delacroix, 2019; Lavoie et al., 2017). Given the growing utilisation of online mechanisms to find a sperm donor and the significance placed on early contact, it is important to understand what occurs in practice. Drawing on qualitative interviews with sperm donors, as well as relevant media coverage of the phenomenon, this chapter considers the experience of donors who meet their RPs online and who have had early contact. It explores why donors choose to donate outside of the formal clinic environment, their expectations from early contact, whether these expectations evolve over time and how these eventuate. It concludes by considering the implications of the trend towards informal donation in a country where formal donation is legally regulated.

4.2   The Mainstreaming of Informal Donation

Known sperm donors have long been part of the fabric of informal donor conception in Australia, particularly within the lesbian and gay communities (McNair & Dempsey, 2002; Dempsey, 2010, 2012a, 2012b; Power et al., 2012). Dempsey (2010, 2012a, 2012b) investigated kinship relationships with gay men who were known "sperm providers" for lesbian women in Victoria. These men conceptualised their role in a variety of ways, from sperm donor, to gay men expressing acts of socio-political solidarity with lesbian women, to co-parent (Dempsey, 2010, p. 1146). Some negotiated their intended role prior to donating, while others allowed relationships to evolve (Dempsey, 2012b, p. 158). The intended involvement in the day-to-day care of the children also varied, with some wanting an active role in the children's upbringing whereas others only wanted to be available for contact with donor offspring. Despite being known to one another prior to the donation, relationships changed over time, and it was noted that post-donation the "parties involved may have very incompatible expectations of these relationships, and that the lived reality of these relationships may deviate from relationships planned before children are born" (Dempsey, 2012a, p. 170). However, the vast majority of relationships appear to have been successfully negotiated, with only a small number of disputes reaching the courts.

As many contemporary social and commercial interactions move to online spaces, it is not surprising that online platforms that directly link sperm donors and recipients have emerged. Consequently, there has been an increase in the number of women conceiving using the sperm of donors previously unknown to them whom they connected with via online platforms (Whyte et al., 2017). The UK-based Human Fertilisation and Embryology Authority, which first noted the phenomenon in 2012, defined online sperm donors as "men seeking to become sperm donors via connection websites … rather than through the regulated routes of fertility clinics and sperm banks" (Whyte, 2019). Recent surveys of global connection-websites that link sperm donors and potential recipients, such as Free Sperm Donors Worldwide and PrideAngel, report membership growth and activity that suggests increased utilisation of online sperm donation.[1] Anecdotal evidence suggests that the use of online platforms for the purpose of donating sperm has also increased in Australia. In 2021, the founder of Sperm Donation Australia (SDA) – Australia's largest Facebook group linking sperm donors and potential recipients – noted that the group had 10,000 members, with 4000 new membership applications in 2020 (Sams, 2021).

Online platforms act like introductory websites (similar to dating sites) that bring parties together. Like dating websites, what transpires face to face after the "introduction" is determined by the parties involved. Some move swiftly to a transaction (the provision of sperm), while others undertake a more gradual pre-donation negotiation phase. While these donors are previously unknown to their recipients, some become "known" through the pre-donation negotiation phase. Further, some men donate to a small number of recipients, while others become prolific donors.[2]

A growing number of women, particularly single mothers by choice (SMC) and lesbian women, who need sperm but not always medical assistance to conceive, choose to use the sperm of donors that they meet online to circumvent the cost, bureaucracy and medicalisation associated with the formal fertility sector (Lever, 2020a). In Australia, where the demand for donor sperm at fertility clinics is often greater than supply, online donors represent increased choice and reduced delay for RPs (Lever, 2020a). As discussed earlier, online donation has similarities with the past practice of known sperm donation in the gay and lesbian communities in Australia, most notably as parties negotiate the provision of sperm and home insemination outside the formal fertility sector. However, some significant differences have emerged. First, the majority of online donors are heterosexual men, many of whom state on their profiles that they prefer to provide sperm via "natural insemination" (i.e., sexual intercourse). These men appear to have quite different motivations than gay sperm donors of the past. Second, because lesbian couples tended to choose gay male friends or acquaintances as donors, a relationship typically existed prior to conception and they were likely to move in similar circles after conception.

---

[1] Free Sperm Donors Worldwide and PrideAngel have more than 2000 and 7000 men registered on these connection websites respectively (Freeman et al., 2016; Whyte et al., 2017). Online donors surveyed were donating regularly (mean number of monthly donations 4.84); to numerous women (mean number of women donated to 15.24); for a medium term (mean duration of donating was 3.19 years); and achieving a mean number of offspring of 6.39 children per donor (Whyte et al., 2017).

[2] Prolific donor denotes a donor who has exceeded the legal limit of donor-conceived children/families in Australia.

There was therefore a social contract of sorts at play, as well as community expectations. By contrast, the new online donor is typically unknown to the recipient and is not likely to move in the same social circles, reducing any sense of obligation between the parties beyond the provision of sperm. Finally, the modern known sperm donor donates to many recipients. He is more likely to be a prolific donor, producing many children across multiple households and with no obligation to inform recipients of the outcomes of donations. By contrast, known donors to lesbian couples usually only donated to a single couple.

Sperm donors in the formal sector have reported varied motivations to donate that included altruism, a desire for procreation/genetic fatherhood, and as a proxy for assessment of their virility (Van den Broek et al., 2012; Cook & Golombok, 1995; Daniels et al., 1996a, 1996b; Riggs & Russell, 2011; Bossema, 2014; Graham et al., 2019). Prior research with known sperm donors in Australia noted the potential for a mismatch in expectations between donors and RPs regarding the roles and responsibilities of donors with regards their DCC and around post-donation contact if not fully discussed and revisited (Dempsey, 2010, 2012a, 2012b).

In contrast, research with online sperm donors suggests that these men choose this platform because it affords them greater agency in negotiating the relationship with their RPs and early contact with the DCC (Bergen & Delacroix, 2019). This is particularly important for donors who perceive themselves as a "father" and want early contact with the DCC. Early contact is generally not possible if they donate via a clinic, where exchange of identifying information is usually limited to the age of majority. As contact between donors and their donor offspring becomes more common and, provided there are few publicised cases of contact going badly, we can anticipate that informal sperm donation will continue to proliferate (Bergen & Delacroix, 2019).

In Australia, only the state of Victoria permits RPs to apply for information about clinic donors and contact with a donor while their child is still a minor. Elsewhere in Australia, early contact can only be achieved via a request to the clinic where treatment occurred. However, fertility clinics are not obliged to provide linking services and only a small number do (Kelly et al., 2019).

While there are risks involved in any fertility treatment – medicalised conception carries health risks associated with the treatment, high levels of intervention due to the propensity to use IVF in Australia (Power et al., 2020), and even clinic-based services may not produce a pregnancy – informal donation poses a new set of risks. Because these transactions occur outside of the formal fertility sector, they are unregulated. Some protections provided by legislation, such as restricting the number of donor offspring or donor families per donor, may be breached. Regulations vary between Australian states but the number of donor-conceived families is limited to either 5 or 10 recipient families per donor. While the laws still apply there is no way to monitor or regulate informal practice. Some informal donors exceed the recommended family limits, a practice which donor-conceived adults are very critical of (Lever, 2020b; Cook & Tomazin, 2021). Informal donation also has the potential to create family law disputes, particularly if there is a mismatch relating to the donor's rights and responsibilities. The legal risk is greatest in the context of sperm donors who have sex with the recipient because the donor is a legal father with all of the rights and responsibilities that flow from that status, including child support liability. In instances where donor insemination is used but there is conflict about the role the donor will play, a known donor has standing to apply for a parenting order if he can demonstrate he is an individual "concerned with the care, welfare and development of a child". Family law does not directly address known donor arrangements, leaving donors and recipients with little guidance about how to negotiate conflict.

Finally, informal donation poses health and safety risks to women. As the phenomenon increases, so too do reports of bad actors coming into the public domain, including reports of assault at the time of the transaction (transfer of sperm to recipient), harassment and fraud (Cook & Tomazin, 2021; Kamenev, 2019). Donors may also falsify test results for sexually transmitted infections and other health issues. While clinic donors may also lie about medical history, clinic testing reduces the risk of false information being provided. Thus, while informal donation has the potential to provide opportunities for donor-conceived children to know their donor, it can also pose legal and health risks for women and children.

4.3 Qualitative Research with Online Sperm Donors

This chapter reports on qualitative interviews with five Australian sperm donors who used informal methods (online platforms, applications or advertisements) to connect with previously unknown recipients. Study participants were required to have had early contact (before the age of 18) with the RPs and their DCC. Purposive sampling was used to recruit donors (Patton, 1990, pp. 169–86). Searches were conducted to identify online sperm donor groups. The online platforms identified were all closed, thus moderators were contacted and asked to post a study recruitment advertisement. Recruitment posts were placed on Sperm Donation Australia (SDA),[3] Pride Angel[4] and Rainbow Families.[5] Study participants were required to have donated in Australia.

Six donors agreed to be interviewed. Four donated only informally, while two donated to recipients met online and via a fertility clinic. One participant who donated online and via a clinic, requested that the part of his interview relating to online donation be redacted, thus his interview has been excluded from this analysis. At the time of interview, participants age ranged from 40 to 51 years (mean age 47.8 years). Four donors were single, and one was married. Three identified as heterosexual, one as gay and one as bisexual. Three were located in Victoria, one in the ACT and one in NSW. All of the donors worked in professional industries and several had postgraduate qualifications.

The interviews were semi-structured and covered three main topics: motivation to be an online donor; experiences of early contact; and perceptions of genetic connectedness. Interviews were conducted in 2020 by phone, recorded, transcribed and anonymised. Pseudonyms were assigned to each of the interview participants. The transcripts were analysed using thematic analysis (Braun & Clarke, 2006).

Given the small sample size, other first-person accounts of online sperm donation within the public domain were reviewed. Four interviews with online sperm donors from the podcast Sperm Donation World (SDW)[6] were analysed. In addition, print, television and digital interviews with a further five Australian online sperm donors were included (Lever, 2020a, 2020b, 2020c; Glover, 2018; Sixty Minutes Australia, 2019). These five donors were not the same as those interviewed on SDW. In the case of donor stories taken from the media, donors are identified by the name used in the original source.

Study limitations include potential sampling biases and small sample size. Participants self-selected to participate in the study and may have done so because they had a particularly negative or positive experience, which may not reflect the experience of all online donors. The small sample size is indicative of the difficulty of recruiting male participants and

---

[3] Sperm Donation Australia (SDA) is a closed Facebook group that links Australian sperm donors with potential recipients.

[4] Pride Angel is a UK-based website with international membership, that assists gay, lesbian, bisexual, trans, queer, intersex persons to form families.

[5] Rainbow Families is an Australian website to assist gay, lesbian, bisexual, trans, queer, intersex persons to form families.

[6] Sperm Donation World (SDW) is a podcast hosted by Adam Hooper the owner/administrator of the Facebook group, Sperm Donation Australia (SDA).

particularly online sperm donors to participate in qualitative research. The challenges of recruiting online sperm donors for qualitative interviews have been identified elsewhere. For example, Bergen and Delacroix (2019) reported findings from a sample of six, while Lavoie et al. (2017) reported on a study of eight online sperm donors. Both teams indicated that they struggled to recruit donors. While some researchers have suggested it may be preferable to have a male interviewer when researching sperm donors (Mohr, 2014), even male researchers have reported difficulty recruiting (Lavoie et al., 2017). Online sperm donors may be reluctant to participate in research due to the perception that researchers are critical of their practice (Lavoie et al., 2017). In the Australian context, some may not want to be interviewed because they know they are flouting Australia's donation laws and are concerned about potential repercussions. This is a justifiable concern given that an online donor who participated in a media interview has been the subject of an investigation by VARTA for allegedly breaching the Victorian offspring limit (Lever, 2020c).

4.3.1   Why Do Donors Choose Informal Online Donation?

Prior research has found that sperm donors choose to donate online for a variety of reasons. Some are motivated by the opportunity to select recipients and have contact with them, often continuing post-conception. Ongoing early contact has been framed as being in the best interests of the children (Hooper, 2018, 2019). Adam Hooper, the founder of the online Facebook group SDA and host of the SDA podcast, suggests that online donation provides donors with a degree of agency that is absent in the clinic context and cites this as a reason why many choose to donate through SDA (Hooper, 2018). Online platforms facilitate contact between donors and recipients, with the ideal that only those "with a similar mindset" will proceed. Prior to proceeding, parties can negotiate the terms of the donation, including the nature and extent of contact. Hooper contrasts this opportunity with what he describes as "a relinquishment of control" when donating via fertility clinics. According to Hooper, donors in the formal fertility sector relinquish the opportunity to influence what happens to their genetic material. "You're giving a part of your DNA to someone, you don't want a child of your own making to come to you at 18 and say, 'I had a shitty childhood. Why did you donate to someone you didn't know?'" (Sams, 2021).

Mayger, an online donor interviewed for the SDW podcast, also emphasised the importance of early contact and being able to influence his donor offspring's development. For Mayger, contact that occurs through the formal sector from the age of majority is too late; "by that stage the child has fully formed their personality, and they have been wondering for 18 years what their donor is like, where the other part of them came from" (Hooper, 2019). Because clinic donors rarely have early contact with their donor offspring, the potential to develop a close and influential connection is lost. Mayger positioned his preference for online donation as being in the best interests of DCC. It was his view that "children deserve to know where they come from … the welfare of the child demands that you meet the sperm donor online, and you donate as a known donor" (Hooper, 2019).

Both Mayger and Hooper frame online donation as preferable because it allows for early contact. This is congruent with advocacy by donor-conceived adults in Australia, who have argued for known donation so that children can grow up knowing their biological origins. This framing of the debate centres the child's genetic relationships, particularly the sperm donor becoming known to the DCC.

4.4 Expectations and Experiences of Contact

The donors interviewed for the study all reported choosing to donate online because it provided them the opportunity to meet their RPs prior to donation and to discuss the anticipated role that they would play post-donation. Pre-donation negotiations did not always result in mutually understood expectations. For some donors their expectations and lived experience were aligned, while others experienced a mismatch. Some described the process from first meeting RPs to donation as progressing too swiftly to fully explore their post-donation role. For other donors on learning that the recipient was pregnant and/or meeting the child, the role that they had conceptualised pre-donation changed and became mismatched with that of the RPs. Some reported positive outcomes, while others experienced disappointment when relationships broke down or they were unable to attain the type of contact that they had anticipated.

4.4.1   Where Expectations Aligned

In some cases, the parties' expectations around roles and responsibilities of the donors, including early contact, were aligned and plans unfolded as anticipated. Pete – who was interviewed for the study – and his recipients achieved an agreement prior to conception that satisfied all parties. While

Pete was previously unknown to the recipients, during the negotiation phase he developed a relationship with his RPs. After agreeing to donate, Pete realised that he wanted to "co-parent". He was initially concerned that his recipients would not agree but he was able to negotiate a role as co-parent. As he explained:

> When we sat down and worked out the plans and worked out how it would be in terms of time and the amount of involvement and influence I'd have in raising the kids, then it became clear that if it worked out ... it would be an ideal situation for somebody like me who really would love to have kids but didn't actually have the ability to have kids with a partner. (Pete, 2020)

Pete's desire to be a father aligned with the RPs' expectations about co-parenting and those remained consistent after the children were born. As Pete noted, "[We] were looking at what's the ideal ... situation for [the children] [which] would be somebody, not a donor but somebody who could be a father as well ... Both women ... wanted their children to have a father figure ... They both really respected the idea of having a father." Pete's current role, in practical terms, involves caring for and co-parenting the children at his own house for half the week (with the children residing with the RPs for the balance of the week). This gives form to how both the parties conceptualised the role of a father.

Pete and his RPs developed a relationship that he felt could withstand the complexities of co-parenting. As he explained, "Basically our focus is the kids, on how to make these kids' lives better". This was further supported by their parenting style, which included trying not to undermine each other. The co-parents had a "tacit agreement that we would never criticise each other in front of the kids ... [and if we had] any problem, we would raise it straight away".

Pete's story is an example of where a carefully negotiated agreement can result in a previously unknown donor becoming "known" and ultimately achieving a co-parenting arrangement. Informal donation, which enabled Pete to inhabit a parenting role from the outset, allowed a single gay man to co-parent with a lesbian couple. This co-parenting arrangement is similar to known sperm donation previously described between gay and lesbians in Australia (Dempsey, 2010, 2012a, 2012b). Such an arrangement would not have been possible through the formal fertility sector.

Craig, who was also interviewed, conceptualised himself as a donor, who wanted to have early contact with his DCC and elected to be an online donor for this reason. He was inspired by the type of extended family network that exists for some egg donor recipients in Australia and wanted to re-create this opportunity for his daughter. At the time of his interview, he had not achieved the level of contact that he anticipated but attributed this to the age of the children and the lack of geographic proximity to the recipient families.

4.4.2   Negotiations and Renegotiations

In some cases, initial agreements around early contact and the donor's role in the child's life changed, evolved or needed to be renegotiated. Thus, while informal donation gave donors agency that was not available in the formal fertility sector, the absence of structure or rules meant that the relationships were constantly in flux. Expectations changed at key moments of the process, such as conception or birth, or when the child matured and became capable of independent interaction. Parties sometimes found themselves feeling differently than they had anticipated, so that their emotional response to the child no longer aligned with their original intentions. At these critical junctures, the donors could make new demands for time with the child. In some instances, the relationship between the parties deteriorated. Thus, despite the rhetoric around informal donation offering donors the opportunity to make a meaningful contribution to their children's lives, some interview participants experienced high levels of conflict. Ultimately, some lost contact with their donor offspring.

Ben – who was interviewed for the study – demonstrates how a failure to communicate expectations early in the process can result in differing views on the role each party will play. Ben was a single, heterosexual man without children of his own. He donated to a lesbian couple, whom he met online. Ben assumed that his recipients would be open to him having a significant role in the child's life, in part based on his interpretation of their advertisement. He said, "the couple, had a long profile ... that [emphasised] the importance of bringing the baby up in a 'healthy' environment. They seemed quite progressive in a way ... I was hoping for a broader community style kind of [parenting] ... [that] they wouldn't object in time to my engagement with the child." However, Ben failed to articulate his desire for significant contact prior to conception and the parties made no formal agreement. As he explained, "There was just a kind of chat about how we'd like to see things go. There was no real detail, other than if the child wants to know me [it can]."

Ben's recipients conceived with their first attempt, which was quicker than he had anticipated: "I thought we would have had a lot more time to get to know each other. But it happened ... really quickly". As soon as he learnt that the RP was pregnant, Ben became emotionally invested in the pregnancy and his self-identity shifted from "donor" to "father". As he explained, "it changed for me when she was pregnant, because I instantly felt a really strong feeling [toward the child] … I concluded that the best thing for the baby and I is to have a relationship from day one."

Ben subsequently met with the RPs to discuss his desire to be a "father". As he explained, "I made the point that I am connected to that child. I am the biological father … and the word 'father' freaked them out, and they got up and walked out." Ben reported that one of the RPs said to him, "You're nothing but the donor". Being reduced to "just a donor" was confronting for Ben. It was not how he perceived his role in relation to the DCC. He said, "I get really offended when people call me the donor. I call myself 'father'. I refer to [the child] as my child."

At the time of the interview, Ben had seen a photo of the child but reported that the RPs had not allowed him to have in-person contact. He felt aggrieved about how the relationship had eventuated and, in sharp contrast to the rhetoric of Hooper, he felt that he had little agency in the situation. Ben believed that there should be reciprocity, however; in his experience, the relationship was "all about the [recipient] parents … They have a right, they have a role, and they have protections … They have actually given up nothing. They have taken and not compromised, and I don't think they understand how it feels."

In her research on known and identity release gamete donors in the UK, Gilman (2018) noted that even in the context of altruistic donation, donors still have an expectation of receiving something in return for the "gift" that they have given. "Bodily donors and recipients frequently do not experience their gift as a 'free' and disconnected act of altruism, as the medical-ethical model arguably encourages. Instead, this gift is conceptualised as relational, creative or expressive of social ties between donor and recipient. … Gamete donors similarly express nuanced and complex views about the meaning of their 'gift'" (Gilman, 2018, p. 705). Gilman suggests that donors are not entirely altruistic and want something in exchange for donating. Ben's expectation was of relational reciprocity for what he had given. When it was not forthcoming, he felt cheated. Perhaps surprisingly, Ben did not pursue any rights in relation to the child. It was his belief that the "system" was stacked against him, though this is not an accurate portrayal of the law.

Art, a single man who was interviewed for the study, reported that his expectations changed over time. Art had donated to multiple families to create 18 DCC over several years. His expectations around involvement with his DCC evolved and on some occasions his expectations were mis-aligned with those of his RPs. In his interview, Art described his expe-riences with two different recipient families which influenced him to reappraise his role as a donor. In one case, the relationship did not unfold as he had hoped, while the other helped him to clarify the relationship he wanted to have with his DCC.

In the first case, the RP, an SMC, birthed twins through Art's donation and had an older child from a different donor. Art had contact with the twins from early in their lives but conceptualised his role as a "significant other", rather than as a co-parent. When the twins were one, he proposed a trip to introduce the DCC to his extended family, who did not live in Australia. Art's need to introduce his DCC to his extended family was at odds with the RP's priorities at the time. She had three children under the age of five whom she was raising without family support. She welcomed practical parenting assistance from Art but declined to go on the trip. Art decided to travel alone, but when he returned, the RP had relocated and established new boundaries in their relationship, including limiting Art's contact with the DCC.

Art described the scenario:

> [She had] three kids, very small apartment, financial uncertainty, father just died. Complete chaos ... and I think she was hoping that I would carry some of the burden for her, and I just didn't do that. I was there joyfully playing with the kids ... She was going through some considerable difficul-ties, and I'm there planning a holiday .... Just before we were due to go she said, "I'm not going on holiday, we're staying here" ... When I came back ... she'd moved on and indicated that she would like a less-contact scenario to be re-established.

This experience that Art described of the RP wanting more practical assis-tance with the care of the DCC, while the donor simply wanted the joy of fatherhood, is echoed in other research with known donors (Dempsey, 2012a, 2012b; Riggs, 2008a, 2008b). In some relationships a source of ten-sion occurred due to different expectations around essentialist gender roles in child-raising, where some donors wanted the "emotional rewards of involvement, but not the responsibility or obligation to care when it does not suit" (Dempsey, 2012b, p. 162).

Following the breakdown in contact with this RP, Art reflected on his relationship with his other RPs and their DCC. Subsequently he devel-oped a close relationship with another donor family, which triggered him to re-evaluate his preferred role with respect to his DCC. The relationship evolved following the breakup of a recipient lesbian couple. One of the

RPs lived in close proximity and Art started having increased contact with her and the DCC. As he spent more time with the child, he began to see himself less as a "donor" and more as a "father". He also began to see himself as having an obligation to his DCC to be more than just a donor. As he explained, "[the children] have an expectation that you will be a 'dad'. And being a dad is something proactive. It's not a status you have, it's something you do. And so just thinking about what that actually means if these kids are wanting me to be a dad."

Art's experience with this family unit was the impetus for his re-evaluation of his relationship with all his donor offspring. Consequently, he engaged in a process of personal development, enrolling in a course on how to become a better father and began to redefine his preferred role in the lives of his DCC. This re-evaluation process led him to believe that he had an obligation to be more involved with his donor offspring.

> To be a dad ... it's a demonstration of a commitment ... [it's] about offering and making offers for availability. That's something I don't tend to do, and it tends to be read as, "He doesn't want to" – "He can be a bit distant". And in actual fact that's my *parenting* style because distant fathers are a bit of a thing in my family ... [and when] there was an expectation that I would be "Dad" ... And so, I'm looking at that and going, "Okay, well, if these kids want me to be 'Dad', then I don't want to be distant" ... and I'm at that moment now where I'm just transitioning ... where I've just deferred mostly to the parents about what they wanted ... now the kids are edging into their tweens, they're going to have their own opinions about things, and so I'm going to start to ask them a little bit more, "What sort of person do you want?" And to the extent that I can provide, then I will.

Art's self-reflection led to a shift in how he conceptualised his role with respect to the DCC. He wanted to make himself "more available" for contact but had not discussed his role realignment with the RPs. Asked how he thought the RPs might respond, Art stated that his responsibility to the DCC superseded the RPs' views: "I do feel like I have a certain duty to the kids to make sure that I am not coming across as a very distant 'dad'". While Art reimagined his role, at the time of his interview it had not been enacted with most of his RPs and their DCC. Ben had a similar response when questioned about the disconnect between his sense of himself as a "father" and the RP's perception of him as a "donor", believing that "donor" did not reflect his intended role towards the DCC. However, neither had actually played active parenting roles for any of their DCC.

The experiences of both Ben and Art are reminiscent of the "underlying, unresolved tension" that Nordqvist and Smart (2014) identify in the relationship between a sperm donor and their donor offspring created by their shared genealogy. As they argue, "The donor is not understood as a parent, nor as family, and yet the genetic contribution means the donor (and his or her relatives) can potentially claim to be connected .... There is constant potential for the donor to fall into the kin category, despite being positioned and conceptualised as 'non-kin'" (Nordqvist and Smart, 2014, pp. 123–4).

For one online sperm donor the intimacy involved in connecting with RPs through the children resulted in role confusion. Nate, a single heterosexual donor interviewed for the study, found himself the object of one of his RP's romantic intentions. The intimacy of being in contact with this RP, who was one half of a lesbian couple, resulted in a blurring of the recipient/donor relationship and ultimately led to the breakdown of his relationship with the children. Nate had initially been encouraged by the couple to spend time with them. He became a regular presence in the lives of his DCC who were teenagers at the time of the interview. As he explained, "[the RPs] basically adopted me. I was effectively part of the family". The RPs subsequently separated. Nate later learned that this was in part due to one member of the couple having romantic feelings towards him. He explained:

> One of the women became like obsessed with me ... She was like just writing me love letters, you know, declaring that she can't go on in life without me ... she says it was there all the time, for her. But I had no idea until she started telling me ... it went on for like I don't know, ten years or something ... [now] they've split up, and the partners – well, they are both blaming me now for not – for being too accommodating or whatever.

When the couple's relationship broke down, Nate was told he could not see the family anymore, including the children, with whom he had a close and longstanding relationship. He attempted to maintain contact with the children, encouraging them to see the scenario from his perspective. As he explained:

> I've got the phone number of one of the kids, but the other kid doesn't have a phone .... I just said to him look, you know, like just – because they are angry with me. I said just don't judge me by what other people are saying ... look at me as an individual and judge me on my own actions, not what other people think of me. Because if they are living with the mother and the mother thinks I'm a horrible person, they also think I'm a horrible person, just because the mother convinces them.

Nate hoped that the children's views towards him would change over time. He attributed their apparent disinterest in him at the time of the interview to their stage of development and anticipated that they might re-establish contact when they were older:

> I am disappointed how it turned out because I have known those kids all their life ... they are 15 and 17 now, so they are growing out of parents in general ... they don't have any interest in the parents they've got, never mind the one who was the donor ... still, I would have been hoping for a much better outcome.

The men interviewed for this study had a variety of experiences, many of which were positive. The majority were able to build some relationship with their DCC through early contact. However, in a number of situations relationships changed or deteriorated, and the donors found themselves separated from their donor offspring.

4.5   Conclusion

The practice of online sperm donation has increased in recent years, in part because of the autonomy it offers donors and recipients. Proponents claim the opportunity for direct contact between parties is advantageous, because it allows parties to negotiate post-donation roles and early contact which is not possible when clinic donors are used. However, the opportunity to interact also created tensions for some donors and their RPs as differing expectations emerged. Our research findings are consistent with prior findings in Australia (Riggs and Scholz, 2011; Dempsey, 2012a, 2012b), which suggest that expectations around early contact vary substantially amongst sperm donors. Some wanted to co-parent or be involved as a "father" in the child's life, while others only wanted to just be a donor. For some, their preference changed during the process of donating and getting to know their recipients and donor offspring. The role preference of some donors aligned with that of the RPs. However, others reported discord in the relationship with their recipients, often due to differing or changed expectations.

In the absence of any regulatory oversight or legal guidance, the donors interviewed for this study felt they had no recourse when conflict arose. These findings point to the vital importance of all parties discussing role expectations prior to embarking on donation, as well as being aware that expectations can change at different times in the child's life. While the size of the sample included in this study makes it difficult to draw any representative conclusions, the interviews suggest that in at least some cases the anticipated benefits of negotiated informal sperm donation may not be realised.

References

Bergen, N., & Delacroix, C. (2019). Bypassing the sperm bank: Documenting the experiences of online informal sperm donors. *Critical Public Health*, 29(5), 584–595. https://doi.org/10.1080/09581596.2018.1492704

Bossema, E., Pim, M., Janssens, R., Treucker, F., van Duinen, K., Nap, A., & Geenen, R. (2014). An inventory of reasons for sperm donation in formal versus informal settings, *Human Fertility*, 17(1), 21–27. https://doi.org/10.3109/14647273.2014.881561

Braun, V., & Clarke, V. (2006). Using thematic analysis in psychology. *Qualitative Research in Psychology*, 3, 77–101. https://doi.org/10.1191/1478088706qp063oa

Cook, H., & Tomazin, F. (2021). "Sperm drought fuels unregulated online market and sex assault concerns", The Age, 22 May. www.theage.com.au/national/victoria/sperm-drought-fuels-unregulated-online-market-and-sex-assault-concerns-20210521-p57uos.html

Cook, R., & Golombok, S. (1995). A survey of semen donation: Phase II – the view of the donors, *Human Reproduction*, 10(4), 951–959. https://doi.org/10.1093/oxfordjournals.humrep.a136069

Daniels, K. R., Curson, R.,& Lewis, G.M. (1996a). Semen donor recruitment: A study of donors in two clinics, *Human Reproduction*, 11, 746–751. https://doi.org/10.1093/oxfordjournals.humrep.a019247

Daniels, K. R., Ericsson, H. L., & Burn, I. P (1996b). Families and donor insemination: The views of semen donors, *Scandinavian Journal of Social Welfare*, 5(4), 229–237. https://doi.org/10.1111/j.1468-2397.1996.tb00149.x

Dempsey, D. (2010). Conceiving and negotiating reproductive relationships: Lesbians and gay men forming families with children, *Sociology*, 44(6), 1145–1162. https://doi.org/10.1177%2F0038038510381607

Dempsey, D. (2012a). More like a donor or more like a father? Gay men's concepts of relatedness to children, *Sexualities*, 15(2), 156–174. https://doi.org/10.1177%2F1363460711433735

Dempsey, D. (2012b) Gay male couples' paternal involvement in lesbian parented families, *Journal of Family Studies*, 18(2–3), 155–164. https://doi.org/10.5172/jfs.2012.18.2-3.155

Freeman, T., Jadva, V., Tanfield, E., & Golombok, S. (2016). Online sperm donation: A survey of the demographic characteristics, motivations, preferences and experiences of sperm donors on a connection website. *Human Reproduction*, 31(9), 2082–2089. https://doi.org/10.1093/humrep/dew166

Gilman, L. (2018). Toxic money or paid altruism: The meaning of payments for identity-release gamete donors. *Sociology of Health & Illness*, 40(4), 702–717. https://doi.org/10.1111/1467-9566.12718

Glover, A. (2018, 15 June). I found my sperm donor on Facebook. www.kidspot .com.au (accessed 24 February 2021).

Graham, S., Freeman, T., & Jadva, V. (2019). A comparison of the characteristics, motivations, preferences and expectations of men donating sperm online or through a sperm bank, *Human Reproduction*, 1(34), 2208–2218. https://doi .org/10.1093/humrep/dez173

Hooper, A. (Host) (2018, 24 December): Jo Donor (Episode 1) [Audio podcast]. In Sperm Donation World Podcast.

Hooper, A. (Host) (2019, 20 January): The Patriarch: John Lyndsey Mayger (Episode 5) [Audio podcast]. In Sperm Donation World Podcast.

Kamenev, M. (2019). Sperm drought. *The Monthly*, August. www.themonthly .com.au/magazine/august-2019

Kelly, F., & Dempsey, D. (2016). The family law implications of early contact between sperm donors and their donor offspring. *Family Matters*, 98. https:// aifs.gov.au/publications/family-matters/issue-98/family-law-implications-early-contact-between-sperm-donors-and-their-donor-offspring

Kelly, F., Dempsey, D., & Frew, C., (2019). The donor-linking practices of Australian fertility clinics, *Journal of Law and Medicine*, 27(2), 355–368.

Lavoie, K., Côté, I., & de Montigny, F. (2017). Assisted reproduction in the digital age: Stories of Canadian sperm donors offering their gametes online via introduction websites. *Journal of Men's Studies*, 26(2), 184–202. https://doi.org/ 10.1177%2F1060826517737047

Lever, C. (2020a, 29 November). Australia's most-prolific sperm donor who fathered 23 children in ONE YEAR is investigated by authorities – after his "hobby" turned into a full-time job because mums love his ethnicity and strike rate. Daily Mail Australia, https://dailymail.co.uk/news/article-8989065/ Married-freelance-sperm-donor-Alan-Phan-investigation-fathering-23-children-year.html (accessed 21 January 2021).

Lever, C. (2020b, 25 September). Australia's chronic sperm donor shortage is causing family heartache. www.kidspot.com.au (accessed 24 February 2021).

Lever, C. (2020c, 1 December). Brisbane sperm donor Alan Phan investigated by VARTA after fathering 23 children. www.7news.com (accessed 21 January 2021).

McNair, R., & Dempsey, D. (2002). Exploring diversity in lesbian-parented families Paper 1: Family formation and women's roles. *Family Matters*, (63), 40–49.

Mohr, S. (2014). Beyond motivation: On what it means to be a sperm donor in Denmark, *Anthropology & Medicine*, 21(2), 162–173. DOI: 10.1080/ 13648470.2014.914806

Nordqvist, P., & Smart, C. (2014). *Relative strangers*. Palgrave Macmillan.

Patton, M. (1990). *Qualitative evaluation and research methods*. Sage.

Power, J., Dempsey, D., Kelly, F., & Lau, M. (2020). Use of fertility services in Australian lesbian, bisexual and queer women's pathways to parenthood. *Australian and New Zealand Journal of Obstetrics and Gynaecology*, 60(4), 610–615. https://doi.org/10.1111/ajo.13175

Power, J., Perlesz, A., McNair, R., Schofield, M., Pitts, M., Brown, R., & Bickerdike, A. (2012) Gay and bisexual dads and diversity: Fathers in the Work, Love, Play study, *Journal of Family Studies*, 18(2–3), 143–154, DOI: 10.5172/jfs.2012.18.2-3.143

Riggs, D. W. (2008a). Lesbian mothers, gay sperm donors, and community: Ensuring the well-being of children and families. *Health Sociology Review*, 17(3), 226–234.

Riggs, D. W. (2008b). Using multinomial logistic regression analysis to develop a model of Australian gay and heterosexual sperm donors' motivations and beliefs. *International Journal of Emerging Technologies & Society*, 6(2), 107–123.

Riggs, D. W. & Russell, L. (2011). Characteristics of men willing to act as sperm donors in the context of identity-release legislation. *Human Reproduction*, 26(1), 266–272. https://doi.org/10.1093/humrep/deq314

Riggs, D. W., & Scholz, B. (2011). The value and meaning attached to genetic relatedness among Australian sperm donors. *New Genetics and Society*, 30(1), 41–58. https://doi.org/10.1080/14636778.2011.552299

Sams, L. (2021, 5 February). Meet the father of 17 who leads Australia's private sperm donor group. *Australian Financial Mail*. www.afm.com.au (accessed 24 February 2021).

Sixty Minutes Australia (2019, 18 February). Sperm donor plans to father 2500 children. www.youtube.com/watch?v=NGhbcTGZmkI.

Van den Broeck, U., Vandermeeran, M., Vanderschuren, D., Enzlin, P., Demyttenaere, K., & D'Hooghe, T. (2012). A systematic review of sperm donors: Demographic characteristics, attitudes, motives and experiences of the process of sperm donation. *Human Reproduction Update*, 19, 37–51. https://doi.org/10.1093/humupd/dms039

Victorian Reproductive Assistance Authority (VARTA). (2018). Annual report. https://varta.org.au/sites/default/files/2020-11/VARTA%20annual%20report%202018.pdf

Victorian Assisted Reproductive Treatment Authority (VARTA). (2020). Annual report. https://varta.org.au/sites/default/files/2021-01/varta-annual-report-2020.pdf.pdf

Woestenburg, N., Winter, H., & Janssens, P. (2016). What motivates men to offer sperm donation via the Internet? *Psychology Health Medicine*, 21(4), 424–430. https://doi.org/10.1080/13548506.2015.1081702

Whyte, S. (2019). Clinical vs. exclusively online sperm donors: What's the difference? *Journal of Reproductive and Infant Psychology*, 37(1), 3–12. https://doi.org/10.1080/02646838.2018.1540864

Whyte, S., Savage, D., & Torgler, B. (2017). Online sperm donors: The impact of family, friends, personality and risk perception on behaviour. *Reproductive Biomedicine Online*, 35(6), 723–732. DOI: 10.1016/j.rbmo.2017.08.023

CHAPTER 5

Parents' and Offsprings' Experience of Insemination Fraud
A Qualitative Study

Sabrina Zeghiche, Isabel Côté, Marie-Christine Williams-Plouffe, and Renée-Pierre Trottier Cyr

5.1 Introduction

For several years, concerns about the regulation of third-party assisted human reproduction have been evident. This is true in Canada, where the government held a public consultation in 2017–2018 aimed at strengthening the law on assisted reproduction (Gruben et al., 2019); in France, where the bioethics law has been revised; and in the United States, where debates are being held on the terms of consent in the context of donor insemination (Byrne, 2019; MacBride, 2021; Tabachnik, 2020). Despite these growing concerns, not only is donor sperm conception receiving less attention (Pennings, Klitzman & Zegers-Hochschild, 2016), several points of contention remain in the debates surrounding its regulation in North America. For example, the lack of consistency across clinics in donation tracking and record-keeping procedures has led to cases of accidental or voluntary substitution of sperm donations (Bender, 2003, 2005; Couture et al., 2014; Cho, Ruiter & Dahan, 2018; Fox, 2017; Miola, 2004). Such substitutions mean that the sperm of the donor selected by the parents or that of the father of the child is not the sperm used for conception.

With the advent of DNA kits, more and more cases of substitution are being uncovered (Madeira, 2019), several going back as early as the 2000s. Dozens of doctors have found themselves in the media spotlight, with several being the subject of high-profile legal proceedings (Agence France Presse, 2019; MacBride, 2021; The Associated Press, 2016), notably in Canada (Paye, 2018; Trépanier, 2020), where a situation involving a doctor who was a pioneer in assisted reproduction made the headlines in recent years. Known for being one of the first to offer services to lesbian couples and single mothers, the doctor had a national reputation.

The first substitution was uncovered in the 1990s when one of his patients discovered that her child was not from the right sperm donor. This would be concluded by a confidential agreement between the doctor and the patient. Ten years later, two former patients sued him, alleging that he had inseminated them with the wrong sperm. During an initial hearing before the Discipline Committee of the College of Physicians and Surgeons of Ontario, he admitted to errors in his management of some inseminations. The College of Physicians and Surgeons suspended him for three months. The following year, he stopped practicing and closed his clinic. The media would reveal in 2016 that one of the children conceived at the clinic in question was (verified through a paternity test) the doctor's biological child. A class action suit was then initiated against the doctor, bringing together more than 200 people (parents and donor-conceived people). In 2019, the Discipline Committee of the College of Physicians and Surgeons of Ontario deregistered the doctor. After five years of legal procedures, the class action resulted in 2021 in a ground-breaking settlement amounting to millions of dollars.

Despite the media attention that the substitution of sperm donation has received, from an academic point of view, this phenomenon has not received the attention it deserves. This chapter proposes to fill this gap by examining the experience of the discovery of substitution by parents and people conceived by sperm donation, based on the Canadian case described above.

5.2   Literature Review

The importance to donor-conceived people of knowledge of their biogenetic origins in the context of conception by sperm donation is relatively well documented. We know how disclosure unfolds according to the stage of life at which it occurs (Canneaux et al., 2016; Golombok, 2015), the family and relational context in which it takes place (Beeson, Jennings & Kramer, 2011; Blake et al., 2014; Nelson, Hertz & Kramer, 2013), as well as its potential fallout in terms of the sense of identity incompleteness associated with not knowing one's donor (Blyth, 2012; Nelson et al., 2013; Rodino, Burton & Sanders, 2011), and the desire to know more about the man's medical history, physical appearance, motivations, or personal aspirations (Blake, Ilioi & Golombok, 2016; Mahlstedt, LaBounty & Kennedy, 2010; Nelson et al., 2013). By contrast, few studies have considered the experience of individuals who discover that they have a progenitor other than the one initially intended.

The limited work on the subject has concerned either the accidental substitution of gametes or embryos (Bender, 2003, 2005; Cho, Ruiter & Dahan, 2018; Fox, 2017; Miola, 2004), or the voluntary substitution of donated sperm, with an emphasis on cases of doctors using their own sperm to inseminate their patients without their knowledge (Chicoine, 2020; Madeira, 2019, 2020; Sharak, 2020). With respect to *voluntary substitution* of sperm donations, only four articles, to our knowledge, have addressed the subject. These are legal articles that aim to deconstruct this act, qualified as "fertility fraud," and to reframe it as a criminal and civil offence, highlighting the ethical principles that it violates, the psychological repercussions that it entails, as well as the reasons it has been difficult to legally condemn (Chicoine, 2020; Madeira, 2019, 2020; Sharak, 2020). Of the nine articles addressing the topic of sperm donation substitution (accidental or voluntary), only one contains empirical data collected from a small sample ($n = 5$) in the context of legal action against the doctor who used his sperm to inseminate his patients (Madeira, 2020).

These studies do not capture the phenomenon of substitution in all its complexity. There are too few of them, most are theoretical, and the only empirical study involves a small sample, documents only one type of substitution, and looks at the issue mainly from a legal point of view.

5.3 Presentation of the Study

Concerns about sperm donation substitution were brought to our attention in an earlier project, STORIES, on the identity integration of people conceived through sperm donation.[1] This project did not set out to investigate sperm donation substitution from the outset; however, the advertisement for the project was circulated in a private Facebook group whose members were affected by the fraudulent behaviour of the doctor in question. Some people from the group then contacted us wanting to discuss insemination substitution.

Data collection was conducted in the winter of 2019 and spring of 2021 in Québec and Ontario,[2] using semi-structured individual interviews lasting approximately 1 hour and 30 minutes. All interviews were audio-recorded and transcribed in full.

---

[1] This research was funded by the Social Sciences and Humanities Research Council of Canada (2018–2022) and received ethical approval from the Université du Québec en Outaouais (#2925).
[2] The research was put on hold during the first few months of successive lockdowns in Canada during the COVID-19 pandemic.

5.3.1   Profile of Participants

In total, 77 participants from 32 families participated in the STORIES project. Among these families, six were affected by the substitution of the father's sperm ($N = 2$) or that of the donor chosen by the parents ($N = 4$), of whom two had discovered that the substituted sperm was that of the doctor. In all, 13 people made up this sample: seven parents (two fathers and five mothers) and six people conceived by insemination (four teenagers, aged between 13 and 16 years and two adults aged 38 and 39 years).

Insemination was used in the context of male infertility ($N = 1$), vasectomy ($N = 3$), sperm freezing after cancer ($N = 1$), and celibacy ($N = 1$).

5.3.2   Data Analysis

A thematic analysis (Paillé & Mucchielli, 2016) was performed on all the verbatim transcripts, using the NVivo qualitative data analysis software. First, the interview outline and project objectives were used to develop the list of (sub)headings that would serve as a data classification tool. Next, a sequenced thematisation was conducted to develop the list of (sub)themes. Thus, a sample of the corpus was analysed to identify a list of themes. This list was recorded in a cross-cutting theme table. The analysis of this table allowed us to first highlight salient thematic clusters and then structure these clusters into more inclusive cross-cutting groups, according to thematic axes. At the end of this analysis process, a first draft of the thematic tree was developed. Once solidly developed, this tree was applied to the whole corpus, and some additions were made during the analysis.

Several themes were identified. For the purposes of this chapter, only the discovery of the substitution will be discussed: the trajectory of the discovery, the emotions associated with the discovery, and the disclosure of the substitution to the children following the discovery.

5.4   Results

5.4.1   Trajectory of the Discovery of Substitution

Two main trajectories were associated with the discovery of substitution. In most cases, the discovery stemmed from suspicions that arose as a result of media reports about the doctor's fraudulent behaviour, particularly those concerning the use of his own sperm. However, in two cases, it was a factor other than the media coverage that led the parents to harbour strong suspicions about the possibility of a substitution. In one case, the parents were informed by the clinic they were working with for their second child that their name was on the list of potential cases of substitution. In another case, it was after a DNA test to verify her daughter's genetic link to another child born from the same donor (the one she initially chose) that the mother discovered the substitution.

Prior to the discovery of the substitution, regardless of the circumstances surrounding it, most parents and children were unsuspecting. Only one mother reported that her husband distrusted the doctor from the first meeting. But, in almost all cases, the trust placed in the medical institution and in the doctor, whose reputation was well established, was a safeguard against doubts. Even when physical differences in children were noted, they were either ignored or explained away by the arbitrary nature of genetics: "My children don't have the same eye color as me … I thought my genes were recessive" (Father_H5). This rationalisation was even stronger *among the children*, who all said they never doubted for a moment the biological link that united them with their father or their siblings (in the case of a differentiated conception): "I did not really have any doubts. I never noticed that my father and I did not look alike" (Teen2_H5).

However, in the case of children conceived with the doctor's sperm, doubts appeared earlier and with more intensity *in the parents' minds*, due to the doctor's phenotypic traits that distinguished him significantly from the parents' physical appearance. In addition, although the parents did not know the physical characteristics of the donor who was to be used, the resemblance to the doctor was obvious to them: "I always knew it was [the doctor]. … As soon as [my daughter] was born, my ex-husband said, 'Oh my God, she really looks like the doctor.' The doctor's secretary told me the same thing" (Mother_H13).

When the doctor's fraudulent behaviour began to be revealed in the media, the first reaction of many people (parents as well as children who had become adults) was to convince themselves that it couldn't possibly concern them: "He [the doctor] has done thousands [of inseminations]. The chances of it happening to me. It can't be" (Adult_H14). Some were convinced of the speculative, accidental, or isolated character of these substitutions.

It was only when the media revealed that the doctor had used his own sperm that doubts really entered the minds of most parents or adult children. The argument that the substitutions were speculative, isolated, or accidental no longer held up: "Everything changed when … they had proof he used his own sperm. That was not an accident. I can no longer believe this was just carelessness; this was intentional wrongdoing" (Mother_H3). It was at this point that many parents decided to have their children tested.

The physical differences observed in the children then took on new meaning:

> I put it aside until we heard that [the doctor] had been accused of using his own sperm. ... I started asking myself: 'Do I see myself in [my] children?' And no, I did not see myself [in them]. ... Then, it became more and more obvious through the years. So, I started to think, in a private way, that it is possible that they might not be [my children]. (Father_H5)

For those conceived with the doctor's sperm, seeing in the media the person whose biological link with the doctor had been established made the physical similarities obvious to them; the possibility of a voluntary substitution could no longer be entirely ruled out. Even though they were convinced they were biologically related to their father before they were told they were conceived through his sperm donation, their physical appearance raised questions: "All my life I have been asked if I was Canadian because of my skin tone"[3] (Adult_H13). Once the media revealed that the doctor had inseminated his patients with his sperm, their physical characteristics were no longer isolated, as others shared them. Doubt then began to enter their minds: "I decided to call the lawyers a few days after [seeing the person in the media] because I was tired of it" (Adult_H14).

5.4.2   Feelings When Discovering the Substitution

5.4.2.1   Steps Prior to Discovery

The period leading up to receiving test results was experienced with great apprehension by parents and adult children. The results would provide crucial information on the nature of filiation, which was not without consequence for the members of these families. For fathers who believed that their children were conceived from their sperm, the mere fact that their biological paternity was being questioned and had to be confirmed was a deeply troubling, even traumatic experience. The paternity they thought they had acquired was put on hold for the duration of the tests: "My insides were in a knot, and you've got anger towards [the doctor] that no matter how this ends, 'You made me do this. I am having to do this because of the mess you have [created]'" (Father_H4).

---

[3] In this quote, the person interviewed means that she does not look Caucasian because of her olive skin.

On the other hand, knowing was not necessarily more comforting than remaining doubtful. By performing the tests and confirming the substitution, the elements on which the family narrative was based collapsed, leaving the family without its foundations: "I didn't want to get confirmation. Once you open that Pandora's box, you can't close it. You can't go back" (Father_H5).

If the process and the results were challenging, so was the wait. Parents lived in anxiety, not knowing when the results would come in, or what they would reveal. The anxiety they felt was commensurate with the issue at stake.

5.4.2.2 *Confirmation of Substitution*

The announcement of the results was like an earthquake for most parents, who reported feeling shock ("I couldn't believe it" [Mother_H5]; "It came as a shock to me" [Mother_SOLO5]) but also anger ("The first few weeks, we spent maybe too much time kind of bitching about the whole situation" [Mother_H4]) and a lot of sadness ("I started crying ... I was inconsolable ... I was a mess" [Mother_H5]).

In addition, many parents explained that they felt betrayed by the doctor they had trusted: "I was cheated ... betrayed by a doctor. A doctor ... I don't just feel betrayed but lied to and then taken advantage of" (Father_H5). What's more, the feeling of being subjected to someone else's choice and learning about it by accident years later was considered by some to be "traumatic".

For those conceived with the doctor's own sperm, confirmation of the substitution occurred in a particular context. The late disclosure of their sperm donor conception had already caused personal and family upheaval, particularly when it became apparent that the donor was anonymous. However, the shock of late disclosure and downfalls of donor anonymity may have softened the shock of the news of the voluntary substitution. In this particular case, the announcement that the doctor was the donor provided answers to identity questions that would have otherwise gone unanswered: "It wasn't such bad news because now maybe I would have some answers, instead of not knowing. It's nice to be able to put a name to [the progenitor] and to know my origins and the medical history" (Adult_H13).

5.4.3 *Disclosure of the Substitution to Children*

The parental disclosure did not concern the people conceived with the doctor's sperm who, being adults when the news of the doctor's fraudulent behaviour broke out, initiated themselves the process of DNA testing.

So, they received confirmation of the substitution before their parents. However, in the case of minor children, it was the parents who learned the news and had to disclose it to their children.

5.4.3.1   Concerns about Disclosure

In cases where there had been a substitution of the father's sperm, the absence of a genetic link between the child and the father, as well as the anonymity of the progenitor of their child, was particularly challenging because it was an arrangement imposed on the parents and not the result of a careful thought process.

Parents were apprehensive about the disclosure of the substitution because they were concerned about how their child(ren) would react to the news of the lack of a biological connection: "I am expecting her to say 'Wait, you're not my dad?' ... I am worried it will confuse her or hurt her a little bit" (Mother_H4). Donor anonymity was also a cause for concern: "I started to read that kids from anonymous donors are much more likely to be drug addicts, they're much more likely to suffer substance abuse. So, then I got thinking that my kids will be damaged if I tell them" (Mother_H5).

These worries were then reflected in the decision about whether or not to disclose the substitution to the children. While parents agreed that disclosure was necessary, they felt helpless about how to go about it. The fear of irreversible psychological repercussions for their children sometimes made them question the merits of disclosure: "If they're damaged, if they're upset ... should I just let them live their childhood?" (Mother_H5). They explained that because they did not choose this mode of conception, they felt helpless; they did not know how to react and what decision to make.

Finally, in cases where parents had decided not to tell their children that they were conceived through artificial insemination, the discovery of the substitution forced them into a double disclosure. Moreover, these parents deplored the fact that the substitution deprived them of the possibility of choosing the terms of the disclosure. They knew that early disclosure was important for donor-conceived children, but by the time they discovered the substitution, their children were teenagers. So, the parents felt robbed of the option of early disclosure: "I didn't have the option to tell my kids when they were young. So, what I had to do was figure out the best way to tell them now" (Mother_H5).

5.4.3.2   The Disclosure Itself

Of the four families with children who were minors, three have disclosed, and one plans to do so in the near future. In the cases in which the substitution was disclosed, two were able to disclose as soon as the child was old enough to talk, and one found out late and disclosed when the children were 14 and 13 years old.

For the parents who disclosed the substitution, the context of the disclosure, as well as the words chosen, was crucial. In one case, the parents waited until they had as much information as possible about the donor and the donor's offspring to minimise the shock to the children, chose a festive moment to reveal the news of the substitution, and tried to remain calm and reassure their children that it would not change their family dynamics: "I had everything planned out so that the shock [would be minimal] … so [our children] wouldn't be wallowing in depression" (Mother_H5). Another mother explained that she tried to ensure that her daughter did not feel responsible for the situation and that the news was balanced by the positive aspects of her life: "I would tell my daughter that the doctor was an idiot and he screwed up and what he did is terrible but at the same time it's not her fault. This is just the situation we found ourselves in" (Mother_SOLO5). Finally, for parents who planned to disclose the news of the substitution in the near future, they explained that they were waiting for the right moment, when the child was a little older, and that they wished to proceed with the disclosure in stages: "She doesn't need to know the messed-up part. The whole [situation with the doctor] will be two or three years down the road" (Father_H4).

Despite the preparation and efforts made by parents to ensure that the disclosure would take place in the best possible conditions, it remained a stressful experience: "It was a very difficult time, which you are never, ever prepared for" (Father_H5).

5.4.3.3 *Children's Feelings Regarding the Disclosure*

Children's feelings varied depending on the nature of the substitution and the age at which they learned about it. In the case of the substitution of the father's sperm, the announcement involves a new fact that affects the family narrative and a central member of the family unit. It also introduces a third person (a stranger) into the equation: "All your life, you think that a person is biologically your father and then you learn that it is someone else you don't know. It's difficult … It's weird sometimes to think that there's someone else you don't know" (Teen_2_H5).

However, in the case of the substitution of the donor's sperm, this means that the information the family thought they had about the donor they chose no longer applies. Not knowing who the actual donor is undermines the child's hope of knowing their origins, background, and potential donor siblings. This situation can be very difficult to deal with: "I feel a bit unnerved because I might have had a chance to meet my father or half-siblings, or more of a chance to. But now, it's kind of almost impossible. So, it's harder to comprehend sometimes" (Teen1_SOLO5).

On the other hand, the fact of having learned it at a young age seemed to protect against the shock that this situation engenders. One of the teens, who said he had always known that he was donor conceived, reported that he was not affected by the news of the substitution. By contrast, children who found out about the substitution later and who had not known they were donor conceived explained the shock they felt upon hearing the news: "At first, it was like a shock. … It's really something you see in the movies. You never expect to learn that about yourself" (Teen2_H5). After the shock, these children said they felt a deep sadness and took some time to integrate and accept this information.

Furthermore, what seems to be decisive in the children's experience is the unknown that the news introduces into the lives of those who do not know whose sperm was used. Children who learned of the substitution late in life experienced it as a shock, but knowing the identity of the donor, even if it was the doctor, seemed to bring them some relief: "I find it less difficult to get used to it because I didn't have to wonder, 'Who is my biological father?' I had the answers to my questions" (Teen1_H5). On the other hand, when the donor cannot be identified, the situation is more difficult to live with: "I'm kind of like a mystery child. Only half of my genetics are known, and then the other half, we don't know what they are …" (Teen1_SOLO5).

5.5   Discussion

Being a victim of sperm donation substitution is a complex experience that varies according to one's position in the insemination process (whether one uses it or is the product of it), the nature of the substitution in question, and the degree of suspicions one had prior to the discovery.

With regard to the substitution, reactions depended on both the source of the intended sperm versus the actual sperm used, as well as the degree of unknown that the substitution introduces. In cases in which there is a substitution of the father's sperm, parents experience grief due to the loss of biological paternity and the ideal of a child born to both parents. For those whose child was conceived by a donor other than the one originally intended, families are forced to give up (temporarily or permanently) the possibility of tracing the man who provided sperm and/or the donor siblings. In such cases, the substitution generates for the parents a feeling of worry about the medical and psychological repercussions for their child and, for the children, a feeling of incomplete identity. However, in the case where the doctor's sperm was substituted for that of an unknown donor, the shock of the substitution experienced by the doctor-conceived people is counterbalanced by the fact that it provides them with information about their origins, which is congruent with the literature on the importance of knowing one's origins (Guichon, Mitchell & Giroux, 2012).

In any case, substitution strongly undermines trust in the assisted reproduction industry. In fact, when the story broke in the media, many refused to believe that they could be affected. Obviously, those who struggled to accept this possibility were the most affected, while those who had strong suspicions about the substitution did not experience a shock of the same magnitude. Furthermore, it should be noted that substitution takes place in a context of challenges related to conception and, consequently, of emotional vulnerability. This has a most devastating effect on parents.

For donor-conceived people, the emotional experience varied according to whether they discovered the substitution on their own – or at the same time as their parents – or whether it was disclosed to them by their parents during adolescence. The later donor-conceived people find out about the substitution, the bigger the shock. We already know that the younger a person is when they learn they were conceived via sperm donation, the better the psychological integration related to this information (Jadva et al., 2009). Research has also shown that the disclosure strategies parents use have an impact on their children's reception of information (Mac Dougall et al., 2007). Therefore, the fact that our young participants learned about the substitution in a parent-controlled setting may have acted as a protective factor. Though it is possible that they did not yet fully understand the ethical issues involved in the situation.

All the participants we met described the announcement of the substitution as a shock. This is a term commonly used by participants in various research studies on the disclosure of conception by sperm donation (Blyth, 2012; Freeman, 2015; Frith et al., 2018; Jadva et al., 2009). Anger, confusion, upset, and the feeling of having been deceived, are also emotions that have been expressed by people who learn of their donor conception unexpectedly (Freeman, 2015; Frith et al., 2018; Jadva et al.,

2009; Madeira, 2020). However, what is specific to substitution is that the deception involves both the parents and the children. They must face this shock together, with each having to deal with their own distress while mobilising their own emotional resources to act as a protective factor for their children. Nevertheless, for some of our participants, the shock of learning the information was accompanied by some "relief". Indeed, the confirmation of the absence of a genetic link can then explain certain questions related to the physical difference observed (Crawshaw, 2018; Jadva et al., 2009).

5.6   Conclusion

This research documented a phenomenon that has been little studied in the literature. However, despite its innovative nature, this research has certain limitations. The size of the sample as well as the variability of the experiments do not allow for definitive conclusions to be drawn about this phenomenon.

However, it does shed some heuristic light on this phenomenon by taking into consideration the subjective experience of the people affected. Indeed, this type of situation is usually treated anecdotally in the media and seems to attract little attention from the scientific community. Nevertheless, many emphasise the need to integrate empirical data into theoretical debates or reflections on bioethics that take into account the difficulties that can be caused, at the psychosocial level, by a sperm substitution (Freeman, Jadva & Slutsky, 2016; Madeira, 2019; Wright, 2016). This is especially important in the context of malpractice. Moreover, social representations of this type of malpractice are inconsistent with the experience of the people affected. For example, some people might believe that the fact that the couple were able to conceive nullifies the circumstances of the conception and delegitimises their grievances (Madeira, 2019). Moreover, when the doctor uses his own sperm, the social prestige associated with his position may be treated as invalidating the claims of the family affected (Madeira, 2020).

The general public, and even the fertility industry, may treat this issue as a marginal phenomenon. However, with the democratisation of DNA testing, this type of discovery could become more widespread (Crawshaw, 2018; Harper, Kennett & Reisel, 2016). It is therefore important to document it to better understand the consequences for the disintegration of the filial or family bond, the possibility of redefining the biological family, and the redefinition of the original parental project.

References

Agence France Presse. (2019, 12 April). Il est surnommé le "docteur sperme" aux Pays-Bas: Jan Karbaat est suspecté d'avoir utilisé sa propre semence dans sa clinique. RTL Info. www.rtl.be/info/monde/europe/il-est-surnomme-le-docteur-sperme-aux-pays-bas-jan-karbaat-est-suspecte-d-avoir-utilise-sa-propre-semence-dans-sa-clinique-1115904.aspx

Beeson, D. R., Jennings, P. K., & Kramer, W. (2011). Offspring searching for their sperm donors: how family type shapes the process. *Human Reproduction*, 26(9), 2415–2424. https://doi.org/10.1093/humrep/der202

Bender, L. (2003). Genes, parents, and assisted reproductive technologies: ARTs, mistakes, sex, race, and law. *Columbia Journal of Gender and Law*, 12, 1.

Bender, L. (2005). To err is human: ART mix-ups – a labor-based, relational proposal. *Journal of Gender, Race and Justice*, 9, 443.

Blake, L., Zadeh, S., Statham, H., & Freeman, T. (2014). Families created by assisted reproduction: children's perspectives. In T. Freeman, S. Graham, F. Ebtehaj, & M. Richards (Eds.), *Relatedness in Assisted Reproduction* (pp. 251–269). Cambridge University Press.

Blake, L., Ilioi, E., & Golombok, S. (2016). Thoughts and feelings about the donor: a family perspective. In T. Freeman, S. Graham, F. Ebtehaj, & M. Richards (Eds.), *Relatedness in Assisted Reproduction* (pp. 293–331) Cambridge University Press.

Blyth, E. (2012). Discovering the 'facts of life' following anonymous donor insemination. *International Journal of Law, Policy and the Family*, 26(2), 143–161. https://doi.org/10.1093/lawfam/ebs006

Blyth, E. (2012). Genes r us? Making sense of genetic and non-genetic relationships following anonymous donor insemination. *Reproductive Biomedicine Online*, 24(7), 719–726. https://doi.org/10.1016/j.rbmo.2012.02.010

Byrne, E. (2019). Texas House passes bill classifying fertility fraud as sexual assault. *The Texas Tribune*. www.texastribune.org/2019/05/16/texas-house-bill-fertility-fraud-crime/

Canneaux, M., Kobilinsky, N., Wolf, J. P., Golse, B., & Beauquier-Maccotta, B. (2016). Information, transmission, secret: quel discours pour les enfants nés par don de gamètes?. *Gynécologie obstétrique & fertilité*, 44(7–8), 410–416. https://doi.org/10.1016/j.gyobfe.2016.05.002

Chicoine, S. (2020). The birth of fertility fraud: how to protect Washingtonians. *Washington Law Review Online*, 95(1), 168–204.

Cho, K., Ruiter, J., & Dahan, M. H. (2018). Protecting fertility clinics against sperm-related fraud: a call to action. *Journal of Assisted Reproduction and Genetics*, 35(6), 1131–1132. https://doi.org/10.1007/s10815-018-1175-8

Couture, V., Dubois, M. A., Drouin, R., Moutquin, J. M., & Bouffard, C. (2014). Strengths and pitfalls of Canadian gamete and embryo donor registries: searching for beneficent solutions. *Reproductive Biomedicine Online*, 28(3), 369–379. https://doi.org/10.1016/j.rbmo.2013.10.020

Crawshaw, M. (2018). Direct-to-consumer DNA testing: the fallout for individuals and their families unexpectedly learning of their donor conception origins. *Human Fertility*, 21(4), 225–228. https://doi.org/10.1080/14647273.2017.1339127

Freeman, T. (2015). Gamete donation, information sharing and the best interests of the child: an overview of the psychosocial evidence. *Monash Bioethics Review*, 33(1), 45–63. https://doi.org/10.1007/s40592-015-0018-y

Freeman, T., Jadva, J., & Slutsky, J. (2016). Sperm donors limited: psychosocial aspects of genetic connections and the regulation of offspring numbers. In S. Golombok, R. Scott, J. B. Appelby, M. Richards, S. Wilkinson (Eds.), *Regulating Reproductive Donation* (pp. 165–184) Cambridge University Press.

Fox, D. (2017). Reproductive negligence. *Columbia Law Review*, 117, 149.

Frith, L., Blyth, E., Crawshaw, M., & van den Akker, O. (2018). Secrets and disclosure in donor conception. *Sociology of Health & Illness*, 40(1), 188–203. https://doi.org/10.1111/1467-9566.12633

Golombok, S. (2015). *Modern Families: Parents and Children in New Family Forms*. Cambridge University Press.

Gruben, V., Cattapan, A., Cameron, A., Busby, K., Baylis, F., Carsley, S., ... & White, P. (2019). Joint Submission to Health Canada on Prepublication of Proposed Regulations to the Assisted Human Reproduction Act.

Guichon, J. R., Mitchell, I., & Giroux, M. (Eds.), (2012). *The Right to Know One's Origins: Assisted Human Reproduction and the Best Interests of Children*. ASP.

Harper, J. C., Kennett, D., & Reisel, D. (2016). The end of donor anonymity: how genetic testing is likely to drive anonymous gamete donation out of business. *Human Reproduction*, 31(6), 1135–1140. https://doi.org/10.1093/humrep/dew065

Jadva, V., Freeman, T., Kramer, W., & Golombok, S. (2009). The experiences of adolescents and adults conceived by sperm donation: comparisons by age of disclosure and family type. *Human Reproduction*, 24(8), 1909–1919. https://doi.org/10.1093/humrep/dep110

MacBride, K. (2021). Fertility doctors used their sperm to get patients pregnant. The children want justice. *Vice News*. www.vice.com/en/article/y3g5qy/fertility-doctors-used-their-sperm-to-get-patients-pregnant-the-children-want-justice

Mac Dougall, K., Becker, G., Scheib, J. E., & Nachtigall, R. D. (2007). Strategies for disclosure: how parents approach telling their children that they were conceived with donor gametes. *Fertility and Sterility*, 87(3), 524–533. https://doi.org/10.1016/j.fertnstert.2006.07.1514

Madeira, J. L. (2019). Uncommon misconceptions: holding physicians accountable for insemination fraud. *Law & Inequality*, 37, 45.

Madeira, J. L. (2020). Understanding illicit insemination and fertility fraud, from patient experience to legal reform. *Columbia Journal of Gender & Law*, 39, 110.

Mahlstedt, P. P., LaBounty, K., & Kennedy, W. T. (2010). The views of adult offspring of sperm donation: essential feedback for the development of ethical guidelines within the practice of assisted reproductive technology in the United States. *Fertility and Sterility*, 93(7), 2236–2246. https://doi.org/10.1016/j.fertnstert.2008.12.119

Miola, J. (2004). Mix-ups, mistake and moral judgement: recent developments in UK law on assisted conception. *Feminist Legal Studies*, 12(1), 67–77. https://doi.org/10.1023/B:FEST.0000026125.37716.d5

Nelson, M. K., Hertz, R., & Kramer, W. (2013). Making sense of donors and donor siblings: A comparison of the perceptions of donor-conceived offspring in lesbian-parent and heterosexual-parent families. In *Visions of the Twenty-First Century Family: Transforming Structures and Identities* (pp. 1–42). Emerald Group Publishing.

Paillé, P., & Mucchielli, A. (2016). *L'analyse qualitative en sciences humaines et sociales.* Quatrième édition. ed. Malakoff. Armand Colin.

Paye, E. (2018). Barwin's babies: the remarkable story of a disgraced Ottawa fertility doctor and those who say they are his children. *Ottawa Citizen.* https://ottawacitizen.com/news/local-news/barwins-babies

Pennings, G., Klitzman, R., Zegers-Hochschild, F. (2016). International regulation and cross-country comparisons. In S. Golombok, R. Scott, J.B. Appelby, M. Richards, S. Wilkinson (Eds.), *Regulating Reproductive Donation* (pp. 39–59). Cambridge University Press.

Rodino, I. S., Burton, P. J., & Sanders, K. A. (2011). Donor information considered important to donors, recipients and offspring: an Australian perspective. *Reproductive BioMedicine Online*, 22(3), 303–311. https://doi.org/10.1016/j.rbmo.2010.11.007

Sharak, S. (2020). Richards v. Kiken and the legal implications of fertility fraud. *American Journal of Law & Medicine*, 46(4), 528–535.

Tabachnik, S. (2020, 9 January). Proposed bill would finally make it a felony for doctors to inseminate patients with their own sperm. *Denver Post.* www.denverpost.com/2020/01/09/fertility-fraud-paul-jones-sperm-doctor-colorado/

The Associated Press. (2016, 12 September). Indiana fertility doctor used own sperm to impregnate patients, court docs say. *CBS News.* www.cbsnews.com/news/indiana-fertility-doctor-used-own-sperm-to-impregnate-women-court-docs-say/

Trépanier, A. (2020, 15 June). Class-action lawsuit against disgraced fertility doctor grows. *CBS News.* www.cbc.ca/news/canada/ottawa/norman-barwin-class-action-16-biological-children-1.5609426

Wright, K. (2016). Limiting offspring numbers: can we justify regulation? In S. Golombok, R. Scott, J. B. Appelby, M. Richards, & S. Wilkinson (Eds.), *Regulating Reproductive Donation* (pp. 185–204). Cambridge University Press.

PART II

*Children's and Adults' Lived Experiences
in Diverse Donor-Linked Families*

CHAPTER 6

The Importance of Donor Siblings to Teens and Young Adults
Who Are We to One Another?

Rosanna Hertz

The growing use of donor sperm to aid in conception has led to curiosity about the existence of donor-conceived siblings, to efforts to trace them through shared donor numbers, and even to the formation of donor-conceived networks (Andreassen, 2017; Cahn, 2013; Hertz and Mattes, 2011). As much as DNA sites, social media, and donor sibling registries have made it easier for offspring of the same gamete donor to locate each other, donor-conceived youth and parents have no clear social script for negotiating what is essentially an unprecedented relationship. Moreover, the status of a donor sibling relative to known kin is quite problematic (cf. Mckinnon, 2015; Hertz et al., 2017; Hertz and Nelson, 2019; Indekeu et al., 2021; and Scheib et al., 2020).

This chapter explores the new forms of relatedness that have emerged with the growing availability and use of donor gametes. Specifically, I ask: how do donor-conceived youth situate their donor siblings in relation to other important relationships in their lives, such as friends and siblings who also live in their nuclear families? How do they actively construct these new relationships with newfound donor siblings and where do they fit within their families?

These questions are important in two respects. First, as Strathern (1992) demonstrated, sex, gender, and heterosexuality are all components of a kinship system in which family and kinship ties are based in "nature" or blood/genes. The accessibility of both donor gametes and information about offspring from those gametes has given rise to tension about the meaning of the terms "sibling" and "family." In the dominant heteronormative view, blood ties are central to the nuclear family – so central, in fact, that the term "sibling" tends to be applied automatically when genes are shared (McKinnon, 2015). And, "family" implies a physical proximity and clearly established kinship. In the case of gamete use to conceive a child neither criteria is fulfilled.

With a growing emphasis on diverse families, family and feminist scholars – such as Powell et al. (2010) and Stacey (2011) – argue that the concept of family that historically privileged a bounded, biological hetero-sexual family must become more varied and fluid. In fact, the commercial reproduction business has created numerous possibilities for new kinship ties based on "affinities offered by technoscience" (Mamo and Alston-Stepnitz, 2015: 525). As Weston (1991: 211) writes in *Families We Choose*, "many come to question not so much the naturalness of a biological tie, but rather the assumption that biogenetic substance in itself confers kinship." As we will see, donor-conceived individuals do deploy ideas and cultural beliefs that a biogenetic connection can be "activated" to facilitate close ties. That is, one can pick and choose among those who share the same donor.

Second, in Euro-American cultures, we often take for granted that bio-genetic connections are the foundation for intimacy or emotional ties. The use of familial language, such as "donor sibling," highlights expectations of emotional closeness simply because donor-siblings are first-order blood relatives. In making this point, I draw upon Jamieson's (2011: 1) charac-terization of intimacy and intimate relationships as a guide: "[I]ntimate relationships are a type of personal relationships that are subjectively experienced and may be socially recognized as close." But "the practice of intimacy" – that is, behaving as an intimate – is what "enables, generates and sustains a subjective sense of closeness." In other words, the discov-ery of donor siblings establishes genetic relatedness but does not explain whether or how a subjective sense of closeness emerges. This is important because, as we will see, many donor-conceived individuals suggest that central preconditions for siblinghood – such as growing up together – need not be prerequisites for feeling emotionally close. I employ the term "donor siblings" because it is the common term currently used to refer to others who share a genetic tie. Younger parents sometimes prefer the shorthand "diblings" as a way to indicate a donor connection but not as conventional siblings (Hertz and Nelson, 2019). Scheib et al. (2020) used "same-donor peers" to indicate similar social position and a shared genetic link through the donor.

To answer core questions about how donor-conceived youth situate their donor siblings in relation to other important relationships (includ-ing siblings who live in their nuclear families), we interviewed children, parents, and donors about their experiences and their perceptions. In this chapter, I present findings from this research with a special emphasis on young people's perspectives because, as I found, they are the front-line participants in a process of social change.

6.1   The Study and Methods

Data for this chapter were originally collected as part of a larger study of donor-conceived families and their network formation funded by the United States National Science Foundation during the years 2014–2017. The study included interviews with 152 different families: 212 parents and their 154 children, ages 10–28, were interviewed separately, usually simultaneously. This allowed each person to tell their own accounts of events and relationships. Twelve donors related to some of these networks were also interviewed. Interviews lasted for 1–2 hours. We only interviewed families where parents had told their children they were donor conceived.

These respondents were drawn from multiple sperm banks and donor siblings' registries. Participants were interviewed across the United States in various cities in the following states: California, Massachusetts, Virginia, Maryland (and D.C.), Minnesota, Texas. When unable to travel to geographic locations we interviewed respondents over video. Since networks (families who purchased the same donor) used Facebook as a way for families to stay connected, I was invited to join several private sites.

The analysis presented in this chapter is based upon a subset of interviews with 62 youth aged 14–28 who had their own social media accounts and who had chosen to establish and maintain contact with their donor siblings. They had met at least one other donor sibling in person. Among the respondents, 36 were girls (median age 17) and 26 were boys (median age 18). The majority of youth were white, identified as heterosexual, and thought their families were middle class. Parents of these youth provided information about their household incomes, and 43 per cent earned below US$100,000. Youth often noted that they would like to meet more frequently in person but that family resources made it difficult. This chapter includes youth raised by single mothers (N = 25), same-sex parents (N = 28), and heterosexual parents (N = 9). Since parents in all family types were enthusiastic about facilitating contact with donor-siblings, these youth felt comfortable with getting to know their donor siblings, and sometimes incorporating them into their lives.

The original 62 interviews were recoded to examine how our respondents viewed their donor siblings: in comparison to siblings in their household; in comparison to friends from school or camp; in terms of how they were described to others (e.g., half-brother/sister, cousin). I wanted to examine how youth situated donor siblings in their lives – as family, friends or a hybrid of both – and how donor siblings fill voids around identity, appearance and whether they felt close to selected donor siblings within their network. In 2021, I conducted ten follow-up interviews with interviewees, who were living at home at the time of the first interview and are currently in college, to learn about changes in their relationships with donor siblings, and how these relationships continued without their parent's supervision.

The results of this analysis are presented in four sections. Each section addresses a different aspect of how youth conceived from the same donor define and experience their new relationship.

6.2 "It's Weird That We Are Related but Don't Know Each Other at All"

The young men and women interviewed found it difficult to explain the relationship they shared with their donor siblings. They may have been close in age and appearance, but they lived in different geographic locations, in families with different surnames, in different family forms, and with and without siblings who shared their parent(s). They lacked a common household that would signal that they were siblings, much less brothers or sisters or half-brothers or sisters. When they did discover their half-siblings, they used genetic "facts," for example visual resemblances, as the basis for claiming each other as some kind of "sibling" (Hertz and Mattes, 2011; Hertz and Nelson, 2019). Family resemblance became a backdrop that is associated with siblinghood. No one asked for genetic testing to confirm what appeared undeniable. As Nordqvist (2017, p. 874) argued "genetic thinking" generates the possibility that this natural connection could become meaningful. Resemblances are used as strategy to construct connectedness.

The discovery of similarities – whether facial features, or quirky mannerisms – is considered "weird" especially when donor-conceived youth did not grow up knowing their donor siblings. Here I give several examples for how donor-conceived youth cope when they confront the reality of an undeniable genetic connection. These moments of first engagement were positive for some individuals but not everyone.

Alice was stunned when she first met nine of her siblings. She felt unprepared for the moment when they met. "I spent a lot of the time just staring at them in disbelief because I have a physical similarity to basically everyone in the group. Not everyone, but most of them. You can find one unifying trait. I was just really consumed by the fact that these were siblings – genetically related to me in a very close way." Alice, who did not know other donor-conceived youth, went on to explain that the "fact" of their donor conception drew her to these "siblings" as she referred to them:

> I guess we have this other unifying concept of the anonymous father. I've never found that in another person before so that's something that brings us together and I guess just that little encapsulation of the feelings and knowledge that comes with that brings it to a different place – just familial.

As much as she took delight in noticing the ways in which they shared traits the mystery of their shared donor was the glue between them.

Similarly, Andy, a high school senior, described the sensation this way: "The fact that we share such similar blood is … a catalyst for getting to know each other." Recalling his first encounters with donor siblings at age 8, Andy described his desire to make a good impression and to puzzle through the situation at the same time:

> The toughest part would be when you don't know what questions to ask. Like you don't know how touchy you can be on a certain subject, how OK certain things are. Because these are your family, and if they were your *normal* siblings that you grew up with, this would be stuff you already shared. Stuff like political orientation or socioeconomic status.

He felt a tension between the biological connection and the lack of social familiarity. He understood that he had to tread carefully trying to figure out how their lives might intersect around culture, politics, social class, or religion. As he looked back at that moment, he reflected upon his concerns that they would not "click" or find common social ground necessary to be something more than just genetically related. He needed to figure out how his life intersected with theirs.

By contrast, Anna, a 10th grader whose quote is the title of this section, initially experienced an affront to her sense of self: "It's weird to see how similar they were to me. The athleticism in some of them, and kind of the way they talked, the mannerisms, it was so weird. I do some weird stuff, like some of my weird quirks, I could recognize that in them, and I was like, 'What the heck? I thought this was mine.'" Things she thought were uniquely hers and made her extraordinary rendered her feeling sort of ordinary. She had always thought that some things were genetically inherited from her donor but she rarely thought that other people, who were strangers, might also be like her. She continued:

> Once again, I'm going to bring up the read a book a day thing, because Samantha does that same thing, and it's so weird. I don't know anybody else who does that besides me and Dan [her twin brother], and now she

> does it too. She reads more than we do, and we read a lot. Yeah, just kind of
> like I see stuff in them that I see in myself, and it's weird, because I didn't
> know them until 3 years ago.

As much as Anna was bothered by the discovery that someone else out-
paced her reading, it operated as an important element in their bond. It
turns out that their donor remarked that he loved reading in his profile.
These youth had independently plucked this information out of the profile, making it something they could implement in their daily life that sig-
nified a connection to their anonymous donor. As "weird" as it was to find
such similarity with their donor sibling, this exchange created a special
bond that compelled Anna and many others to want to know more about
peers who were otherwise strangers.

Shared genes may have prompted curiosity and outreach but they did
not always convert into a lasting connection. By contrast to Andy, Lee,
age 19, concluded that genes were not enough to maintain ties. He found
physical resemblance but not common ground on which to build meaningful relationships: "It was kind of creepy actually, 'cause we were all about
the same age and we all had similar facial structure. [But it] never felt like
they would be the people who would be in my friend group. We all seemed
to have really different personalities." Eliza, age 21, recalled that her initial
curiosity faded over time: "I think of them as pretty much what they are:
people who happened to have gotten the same sperm donor. I don't feel any
more attached to them than I would any other person I'd meet, basically."

Encounters with others who share genes but not history call into question the heteronormative notion of blood ties constituting a superordinate
social relationship. Blood ties are important, but our interviewees suggest
that their initial role is to catalyze an exploration. Finding meaning in
terms like sibling or donor sibling takes both justification – or, perhaps
better put, perceived benefit – and persistence, as we see in the next section.

6.3   "I Find Pieces of Myself through My Donor Siblings"

For the majority of respondents, the first occasion to connect with donor
siblings was highlighted by the discovery of physical resemblances and
shared personality traits, a way to expand their biological knowledge
(Firth et al., 2018; Hertz et al., 2017; Hertz and Nelson, 2019; Scheib et al.,
2020). Their contact occurred prior to contact with the donor. Pretty
quickly, however, recognition manifested itself in other, more substan-
tial ways: finding explanations for parts unknown to themselves, seeing
themselves reflected in their donor siblings, and crafting a narrative to

explain themselves to a world unfamiliar with the donor route to conception. Moreover, recognition involved collaboration; that is, the insight may have been individual but it was facilitated by active conversation about similarities and differences and their origins. In effect, donor siblings prompted self-awareness.

Face-to-face encounters were especially important for kids who either did not have siblings or who did not share the same donor. For instance, Janey, age 17, said that meeting her donor sibling helped her understand the dramatic difference in height and build between herself and her mother. She explained: "Meeting my donor sibling was when I stopped feeling weird and different." This was an important time for her as a teenager, she went on, because she felt insecure about her body. Without even a photo of her donor it was difficult to understand that she physically favored her "paternal side." She even wondered if she was adopted. Once she met her donor sibling her height made sense to her as she found a bodily connection that explained a biological fact. Sam, raised by a single mother, was delighted to meet a donor sibling when he was a high school freshman because "she's the connection I have to my father, especially not having a photograph of my father, she's the next closest thing I could possibly have." Sam discovered in her what he felt to be an absent part of his identity, something more tangible than his imagined version of the donor. First, donor conception meant he lacked paternal kin which bothered him: meeting his half-sibling began to fill this void. Second, their moms reinforced their siblinghood by always commenting on how much they resembled one another, reinforcing that they belonged together.

Engagement with donor siblings provided the opportunity for self-discovery but it also helped many explain themselves to peers at critical developmental stages. For example, Jocelyn, Sam's half-sibling, felt ostracized when her 7th grade classmates at a Catholic school in Virginia learned that her mom conceived her with the help of a sperm donor. Jocelyn was devastated when her classmates referred to her as the "test tube baby" at a point in time when she just wanted to be like everyone else. As she put it: "[I wanted to be] normal and cool in an atomic family and I didn't have that. My friends couldn't understand being donor-conceived." Then in her sophomore year in high school she met her donor sibling and felt she had finally found someone who could understand her circumstances: "Meeting Sam changed all that. I was finally happy to find someone else that I could connect with about that kind of stuff." She found someone else like herself to talk with and, most important, she and Sam decided that their relatedness was "way cooler" than her friends "atomic" family lives. In fact, including each other within their immediate family orbit exploded traditional ideas about family membership.

Ella, born in Texas to heterosexual parents, offered a parallel example of how interaction with donor offspring helped craft a personal narrative. She wanted to keep her donor conception a secret in their politically conservative community but found her donor siblings instrumental in helping her develop a sense of comfort with her identity: "Once I met my siblings I stopped covering [up] and I explained to people who had always assumed that my dad was my biological father saying, 'No, actually I'm not related to this person or this person. I am actually donor-conceived.' It was a sort of a coming out experience." In both instances, teenage girls felt that meeting donor siblings gave them both the words and the courage with which to normalize their experiences.

In some instances, getting to know donor siblings opened the door to appreciating different kinds of families and observing relationships not found in one's immediate family. A case in point is Julia. Raised by a single heterosexual mother who married and then divorced when she was young, she had not observed a loving relationship within her own family. Through her donor sibling's parents who were lesbian, she met a loving couple. In a recent interview, Julia, now 21, commented about what she learned about love and comfort from observing her donor sibling's moms:

> It was really wonderful for me personally – exploring my sexuality after being with two parents who loved each other so much regardless of sexual orientation. It was just wonderful … They just obviously just love each other and have chosen each other as their life partners. Honestly that's something that's different than a lot of heterosexual couples I know.

By contrast to her home state, her donor sibling's family flourished in a geographic location where lesbians were welcomed. Her visits opened up the possibility for her to learn about sexuality and partner preference in ways she had not observed in her mother's relationships with men.

The key insight here is that acquisition of donor siblings can be satisfying and fill voids around identity, appearance, and siblinghood. These donor siblings embody aspects of the donor, allowing them to explore parts of their identity based on shared genetics. They feel affirmed through one another as they become more comfortable with their donor-conception status. Moreover, they have the opportunity to observe and participate in families they were unlikely to meet otherwise. The ability to question without judgment and to observe without restraint turns out to be an important part of giving meaning to an unfamiliar relationship – for all participants.

6.4 "Just Because They Have the Same Genetics, Does That Mean They're My Family?"

Unprecedented relationships are often scripted the first time using conventional ideas and experiences. Garfinkel (1967) referred to this use of knowledge as "indexing" or sorting things and people into categories we already know. When indexing does not work – when, for example, the category does not do justice to the experience – new categories may come into being. But they rarely survive without repetition and repetition often requires dedicated effort, creativity, and even courage. Developing a relationship with these genetically close but strange individuals involves bridging categories that are familiar but not always compatible.

Interviews with this group of young men and women revealed that definitions and labels proved to be extremely important in three stages of donor sibling interaction: the buildup, first contact and relationship building. During these stages kids grappled with using what is known and familiar to them in friendships and families to incorporate a new category of people in their lives. Based upon the evolution of these interactions, indexing either "succeeded" by reaffirming conventional labels of friend or family or it "failed" in that it led to new categories. In the following section I provide examples of both and explore possible explanations for the difference in outcomes.

6.4.1 Buildup

The first stage is the buildup to communication or meeting, as children (and often parents) try to answer questions such as, what do they want to come of this meet up? What are they expecting? Or as Oliver put it: "Just because they have the same genetics, does that mean they're my family?" In this stage, expectations build as youth use their understanding of familial roles and friendships to imagine possible relationships with their genetic kin.

Youth in this study had vastly different expectations. Gabriella, who had no siblings within her immediate family, was "hoping that I would find maybe like a true brother or sister – like where you're really close with them." Marc, by contrast, had a brother and a stepsister and "thought that it would be like a fun new friend group." In this stage, the language and constructs they rely on typically reflect what these teens hope to get out of their engagement. Marc added, "I don't really need more family than I already have." In other words, teens use the definitions of friend versus family to set boundaries on their obligations and commitment to their donor siblings. Those who use the language of family may expect more serious, intimate relationships to develop, while friendship can be distancing, allowing for fun and perhaps intimacy without the intensity or reciprocity that familial relationships imply.

6.4.2   First Contact

In the second moment, first contact, the youth's imagined relationships are challenged as they collide with the real people attached to their fantasies. This stage is significant because teens are introduced to new emotional and social connections with their donor siblings. These interactions provide them with a new lens through which to understand how these people may fit in their lives. Instead of using friendship and family as abstractions through which to assign types of obligation, they now have the opportunity to compare these feelings to the attachments they already have with "real" friends and family. They also use tools such as age, gender, and similar interests to probe these connections and determine who they feel closest to. For example, Ethan explained how he was keen to get to know a male donor sibling: "I grew up in a house very much dominated by females, and so I tried to reach out to Max in particular." However, he went on, "That didn't really work out because Max and I don't really have much in common." Undeterred, he and his twin, Julia, did ultimately establish a relationship with another sibling, Iris, with whom they shared a great deal in common.

6.4.3   Relationship Building

Heavily influenced by first contact, definitions related to who these siblings are to interviewees develop more fully in the relationship building period that follows. For those who were disappointed by the meet up, did not feel connections or felt only limited attachment, this stage may be more casual. Liza, age 19, felt that it was enough to simply have made contact: "It's important for me to know them and to know that they are their own people and they exist in the world. I don't have to like them, but they are still there and they're not ideas of people, they are real human beings." For those who clicked and hoped to grow these relationships, it involved further face-to-face meet ups and potentially establishing relationships with their donor sibling's family, as well.

While these stages help children to understand their connectivity, many ultimately find themselves in a hybrid territory where donor siblings are neither just friends or completely family. Oliver explained that as much as he liked all five kids he met he picked only two to call "siblings." These two kids are not family because they share the same donor but because they have "*become* family" – similar to his "closest best friends" who were "random people I basically met and they became close enough to me that they crossed that same bridge." The *bridge* is important because he felt obligated to the two high school friends whom he has selected to "crossover" from friends to family. He characterized this as a conscious process: "I had months of kind of being able to let myself say, 'Listen, you need to be able to dismiss this idea of what is traditionally family.'" By contrast, for kids who weren't looking for (or weren't prepared for) familial intimacy, donor siblings would never cross this bridge.

The kids who develop relationships are more open to creating a notion of siblinghood that doesn't require that they grow up together. However, even in Oliver's case, the notion remains a private one – shared only by those whose interactions have given it meaning.

Making it public (or keeping it private) turns out to have a lot to do with how kids choose – a topic to which I now turn.

6.5   Deciding among My Siblings? Picking and Choosing

After making a connection, youth are challenged to decide whether to view their donor siblings as family, friends, or a hybrid. Some we interviewed chose people who matched their expectations of an idealized family; others took a more social approach, selecting based on friendships they already had. However, the plurality ended up employing a combination of these two, affirming the idea that donor siblings fall into an interstitial space.

In instances where imagined family structures were used as a selection screen, children began with what an idealized sibling looked like to them. Analyzing conventional sibling relationships, Katherine Davies (2015) argued that siblings erect their relationships through stories that make comparisons between themselves and their brothers/sisters. Jocelyn, quoted earlier, was 15 when she met her donor sibling, Sam. She explained their motivation to continue their relationship.

> I think in high school especially, we had a really big sense of competition, because we're both very smart. But he tried harder than I did. He just seemed so impressive, and I wanted to impress him. To be an older sister he could be proud of. That sense of wanting to make each other proud also helps to connect us.

Table 6.1 *Raised with siblings and feelings about donor siblings*

	No siblings (n = 34)	Siblings (n = 28)
Number of siblings in house (M, range)	N/A	1.5, 1–4
Number of donor siblings (M, range)*	8.5, 1–41	11.8, 1–41
Intimacy with donor siblings		
Not close to donor siblings	10 (29.4%)	10 (35.7%)
Close to at least one donor sibling	24 (70.6%)	18 (64.3%)
Immediate family members		
Only considers siblings in household as immediate family	N/A	20 (71.4%)
Considers donor siblings to be immediate family	17 (50%)	7 (25.0%)
Did not respond	0	1 (3.6%)

*Includes only those that have revealed their identities. Others may be listed on registries but are unwilling to connect with donor siblings. Still others may not be listed.

Oliver (discussed above) anticipated that two of his donor siblings would fulfill a conventional family script he admired and wanted as part of his life: "They fit the roles that I was looking for: a younger brother who looks up to me, and an older sister I look up to." He embraced a sense of familial belonging only with these two donor siblings, not the others in his network. Like Oliver, respondents who did not grow up with siblings in their household but entered a network with a large number of donor siblings were more likely to say they felt close to more donor siblings than those who grew up with household siblings (70.6 per cent versus 64.3 per cent – see Table 6.1). But, even in their selection the affinity they felt and the criteria they chose approximates the size of a typical sibling group in the United States.[1]

In instances in which kids began with the expectation of finding a "friend," the choice process followed a familiar script, that is, guided by a search for someone who shared their interests or hobby. The central dynamic was one of mutual fulfillment, that is, a recognition that pursuit of a shared interest would "naturally" be mutually satisfying. For example, Ethan considered himself quite shy and socially awkward; nonetheless, he hoped to find in his network of donor siblings a "guy friend" to become close to, who shared more intellectual pursuits. His solution was to employ his twin, Julia, to help him navigate both online and face-to-face encounters. That's how he and Iris became friends over a shared love of historical fiction.

---

[1] In the United States, families with children have an average of approximately two per household (1.86): Census, www.census.gov/data/tables/time-series/demo/families/states.html

Bids for friendship did not always succeed. For example, Gabriela met her donor siblings at what she described as an "awkward stage" – her early teens – and to her mind that made the first connection more difficult. Looking back, she realized that meeting them at this age impeded her hopes of becoming lasting friends; at age 15, she felt pickier about friendships and already had a life of her own, so she did not fully exert herself, and neither did her donor siblings. To her, a classic friendship would have involved kids who had grown up together through awkward stages. Similarly, Alyssa was hoping for a strong bond between donor siblings especially now that they were on their own and in college but found that they didn't have time to reciprocate her efforts. She exclaimed, "It'd be nice if they would try to plan things with me, too, because it can be hard and sometimes I can feel a bit rejected when they just ignore me." Disappointment might prove frustrating, as it did for Gabriela and Alyssa, but it helped many to refine their expectations and, ultimately, their definition of siblinghood.

Of particular interest are the expectations and experiences of kids raised without siblings. Many of these youth told us that they wished for siblings and thus were excited to be introduced to other children from the same donor. Having no experience at the performance of siblinghood, they had difficulty understanding social obligations and expectations in this context. They had to start from scratch, unable to use personal knowledge as an index, to help guide these new sibling relationships. The absence of a frame or index, in Garfinkel's terms, gave them more work to do. Joy, age 18, put it this way: "I don't even have a lot of boy cousins and I obviously don't have any siblings so I never had a brother relationship (besides my really good guy friends). So, it was really hard to establish that brother-sister relationship." Henry, interviewed at age 19, seconded Joy's point: "I wanted to meet them and all that, but I didn't understand what it would mean to meet them or what it would mean to be their brother." He recalled meeting the first of his many donor siblings when he was 13: "Mary hates pigeons. It's awful, to the point in which the first time we saw pigeons, which are everywhere in New York, and I mean everywhere, she hid behind me and was terrified. I'm all like, what is happening? I learned that this person, who had just met me, was already seeking security from me. Clearly, that's a big commitment for something that you haven't done for the past 13 years of your life." Henry's example not only points to how unprepared he was for sibling expectations that Mary had about older brothers but also that, like Joy, he felt at a loss having little to guide him as he entered a new role.

On the other side, most young people who grew up with siblings did not think of donor siblings as their immediate family (see Table 6.1). Some, like Eliza, set high expectations for what it would take for someone to become family. Eliza grew up with a twin and was unwilling to embrace a deep connection with her donor siblings. She advised kids new to the donor sibling network: "Don't go in thinking that you're going to have a new family or anything, because that's not what this is about at all." By contrast, Julia and her brother Ethan acknowledged that physical proximity made a difference when it came to the day-to-day interactions; but they also fully embraced Iris as immediate family. Ethan explained: "Even if I don't see Iris for two years we pick up as if it didn't matter ... we see each other for like a week and we're best buds." They placed Iris within the orbit of their immediate family, while their ten other donor siblings belonged in an outer orbit of distant kin. In effect, youth raised with siblings have mixed expectations of the place of donor siblings in their lives.

Follow-up interviews with a subset of respondents gave a clear indication that initial designations of siblinghood do not always hold fast. For example, Joy's initial interaction involved Nick, the one kid her moms had unearthed who shared the same donor. Joy reported trying hard to connect with Nick but summed up the results as "awkward" because it was a stretch to find much in common. She was prepared to limit their relationship to occasional text messages until an avalanche of donor offspring appeared online and she suddenly had a choice. Almost immediately, she hit it off with Beth because "we are a lot alike because we are both really silly and also we are into the same social media, as dumb as that sounds." Joy began to describe their relationship in sibling terms. Her takeaway from Nick and Beth was that it was possible to pick and choose: to see which connections evolved and which did not.

6.6   Conclusion

Four findings stand out from my analysis of interviews with donor siblings:

First, children actively "index" new-found siblings using relational categories and roles both familiar and imagined. Kids who come from families where they already have brothers and/or sisters (including other donor offspring) tend to have ready-made roles to slot new entrants into. Others, raised solo, are initially challenged to define a role for a new arrival. Some will borrow from what they know of heteronormative models to create an initial set of expectations like, for example the pattern of obligations older children have to younger ones. Others will imagine a relationship – of intimacy or companionship – and employ it until it isn't reciprocated or otherwise proves a mismatch.

Second, whatever their expectations of donor siblings, children discovered that a central feature of the heteronormative model did not accord with what they were experiencing. That is, the discovery of multiple offspring – numbering perhaps in the dozens and sometimes already organized into networks – upset traditional notions about the size of a family. Notions of intimacy and obligation in a bounded, nuclear family were immediately called into question by the sheer number of potential new members.

Third, in the face of undefined roles and larger numbers, children (sometimes with the help of their parents) experimented with how they named their relatives and how they did the work of siblinghood. For most, a hybrid between brother, sister, friend, and acquaintance emerged. When bids for more intimate relationships were rebuffed or otherwise faltered, kids tended to accept a less intense alternative. But in many instances, children did find a way to "bridge" the definitional gap and arrive at a stable script for their relationships.

And, finally, the overarching process of "enacting" siblinghood and "sustaining" a sense of closeness to them, I observed by way of the interviews – aided significantly by follow-up interviews done several years later – revealed that even the "hybrid" category was still undergoing redefinition. That is, the increased use of donors by single mothers and queer families, the rapid growth in the number of donor sibling registries attached to sperm banks resulting in the formation of donor sibling networks at younger ages have all contributed to a routinization of the idea of donor siblinghood. We can expect that in the future children born from donor gametes will encounter more formalized options.

Two significant questions follow from this research and deserve further investigation. First, it is not yet clear whether the processes I explored will cause a fundamental shift – much less a reformation – of the heteronormative model of family. Certainly, the growing familiarity of what I have described as the hybrid notion of donor sibling will provide comfort and tethering for a rapidly growing category of donor-conceived families; but it is not clear whether the recognition of the importance of networks of donor siblings will lead to a revision in the definition of family.

Second, there is an important policy implication here: In this research the number of known donor siblings varied enormously from 1 to 41 (see Table 6.1). Without global consensus and regulations that limit the number of offspring produced from a given donor, it will not be possible to form meaningful relationships between donor siblings. As much as these interviewees recognize newcomers as "genetically related," those who come forward (or discover their donor-conception late) are likely to be marginalized, relegated to the Facebook page, but hardly embraced as intimates.

Acknowledgements

Thank you to the Knapp Center for funding Aiyana Smith, who was an outstanding research assistant. Thanks to Caroline Witten for help with quantitative data analysis and to Robert J. Thomas for critical comments.

References

Andreassen, R. (2017). New kinships, new family formations and negotiations of intimacy via social media sites. *Journal of Gender Studies, 26*(3), 361–371. https://doi.org/10.1080/09589236.2017.1287683

Boyd, D. (2014). *It's Complicated: The Social Lives of Networked Teens.* Yale University Press.

Cahn, N. R. (2013). *The New Kinship: Constructing Donor-Conceived Families.* NYU Press.

Davies, K. (2015). Siblings, stories and the self: the sociological significant of young people's sibling relationships. *Sociology, 49*(4): 679–695.

Frith, L., Blyth, E., Crawshaw, M., & van den Akker, O. (2018). Searching for 'relations' using a DNA linking register by adults conceived following sperm donation. *BioSocieties, 13*(1), 170–189. https://doi.org/10.1057/s41292-017-0063-2

Garfinkel, H. (1967). *Studies in Ethnomethodology.* Prentice-Hall.

Hertz, R. (2009). Turning strangers into kin: Half-siblings and anonymous donors. In M.K. Nelson and A.I. Garey (Eds.), *Who's Watching?: Daily Practices of Surveillance among Contemporary Families.* Vanderbilt University Press, pp. 156–174. https://doi.org/10.2307/j.ctv17vf76w.13

Hertz, R. & Mattes, J. (2011). Donor-shared siblings or genetic strangers: New families, clans and the internet. *Journal of Family Issues, 32*(9), 1129–1155. https://doi.org/10.1177/0192513x11404345

Hertz, R., & Nelson, M. K. (2019). *Random Families: Genetic Strangers, Sperm Donor Siblings, and the Creation of New Kin.* Oxford University Press.

Hertz, R, Nelson, M. K., & Kramer, W. (2017). Donor sibling networks as a vehicle for expanding kinship: a replication and extension. *Journal of Family Issues, 38*(2), 248–284. https://doi.org/10.1177/0192513x16631018

Indekeu, A., Bolt, S. H., & Maas, A. J. B. M. (2021). Meeting multiple donor half siblings: psychosocial challenges. *Human Fertility*, 1–12, https://doi.org/10.1080/14647273.2021.1872804

Jamieson, L. (2011), Intimacy as a concept: explaining social change in the context of globalization or another form of ethnocentricism? *Sociological Research Online*. 16(4), 151–163. Org.uk/16/4/15.html>10.5153/sro.2497

Mamo, L., & Alston-Stepnitz, E. (2015). Queer intimacies and structural inequalities: new directions in stratified reproduction. *Journal of Family Issues*, 36(4), 519–540. https://doi.org/10.1177/0192513x14563796

McKinnon, S. (2015). Productive paradoxes of the assisted reproductive technologies in the context of new kinship. *Journal of Family Isses*, 36(4), 461–479 https://doi.org/10.1177/0192513X14563799

Nordqvist, P. (2017). Genetic thinking and everyday living: on family practices and family imaginaries. *The Sociological Review*, 65(4): 865–881.

Powell, B. Blozendahl, C., Geist, C., & Steelman, L.C. (2010). *Counted Out: Same-Sex Relationships and American's Definitions of Family*. New York: Russell Sage Foundation.

Scheib, J. E., McCormick, E., Benward, J., & Ruby, A. (2020). Finding people like me: contact among young adults who share an open-identity sperm donor. *Human Reproduction Open*, 2020(4) 1–13. https://doi.org/10.1093/hropen/hoaa057

Stacey, J. (2011). *Unhitched Love: Marriage, and Family Values from Western Hollywood to Western China*. New York: New York University Press.

Strathern, M. (1992). *Reproducing the Future: Anthroplogy, Kinship and the Assisted Reproductive Technologies*. London: Routledge.

Weston, K. (1991), *Families We Choose: Lesbian, Gays, Kinship*. New York: Columbia University Press.

CHAPTER 7

The Experiences of Donor-Conceived People Making Contact with Same-Donor Offspring through Fiom's Group Meetings

Astrid Indekeu and A. Janneke B. M. Maas

7.1 Introduction

More and more donor-conceived people are interested in, and in contact with, same-donor offspring,[1] defined as those conceived using the sperm or egg of the same donor (Indekeu et al., 2021b). Increased openness regarding donor conception, the establishment of donor registers and the impact of the Internet (e.g. social media, online searchers, direct-to-consumer online DNA testing) have created increased possibilities to seek and contact donor relatives. For example, voluntary services were established so donor-conceived people could seek information about the donor – for example, the Donor-Conceived Register (DCR) in the UK, the Fiom KID-DNA Database in the Netherlands, and the Voluntary Register in Victoria, Australia (Crawshaw et al., 2016). Through these registers, donor-conceived people could directly or indirectly also discover information about same-donor offspring. Other initiatives focused more specifically on finding information about same-donor offspring. Some of those are private, offspring and/or parent led organisations, such as Donor Sibling Registry (US-based, but international in scope) or MyDonorFamily (Denmark), while others are provided through a fertility clinic or gamete bank, such as The Family Contact list at The Sperm Bank of California (TSBC). Also, online genetic genealogy services, developed for purposes other than donor-linking, such as FamilyTreeDNA, MyHeritage and 23andMe are increasingly used to successfully identify donor relatives (Crawshaw et al., 2016). Finally, some countries have introduced a legal right to access information about same-donor offspring. For example, in the UK, the entitlement for donor-conceived individuals conceived after April 2005 to access identifying information about the donor at the age of 18 was

---

[1] In this chapter we will use the term 'same-donor offspring' without giving a specific social meaning to this genetic connection.

extended in 2009 to include a right to seek identifying information about same-donor offspring (Human Fertilisation and Embryology Act 2008). This led to the Donor Sibling Link (DSL, UK), a service established by the Human Fertilisation and Embryology Authority in 2010. In the Australian state of Victoria, the Voluntary Register permits information exchange between donor-related parties, including same-donor offspring and the parents of same-donor offspring when the children are minors (Assisted Reproductive Treatment Act; Johnson et al., 2012).

First reports on the outcomes of contact between same-donor off-spring are generally positive (Blyth, 2012; Freeman et al., 2014; Hertz & Nelson, 2019; Hertz et al., 2017; Jadva et al., 2010; Scheib et al., 2020). Moreover, 'the discovery of same-donor offspring relationships is commonly viewed as more straightforwardly beneficial than connecting with a donor' (Freeman et al., 2014, p. 286; Scheib et al., 2020). However, looking more closely at these new connections, two questions arise. First, what does it means to share genes with 'strangers'? Is a social relationship presumptively imposed on these new genetic connections and if so, how is kinship made and maintained and maybe unmade? Our findings suggest that genetic connections alone do not make kinship feel 'natural'. Instead, it appears that work has to be done to create the emotional feeling of familiarity and belonging with these new connections. Same-sibling connections are typically experienced in a continuum, moving from strangers, to acquaintances, to friends, and then to extended family and close family (Bolt et al., 2021; Hertz, 2017; see also Chapter 6 by Hertz in this volume). The second question to arise is what happens when donor-conceived people meet *multiple* same-donor offspring or join large same-donor offspring groups? This question will be the focus of this chapter.

Prior to the enactment of assisted reproductive technology (ART) laws in a number of jurisdictions, no limit was placed on the number of donor-conceived offspring per donor. Some countries still do not have limits, while others have professional guidelines that are however not enforced by the law (e.g. the United States). However, even in countries with ART regulation and limits on offspring per donor, the practice of international sperm banks sometimes causes large networks of same-donor offspring to be created. This is because international sperm banks ship to multiple countries, so while they may comply with the limit in each receiving country, the overall number of offspring may exceed the limits. Furthermore, in recent years, there has been a sharp growth in the number of 'online sperms donors', men who donate outside the regulated routes of fertility clinics and sperm banks (Freeman et al., 2016). Reports are published on groups of 150 or more same-donor offspring (Mroz, 2011, 2021). These new developments have raised debates about the psycho-social consequences of being part of same-donor offspring networks (Scheib & Ruby, 2009).

Large groups of same-donor offspring often evoke a lot of emotions, such as distaste towards a prolific donor and concerns about harm for those involved, such as the increased risk of consanguineous relationships (Freeman et al., 2014; Wright, 2016). Less is known about how donor-conceived people themselves experience and manage these multiple new genetic connections. In addition to the size of some of these networks, donor-conceived people are confronted with the *constantly expanding* nature of same-donor offspring networks as new members join (Blyth, 2012). Moreover, as same-donor offspring belong to different families, they are challenged to manage being part of various scattered same-donor offspring networks (Hertz et al., 2017). Finally, given the international nature of the fertility industry, donor-conceived people will be part of "assisted world families" (Hudson, 2017) – genetic families that are geographically spread out over the world.

This chapter presents empirical findings on psycho-social research with donor-conceived people who met multiple same-donor offspring in group-meetings guided by Fiom's counsellors. A full description of these findings can be found in Indekeu et al. (2021b) and Bolt et al. (2021). This chapter, however, explores more deeply Fiom's approach to these group meetings. It concludes by discussing the opportunities and challenges presented by contact between multiple same-donor offspring and reflecting on a possible role for policy/regulators.

Findings in this chapter derive from a qualitative study conducted by Fiom in the Netherlands. Fiom is a Dutch organisation that has provided independent information and support in the search for birth and biographical origins since 1930. In 2010, together with Canisius-Wilhelmina Hospital (CWZ), Fiom founded a voluntary DNA database (Fiom KID-DNA Database) for those conceived via gamete donation or who had donated prior to 2004. In 2004, the Netherlands enacted the Information Donor Insemination Law (Wet Donorgegevens Kunstmatige Bevruchting) (Janssens et al., 2006) which required that only identifiable donors be used in the Netherlands. Fiom was assigned to provide a professional support service for donor-conceived people when accessing identifying information about the donor (starting at age 16). On 30 April 2022, a total of 2,533 donor-conceived people and 880 donors had registered in the Fiom KID-DNA Database. Forty-six per cent ($n = 1,174$) of donor-conceived people have been linked with one or more same-donor offspring. While

Fiom's database focuses on linking donor-offspring and the donor, it also revealed several same-donor offspring networks. As of April 2022, there are 56 same-donor offspring networks (≥4 same-donor offspring) in the Fiom KID-DNA Database. The donor is known to 41 of these networks. The size of these networks is continuously growing, with the largest network consisting of 76 people. Some of the networks in the Fiom KID-DNA Database have additional connections with other same-donor offspring who are registered at a direct-to-consumer genetic database but not at the Fiom KID-DNA Database. These connections are not included in the Fiom data. This means that donor-conceived people can be confronted with networks that are even larger than we identify in the Fiom KID-DNA Database.

Guided group meetings has been a long-standing offer by Fiom, although in the past they were mainly offered to adopted people. Guided group meetings helped in the recognition and acknowledgement of adoptees' experiences and offered support as they moved through the process. In the context of donor conception, guided group meetings were set up specifically for donor-conceived people conceived from the same donor. This was because donor-conceived people requested this themselves (for example, a network of same-donor offspring with a specific context that caused much emotional turmoil and need for support). Sometimes it was offered to them by the Fiom social worker (e.g. when multiple same-donor offspring were at the same time identified from the Fiom KID-DNA Database). Group meetings at Fiom are generally offered once to each network to introduce members of the network to each other. Subsequently, the members can freely decide to continue meeting each other in group settings or not. When new matches are identified within an existing network, Fiom social workers explore with the new donor-offspring if and how they want to be introduced to the same-donor offspring network. A guided group meeting is free of cost for the participants as the support is funded by the Dutch government.

The study adopted a qualitative approach to understand how meeting multiple same-donor offspring, and the support provided to them, were experienced. Data were collected through individual qualitative interviews. All study-participants were a member of a same-donor offspring network identified by the Fiom KID-DNA Database and took part in a group meeting organised by Fiom counsellors between May 2017 and February 2018. A total of 82 donor-conceived people participated in the meetings (30 per cent male, 70 per cent female) and 19 people were willing to be interviewed. Interviews took place between April and June 2018

Table 7.1 *Number of same-donor offspring in each network*

	Network 1 (n)	Network 2 (n)	Network 3 (n)	Network 4 (n)	Network 5 (n)
Month of first group meeting	2017 May	2017 June	2017 June	2017 October	2018 February
Network size at first group meeting	18	19	12	27	7
Network at recruitment time April 2018	34	19	12	31	7
Network in April 2022	76	47	22	57	14
Increase group size over 4–5 years	322%	147%	83%	111%	100%

and addressed the following topics: (i) motives for searching for same-donor offspring; (ii) expectations about contact; (iii) feelings prior to, during and after the group meeting; and (iv) experiences of the support they received.

The nineteen study participants came from five same-donor offspring networks. These five networks each had one group meeting guided by a Fiom counsellor. The networks ($n = 5$) of same-donor offspring consisted of 7–27 donor-offspring at the time of the meetings, extending to 7–34 at the time of recruitment and to 13–67 by September 2021 (see Table 7.1). Both male and female donor-conceived people participated in the group meetings, but only female donor-conceived people participated in the study. Study participants were 15–42 years old (Mean ± SD = 30 ± 8.6). Donor-conceived people in the networks in this study did not meet until they were at least adolescents, but most were adults. Study-participants were born into different household types: 13 into a heterosexual couple, 3 into a solo-mother and 4 into a lesbian couple household.

7.2 Donor-Conceived People's Experiences of Meeting Multiple Same-Donor Offspring

Study-participants mentioned several positive experiences and consequences when finding and meeting same-donor offspring. For example, through comparison and looking for shared or unique physical and/or personality traits, participants gained information about themselves (such as medical information) and gained indirect knowledge about the donor. This was especially valuable for those who had no information about the donor or who did not resemble their own family. In addition to the obtained knowledge, many experienced feelings of recognition and belonging when meeting same-donor offspring. By meeting and hearing from other donor-conceived people they felt recognised and acknowledged in their own experiences of being donor-conceived. Other research (Scheib et al., 2020) has described the significance of 'finding people like me'. Associated with this feeling of recognition is a sense of belonging. So the feeling of belonging was not only connected to sharing a genetic connection, but as well to the emotional support found in connecting with others who are also donor-conceived. While recognition could be immediate, belonging would take time and effort (Bolt et al., 2021). Our research explores a short time frame of a maximum of one year, and is thus not able to comment on the ways these new relationships develop in the future.

Like Blyth (2012) has argued, our observation strengthens the idea that the value of connecting with same-donor offspring does not lie only in the knowledge same-donor offspring gain from each other, but also in the interactions with each other. Like others (Freeman et al., 2014); Hertz, Chapter 6 in this volume; Montuschi & Ellis, 2020), participants in our study also seemed to experience less ambivalence in meeting same-donor offspring than the donor. However, even when the interactions with same-donor offspring are highly valued, searching for and meeting donor relatives is also acknowledged as a challenging process.

Most participants (13/19) had not thought about same-donor offspring when they started searching for their donor. However, a minority (4/19) were solely interested in contact with same-donor offspring, while 2/19 wanted to confirm if their sisters, who they were being raised with, were full-genetic siblings. It is not uncommon for donor-conceived people to not initially think of same-donor offspring. This is because parents and donor-conceived often think of the donor as the person who donated to them or whose donation led to their existence (and maybe that of the siblings they grew up with). At first, they do not generally think about 'the other families' the donor helped to create.

Finding same-donor offspring when 'unprepared' is challenging. However, being confronted with a large number of same-donor offspring raises more complex issues. For some this is a positive experience ('I am happy with so many brothers and sisters'), while others experience it with ambivalence. Recognition and belonging could be positive but having many same-donor offspring could also be associated with a feeling of loss of specialness or uniqueness due to being 'one of so many' (Indekeu & Hens, 2019; Montuschi & Ellis, 2020). Additionally, multiple same-donor offspring can also evoke emotions related to the donor, such as 'the yuk'-factor of an unlimited donor (Freeman et al., 2014). This again might impact how donor-conceived people think and feel about their own personal life story.

While interactions between the same-donor offspring were highly valued, it was challenging to manage the contact with a large number of same-donor offspring. Each member could have different expectations about the contact and different ideas about privacy. Besides managing their own feelings regarding these new contacts, donor-conceived people had to cope with group dynamics and group pressure (Indekeu et al., 2021a). Study-participants also struggled with the continuous expansion in numbers, as it created new dynamics within the group.

Interactions between same-donor offspring could lead to various relationships and feelings of belonging (Bolt et al., 2021), but study-participants also mentioned feeling guilty about not being able to connect with everyone or feeling fearful for falling out the group. They wanted to be in closer contact with their donor relatives, but were puzzled about how to fit these multiple new relationships into their existing relationships, particularly as they realized that establishing (and maintaining) relationships takes effort and time (Bolt et al., 2021). Job and family demands often intervened. The following participant describes the frustration she experienced when confronted with 34 same-donor offspring and figuring out how to get to know them and feel part of the network:

> I want to get rid of this feeling of powerlessness. It makes me sad. I don't want that, I want to learn to deal with it. I don't know how. I can just schedule 34 appointments on a Sunday, and that will occupy me for a year, but it doesn't work that way. I don't know who should help me, someone from Fiom, a psychologist or someone else. It drives me crazy. I want to belong somewhere and I am happy that I have found them. But how do I continue to belong? How do I avoid getting excluded? (Network 1, age 42)

In our study, donor-conceived people were generally in contact with multiple same-donor offspring (n = 8 to 31) and met frequently in group settings rather than having individual contacts with some members of the network as described in previous studies (Blyth, 2012; Hertz et al., 2017; Jadva et al., 2010; Hertz, Chapter 6 in this volume). It is important to notice that it is unclear if the networks continued to meet in group settings over the years. Some factors might have enhanced a group-feeling, such as being identified from the start as a group rather than gradually and individually being linked to each other, making contact from the start in a group setting, or geographical closeness. Another possible influencing element might be the use of a 'siblingship' framework. Most participants described these relationships in terms of 'half-siblings'. This can also be seen in policy documents ('sibling-registries'), parents talking about 'searching for your siblings', and use of sibling language in media-reports. However, the word sibling is linked with various feelings, expectations and norms about responsibilities and obligations associated with kinship-relationship. While disengaging from relationships with strangers might be quite easy, it is likely more difficult to do so for a relationship within a kinship-context.

7.3 Fiom's Practice of Running Group Meetings for Same-Donor Offspring

While some jurisdictions have professional practice guidelines for supporting *individual* contact between donor and donor-conceived person (e.g. ANZICA, 2012), no such professional guidelines exist for supporting contact between multiple same-donor offspring. In the absence of guidance, Fiom developed an approach for facilitating and supporting contact between multiple same-donor offspring that include recognition of the challenges associated with the specific context of same-donor offspring networks.

In general, group meetings at Fiom are offered once to each same-donor offspring network to introduce members of the network to each other. Alternatively, a group-meeting can be requested by the network itself. Subsequently, the members can decide to continue meeting each other in group settings, but these meetings will not be guided by Fiom. More recently, fewer new same-donor offspring networks have been identified in the Fiom KID-DNA Database. Instead, new members of an existing network are being identified. Professional support is now more focused on introducing new members to an already existing network, rather than facilitating group meetings.

In describing the practice of running group meetings, we will use a slightly adapted version of the model proposed for support groups by Schopler and Galinksy (1993) in which they describe external and internal elements (environmental conditions, participant characteristics and group conditions) that are considered important determinants of group interactions and outcomes. For professionals guiding such group meetings, it is important to have knowledge of and insight into these factors, as well as to have knowledge about donor conception.

7.3.1   Environmental Conditions

Except for one person, all group attendees lived in the Netherlands and their geographical closeness facilitated in-person group meetings. For same-donor offspring living in large countries or in different countries (e.g. when conceived by a sperm donor from an international sperm bank), in-person meetings would be cost prohibitive (not only financially, but also in terms of time and energy). However, even in a small country like the Netherlands distance was a hindrance to meeting regularly in person. Many donor-conceived people would therefore engage more with same-donor offspring living closer to them.

The group meetings guided by a social worker from Fiom were free of charge. Thus, besides travel costs, there was no additional financial burden. The location of the meeting seemed an important element in the success of a meetings. Group meetings were held at the Fiom building, an old, three-storey townhouse in the middle of a provincial town. For some, Fiom's association with the government made the location too clinical and unsuitable for such an emotional event. For example, some participants felt a restaurant was considered a better location. However, others regarded a public place such as a restaurant as unsuitable for such a personal event. Furthermore, large same-donor offspring networks attract high media attention, in which various and often challenging representations of the situation are published. Media reports impact the group meetings and may affect group dynamics; for example, by intensifying already existing emotions or by dividing the network as representations might not be shared by all network members.

7.3.2   Participant Characteristics

7.3.2.1   Composition

Mainly women (70 per cent) participated in the group meetings. A similar gender-ratio is seen within the registrants of the Fiom KID DNA-Database. The group meetings were otherwise characterised by a great variety in age (15–43), family type (two-mother, solo-mother or father/mother household, with siblings or not), being early or late informed about the donor conception, education, relationship status, region of residence and so on. All these characteristics shape participants' perceptions and views on being donor conceived and the shared genetic connection. They may also affect the expectations they have regarding the other members of the network, what they expect from a group meeting and how bonds will be formed.

7.3.2.2 Size

The size of same-donor offspring group meetings is a challenging feature in two ways. Firstly, in contrast to most other group meetings (either support, therapy or self-help groups) where an organiser often sets a limit on the size of the group, this is not possible in group meetings for same-donor offspring networks. The size of the same-donor offspring network determines the size of the group meeting. The number of participants can already be significant at the time of the first meeting. Secondly, same-donor offspring networks almost always increase as new same-donor offspring are identified (see Table 7.1). The continuous expansion can be a challenge for the network and new members, as well as for the professional with oversight of the group. In a continuously growing network over time, it is difficult for the professional to stay abreast of the dynamics within the group. Yet this can be important information when supporting new members joining the network.

7.3.3 Group Conditions

Group conditions mediate the environmental conditions and participants' characteristics and directly affect group outcomes. Group conditions refer broadly to the goals, structural form, and development of the group.

7.3.3.1 The Goal of the Group Meeting

Identifying the goal of the group meeting was not easy. The large networks of same-donor offspring that were identified from the Fiom KID-DNA Database revealed that members could have different expectations. For example, one network was confronted with the news that the fertility doctor who had treated their mothers had been the donor himself, causing much emotional turmoil within the network and a need for support in coping with the situation. In another case, multiple same-donor offspring were identified at the same time which required a large number of groups members to meet each other simultaneously, rather than getting to know each other successively. Support was requested for setting up and facilitating contact between attendees. Moreover, even where there was a shared general goal (e.g. to meet each other) individuals could have very different underlying motivations (e.g. curiosity, to get information about themselves, to meet family, to extend their family, as is also described in Scheib et al., 2020 and Indekeu et al., 2021a) creating different expectations. Consequently, the group meetings typically had a double goal: facilitating contact between same-donor offspring and offering support (offering information about DNA matching, receiving acknowledgement and recognition for their experiences).

7.3.3.2   The Structural Form

The structural form of a group system is defined by its group operating procedures and meeting format, roles, norms and culture, and bonds.

Group operating procedures and meeting format: Initially the group meetings followed a structured format. A Fiom social worker would welcome the participants and explain the course of the meeting. This was followed by guided contact moments. At first, due to the size of the group and duration limits of the meeting, a 'speed-date' set-up was followed in which all participants would meet each other for a short period of time. This approach left some people unfulfilled because they were unable to get to know each other better. Therefore, the speed-date approach was abandoned and a new contact approach with longer contact moments in smaller groups (4–5 people), followed by time in which people could freely interact with others in the group was introduced. The contact moments were followed by an information session explaining DNA matching, with the possibility to ask questions.

In the more recent situation where new members wanted to be introduced to an existing network, initially, professionals would work with a 'contact person within the network'. The new member was introduced to the contact person and they would introduce the new member to the network. This put a lot of responsibility on one person and could be emotionally demanding, depending on the dynamics within the group. Moreover, as groups continuously expand, managing the introduction of new members became practically undoable for one person. However, this format was recently adapted and now profiles are exchanged. When a new same-donor offspring is identified and wants contact with the network of same-donor offspring, the social worker will ask the new member to fill in a profile and will ask members of the network if they want to share a profile. These profiles are exchanged, and the new member will choose four people they want to contact first. The new model means that responsibility is now shared by Fiom's social worker, the new member and the network.

Roles: Initially Fiom's social worker's main role was that of a facilitator of contact between members of a same-donor offspring network. It was Fiom's responsibility to develop some structure (e.g. meeting format) that would ease contact building between the members of the same-donor offspring network. However, after the initial group meeting (or individual contact with the network) it is left to the members of the network to decide if and how they want to proceed with the contact.

Over time and through experience Fiom counsellors gained more insight into the questions and needs network members had, and the influence of group dynamics became more visible. As a result, the supporting role grew in importance against the facilitator role. Over time, new members were increasingly identified individually, rather than in groups as they had been at the start, and individual preparation and support to cope with group dynamics became a standard part of the professional guidance. Support helped individuals to prepare themselves to meet multiple same-donor offspring and included: support with informing new members about how group dynamics and processes worked, discussions about own pace and pace of the group, differences that can occur in the group, strengthening coping-mechanisms to handle group dynamics, and reflecting on expectations, feelings that could be triggered by the group and process, as well as staying available for individual questions. Follow-up calls after the meeting were perceived as valuable as they give donor-conceived people the opportunity to talk things through afterwards, which helped them cope with and manage emotions evoked by the meeting. In contrast to situations of contact between a donor and donor-conceived person, Fiom's social workers do not play a mediating role either in a group meeting or between members of the same-donor offspring network. However, they do support members individually when asked for help with issues specifically triggered by meeting multiple same-donor offspring.

For example, donor-conceived people often described being challenged and overwhelmed by the size of the network and request a framework for how to cope emotionally with all these new contacts. Meeting an existing group as a new member can be daunting: concerns can arise about whether one will fit in or be accepted. Existing group dynamics can influence how new members are welcomed as well. Questions also arose around how to cope when their own experiences, needs, focus, pace were different from those of the group ('I feel like a spoilsport'). For some, a group setting and being part of a network had a strong cohesive effect, but this left little room for individual choices within the network. Professional support could help safeguard space for individual choices within the network/group setting:

> Maybe it is good to clarify that you aren't obligated to anything. To be told that you don't have to be (best) friends with every half-sibling. (Network 3, age 20)

While the role and responsibilities of the social worker are fairly clearly defined, they are regularly reviewed as same-donor offspring express different needs/views on professional support. Some donor-conceived people had good external support and did not feel a need for additional professional support, while others experienced professional support as too protective ('patronizing'). Others found it beneficial. As same-donor off-spring networks continuously expand (see Table 7.1) so group dynamics and group balances are constantly changing. Some donor-conceived people appreciated support only at the first group meeting and felt that afterwards it should be left up to the group.

> Fiom is not responsible for how the group works. You offer the opportunity to meet each other, and then personally I think your work stops. ... After your initial support it is up to the group itself, how they stay in contact etc. ... I don't think there's a job for Fiom after that. (Network 4, age 30)

Others did not support leaving the group to find its own way and would have preferred ongoing support to guide group processes:

> Don't leave such a large group on its own and expect that it will be all right. My mother is a teacher and she assures me that it is about group processes and it will take time. For me, it feels like Fiom offers support at the beginning but afterwards, nothing. (Network 2, age 34)

Others felt more ambivalent about ongoing involvement:

> I might have expected that the meeting would be a little more guided ... On the other hand, I didn't want to be taken by the hand, if you get me .... (Network 5, age 27)

Norms and culture: Norms and culture shape group interaction. Confidentiality is often a discussed and valued norm in group meetings. Explicit explanation and advice were given on the use of social media, so as to protect each other's privacy, as not everyone had informed their social network of their conception story or wanted to be so open about their experiences.

Bonds: The strength of group bonds is commonly seen as a determinant for success of the group. Strong bonds are often created by sharing a certain concern, feature or problem and can work to override individual differences. As mentioned earlier, participants' characteristics varied, creating divergent views on the shared feature (being donor-conceived, the genetic tie). These divergent views meant that bonds were experienced differently. This meant that some participants experienced immediate strong bonds, while others did not. This divergence was captured in how a group picture was experienced at the end of a group meeting:

> It might be better to make separate photos of people [instead of a group photo]. You shouldn't be forced into a group of 'we belong together'. 'Cause obviously that's not the case. Only DNA – technically, but otherwise we are not a group. Personally, I would like pictures of each individual separately, but not in a group together. (Network 2, age 34)

As contact proceeded and networks evolved, smaller subgroups were formed, often defined by certain shared features such as age, place of residence, shared norms and values or social behaviour (Bolt et al., 2021). Bonds might also change over time.

7.3.3.3   Development
History and stage of the group: In a group meeting, there were instances where some participants already knew each other due to previous connections via social media or online DNA databases. For these participants, familiarity already existed, but for others the absence of these relationships reinforced their difference. Fiom offers one group meeting to each network, but due to the ongoing introduction of newly identified members to the network and subsequent requests for support, Fiom often remains in contact with the network. The continuous expansion of the network requires constant adaptation and finding a new balance within the group. Members could stay engaged, disengage or form subgroups.

7.4   Is There a Role for Regulators/Policy Makers?

ART regulations are often introduced or revised following new developments in society. In this context, we can ask ourselves if there is a role for regulators/policy makers in light of our findings regarding contact between same-donor offspring. The approach depends on what view we take of the role of the state in regulating such matters. Two possible ways of conceptualising the state are: a laissez-faire state and a stewardship state (Wright, 2016). In a laissez-faire state, as much as possible is left to personal choice and negotiation between individuals. Under such an approach, regulation is unnecessary; donor-conceived people can identify each other using social media or international DNA databases. By contrast, a stewardship state is facilitative in nature, making it possible for people to do things. For example, a facilitative state might introduce structures that enable donor-conceived people to find same-donor offspring. As a consequence of facilitating certain activities (and not others) they give importance to certain values, such as the importance of genetic ties between same-donor offspring.

The Dutch government takes a stewardship position when it comes to the identity rights of the donor conceived. Donor anonymity is prohibited, a national central register (SDKB) was established that contains the identifying information of donors and offspring since the enactment of the law in 2004. It also provides a voluntary DNA database, established to enable finding information about a previously anonymous donor. Registration in the DNA database and DNA testing are funded by the Dutch government and thus free of cost for donors and donor-conceived people.

The situation is somewhat different when it comes to information about same-donor offspring. The Fiom KID-DNA-Database was established so donor-conceived offspring could find the sperm donor. Therefore, the Fiom KID-DNA Database uses a technology that focuses on revealing paternity kinship. However, this technique is inadequate to demonstrate kinship between same-donor offspring. Only when the donor is found, or after a certain number of same-donor offspring have registered, can same-donor offspring be identified. Dutch donor-conceived people, who do not know the donor and who want to find same-donor offspring, have to search via social media or register with a commercial online DNA database. However, in 2020, law reform was proposed that would entitle donor-conceived people to access identifying information about same-donor offspring. The amendment would apply to all donor-conceived people conceived after June 2004. For those conceived prior to June 2004, the central register, where requests are submitted, would contact the clinic to see if any information about the donor and his donations is still available. This might help in locating same-donor offspring. If not, the donor-conceived person will be referred to the Fiom KID-DNA Database or online DNA databases. On the other hand, the Dutch government facilitates contact between same-donor offspring, as they fund the professional guidance offered at a first group meeting of same-donor offspring.

The proposed amendment of the Dutch Information Donor Insemination Law is in line with the amendment in 2009 of the Human Fertilisation and Embryology Act 2008 in the United Kingdom. This led to the Donor Sibling Link, a service established by the Human Fertilisation and Embryology Authority in 2010, enabling donor-conceived people aged 18 or over to exchange contact details with same-donor offspring, with mutual consent. In the Australian state of Victoria, the Voluntary Register was also created to allow for information exchange between donor-related parties, including same-donor offspring who have reached adulthood (Johnson et al., 2012). The Victorian Register also permits parents of donor-conceived children to consent to contact with same-donor offspring for their minor child.

While the amendment to the law would entitle donor-conceived people to access identifying information about same-donor offspring, the proposal has some constraints. First, identifiable information can only be exchanged after mutual consent. This is different from the situation where information about the donor is requested and where the interest of the donor-conceived person is given more weight than that of the donor. In the context of same-donor offspring both their interests are seen as equal. Secondly, it does not give access to information about children from the donor that are not donor-conceived, even though they are equally genetically related. Moreover, the law only refers to same-donor offspring who are registered in the Dutch central registry, which contains data from donors whose sperm is used in treatments in Dutch clinics and donor-conceived people who are conceived in Dutch clinics. The law does not address same-donor offspring conceived outside the Netherlands. So a limitation is created by the law as donor-conceived people will only have access to identifying information about same-donor offspring *conceived in the Netherlands*. This restricts the access to a limited group of same-donor offspring.

Thirdly, requesting identifying information from same-donor offspring is allowed from the age of 16, similar to a request for information about the donor in the Netherlands. This limit prevents younger donor-conceived people from getting access to information about the donor via an older same-donor offspring, at least in practice. The law does not take into account the situation of younger siblings living within the same family.

Finally, mismatches between the language of the law and 'real life' are observed. While the Dutch law uses the clinical language of 'offspring conceived by donations from the same donor', parents, donor-conceived people and the media often use words like 'half-siblings' or 'siblings' to refer to the same relationship. Using kinship language often indicates certain views and expectations. One of those is the expectation that siblings know each other from a young age. Other research (Kelly, 2016; Freeman et al., 2016) and our own experiences indicate that parents often search for their child's 'half-siblings' when the child is still very young and treat these relationships as familial. However, in their search for their children's donor-conceived half-siblings, some parents are confronted with a large number of half-siblings and express concern that this information will negatively affect their child. As these are still pioneering relationships, and little follow-up data have been collected yet, it is difficult to know what psycho-social significance these new genetic connections will be ascribed over time. It will be important to continue research in this field to see if law and societal developments stay aligned.

7.5   Conclusions

At first glance, relationships with same-donor offspring might seem more straightforward than connecting with the donor, as they may be understood as free of obligation and more equal. However, these relationships may be accompanied by challenges, and are perhaps less voluntary and equal than one might initially assume. Professionals at Fiom supporting same-donor offspring networks have noted unique issues among same-donor sibling groups compared to those that emerge from contact between donor-conceived people and the donor. Finally, the pace of developments in the field, and the growing trend in exporting sperm to other countries, create new challenges for regulators. Follow-up research is needed to explore how same-donor offspring relationships, and the meaning attributed to them, develop over time.

References

ANZICA (2012). Guidelines for professional standards of practice: donor linking counseling. www.fertilitysociety.com.au/wp-content/uploads/20120504-anzica-guidelines-donor-linking-final-version.pdf

Blyth, E. (2012). Discovering the 'facts of life' following anonymous donor insemination. *International Journal of Law, Policy and the Family*, *26*(2), 143–161. https://doi.org/10.1093/lawfam/ebs006

Bolt, S. H., Notermans, C., van Brouwershaven, A. C., Maas, A. J. B. M., & Indekeu, A. (2021). The ongoing work of kinship among donor half-siblings in the Netherlands. *BioSocieties*. https://doi.org/10.1057/s41292-021-00259-z

Crawshaw, M., Daniels, K., Adams, D., Bourne, K., van Hooff, J. A. P., Kramer, W., Pasch, L., & Thorn, P. (2016). Emerging models for facilitating contact between people genetically related through donor conception: a preliminary analysis and discussion. *Reproductive Biomedicine & Society Online*, *1*(2), 71–80. https://doi.org/10.1016/j.rbms.2015.10.001

Freeman, T., Jadva, V., & Slutsky, J. (2016). Sperm donors limited: psychosocial aspects of genetic connections and the regulation of offspring. In S. Golombok, R. Scott, J. B. Appleby, M. Richards & S. Wilkinson (Eds.), *Regulating Reproductive Donation* (pp. 165–184). Cambridge University Press. https://doi.org/10.1017/CBO9781316117446

Freeman, T., Jadva, V., Tranfield, E., & Golombok, S. (2016). Online sperm donation: a survey of the demographic characteristics, motivations, preferences and experiences of sperm donors on a connection website. *Human Reproduction*, *31*(9), 2082–2089. https://doi.org/10.1093/humrep/dew166

Hertz, R., Nelson, M. K., & Kramer, W. (2017). Donor sibling networks as a vehicle for expanding kinship: A replication and extension. *Journal of Family Issues*, *38*(2), 248–284. https://doi.org/10.1177/0192513X16631018

Hertz, R., & Nelson, M. K. (2019). *Random Families: Genetic Strangers, Sperm Donor Siblings and the Creation of New Kin*. Oxford University Press. https://doi.org/10.1093/oso/9780190888275.001.0001

Hudson, N. (2017). Making 'assisted world families'? Parenting projects and family practices in the context of globalized gamete donation. *Sociological Research Online*, *22*(2), 48–58. DOI: 10.5153/sro.4246

Indekeu, A., Bolt, S., Maas, A. (2021a). Meeting multiple same-donor offspring: psychosocial challenges. *Human Fertility*, *25*(4), 677–687. https://doi.org/10.1080/14647273.2021.1872804

Indekeu, A., & Hens, K. (2019). Part of my story: the meaning and experiences of genes and genetics for sperm donor-conceived offspring. *New Genetics & Society*, *38*(1), 18–37. https://doi.org/10.1080/14636778.2018.1549476 Open Access

Indekeu, A., Maas, A. J. B. M., McCormick, E., Benward, J., & Scheib, J. (2021b). Factors associated with searching for people related through donor conception among donor-conceived people, parents and donors: a systematic review. *F&S Reviews*, *2*(2), 93–119. https://doi.org/10.1016/j.xfnr.2021.01.003

Jadva, V., Freeman, T., Kramer, W., & Golombok, S. (2010). Experiences of offspring searching for and contacting their donor siblings and donor. *Reproductive Biomedicine Online*, *20*(4), 523–532. https://doi.org/10.1016/j.rbmo.2010.01.001

Janssens, P. M. W., Simons, A. H. M., Van Kooij, R. J., Blokzijl, E., & Dunselman, G. A. J. (2006). A new Dutch Law regulating provision of identifying information of donors to offspring: background, content and impact. *Human Reproduction*, *21*(4), 852–856. https://doi.org/10.1093/humrep/dei407

Johnson, L., Bourne, K., & Hammarberg, K. (2012). Donor conception legislation in Victoria, Australia: the 'Time to Tell' campaign, donor-linking and implications for clinical practice. *Journal of Law and Medicine*, *19*(4), 803–19.

Kelly, F. J., & Dempsey, D. J. (2016). Experiences and motives of Australian single mothers by choice who make early contact with their child's donor relatives. *Medical Law Review*, *24*(4), 571–590. https://doi-org.kuleuven.e-bronnen.be/10.1093/medlaw/fww038

Montuschi, O., & Ellis. J. (2020). *Continuing the Conversation: Talking with Young People and Adults 12yrs and Up*. Donor Conception Network.

Mroz, J. (2011). One sperm donor, 150 offspring. *New York Times*. www.nytimes.com/2011/09/06/health/06donor.html

Mroz, J. (2021). The case of the serial sperm donor. *New York Times*. www.nytimes.com/2021/02/01/health/sperm-donor-fertility-meijer.html

Scheib, J. E., McCornick, E., Benward J., & Ruby, A. (2020). Finding people like me: contact among young adults who share an open-identity donor. *Human Reproduction Open*, *2020*(4). https://doi.org/10.1093/hropen/hoaa057

Scheib, J. E., & Ruby, A. (2009). Beyond consanguinity risk: developing donor birth limits that consider psychosocial risk factors. *Fertility and Sterility*, *91*(5), 91, e12. https://doi.org/10.1016/j.fertnstert.2008.12.071

Schopler, J. H., & Galinsky, M. J. (1993). Support groups as open systems: a model for practice and research. *Journal of Health and Social Work*, *18*(3), 195–207.

Wright, K. (2016). Limiting offspring numbers: can we justify regulation? In S. Golombok, R. Scott, J. B. Appleby, M. Richards & S. Wilkinson (Eds.), *Regulating Reproductive Donation* (pp. 185–204). Cambridge University Press. https://doi.org/10.1017/CBO9781316117446

CHAPTER 8

'It's All on Their Terms'
Donors Navigating Relationships with Recipient Families in an Age of Openness

Leah Gilman and Petra Nordqvist

8.1 Introduction

In the last two decades, there has been a significant cultural shift in perceived 'best practice' in donor conception. Secrecy and anonymity used to be viewed as appropriate strategies for managing the relational 'complexities' resulting from the use of donated gametes. However, in recent decades there has been a shift in the UK and some other jurisdictions in the global North (Sweden, the Netherlands, Germany and certain states in Australia) towards seeing 'openness' – that is, disclosure and donor traceability – as necessary for the well-being of individuals and relationships in this context (Gilman and Nordqvist, 2018; Klotz, 2014). In contemporary Britain, parents are strongly encouraged to tell any child born through donor conception the circumstances of their conception from a young age (BICA, 2019). The ability of donor-conceived people to access this information about their conception is often perceived as a 'human right' (Besson, 2007; Blyth and Farrand, 2004; Frith, 2001).

This set of ideas, which we describe as an 'ethic of openness' was marked, in the UK, by the abolition of donor anonymity in favour of a donor identity-release policy. Children conceived after 1 April 2005 in clinical donor egg, sperm or embryo treatment have the right to identifying details about their donor(s) on turning 18. Hence, egg and sperm donors whose gametes are now used in UK clinics do so with the knowledge that they could one day be traced. There is another group of donors who donate to someone personally known to them; such donation practices can, in the case of sperm donation, take place entirely outside the clinic context. A known donor can be a person previously known to the recipient(s) (e.g. a brother or friend) but it also refers to a person who the recipients have gotten to know for the purposes of donation. These 'matches' may be facilitated through various websites (e.g. Pride Angel) or Facebook groups. Although the circumstances of clinical identity-release donation and known donation differ, both are shaped by this emerging 'ethic of openness' and create circumstances in which donors' identities are or can be known.

This chapter asks what this new ethic of openness in reproductive donation means for contemporary donors (both identity-release and known) in terms of how they view and navigate what it means to be a donor. Our research with UK egg and sperm donors (more details below) suggests that donors now occupy an ambiguous and somewhat contradictory role in relation to recipient families. On the one hand, and like their former anonymous counterparts, donors are expected to 'know their place' as legal and social non-parents and to uphold the status of their recipient(s) as the only 'real parents'. On the other hand, and unlike their anonymous forebears, they are also expected to 'be available' to the people born from their donation (Nordqvist and Gilman, 2022). The latter because the ethic of openness is formulated around the understanding that knowledge of 'where you came from' (here including the identity of the donor), is, or could be, crucial for people's sense of identity and their 'ontological security' (Carsten, 2000). In contemporary Britain, 'good donors', whether or not they donate via clinics, are expected to embody both of these moral relational norms (Graham, Mohr, and Bourne, 2016). However, this puts donors in a contradictory position because the imperative to 'know one's place' whilst also 'being available' pulls donors in opposite directions, both towards and away from connections with recipient families generally and donor offspring more specifically. This chapter explores how donors understand this paradoxical role, how they work to resolve it and its consequences in terms of their own personal and relational lives.

8.2 The Curious Connections Study: Investigating How Donors 'Do' Openness

There has been considerable research into the impact of openness on donor-conceived people and their families – including the proportions who disclose (Applegarth et al., 2016; Crawshaw, 2008; Freeman and Golombok, 2012), the challenges for parents in disclosing (Grace and Daniels, 2007; Nachtigall et al., 1998; Nordqvist, 2014, Nordqvist and Smart, 2014) and the well-being of children and parent-child relationships following disclosure (Nachtigall et al., 1997; Ilioi et al., 2017). However, these studies focus on the recipient family and there has been little research into the ways in which *donors* 'do' and experience the shift to greater openness in donor-conception policies and practices. Few qualitative studies have considered

how sperm and egg donors navigate 'open' and traceable forms of donation (although see Almeling, 2011; Dempsey, 2010; Mohr, 2018).

The Curious Connections study at the University of Manchester (UK),
funded by the Economic and Social Research Council (ESRC) (grant number
ES/N014154/1, PI Petra Nordqvist), sought to address precisely this question.
We conducted 88 in-depth interviews with 52 donors (1 embryo donor, 26
sperm donors and 25 egg donors), 23 relatives of donors and 18 fertility counsellors and donor coordinators, working for UK clinics.[1] In this chapter, we
focus on data collected during the interviews with donors but our analysis of
their words and experiences is informed by the dataset as a whole.

The donors we interviewed were living in the UK at the time of interview. The vast majority had donated since 2005 when identity-release legislation was introduced in the UK. Four had donated under conditions of
anonymity, about two thirds had donated as identity-release donors and
over 40 per cent had donated as known donors. Many had donated more
than once, sometimes migrating from one donation pathway to another.
Participants came from diverse backgrounds in terms of social class, sexual
orientation, gender, though all but two donors identified as white.

During interviews, we explored the significance of donation in donors'
everyday lives and relationships, past, present and in an imagined future.
We asked how they became a donor, if, when and how they had discussed
the donation with others, their thoughts about relationships with recipients and people conceived from their donation and their expectations in
relation to any (current or future) contact with recipient families. Please see
Nordqvist and Gilman (2022) for a detailed account of the study methods.

8.3 Assigning Relational Authority to Recipient Families

In the context of ambiguity about their role and contradictory moral
imperatives to both 'know their place' and also 'be available', sperm
and egg donors typically articulated a commitment to letting recipient
families decide what their role as donors would be. This was the case for
both identity-release and known donors, with the former group generally emphasising that they would, and rightly should, allow the donor-
conceived person to lead this relationship and the latter allowing a more
prominent role for the recipient parents, as custodians of their child's 'best
interests', to define and shape relationships. We refer to this practice of

---

[1] The numbers in each group do not total to 88 because 5 participants were both donors and relatives
of donors.

empowering (or attempting to empower) others to lead a relationship as a process of assigning relational authority (Nordqvist and Gilman, 2022). Assigning relational authority to recipient families, particularly donor off-spring, was seen as the right and proper way to be a donor.

'Letting others lead' was enacted in slightly different ways for each group. We found that identity-release donors were often reluctant to express any preference regarding the possibility of future contact with someone conceived from their donation. As one egg donor, Becky, explained:

> I'm not saying, 'it would be better if they got in touch or it would be better if they didn't.' I think it would be better if they … were able to do what was right for them. (Becky, egg donor, identity-release donation)

Like Becky, participants who had undertaken identity-release donation emphasised that whether or not they ever met their donor-conceived offspring was rightly the decision of the donor-conceived person; their role, as good donors, was to 'be available' and prepared for such an eventuality without actively pursuing it. What form any contact might take and the overall character of any relationship that developed were also seen as decisions which their donor offspring should be allowed to make and which they should follow:

> Yeah for me I think I would want … I want them [donor offspring] to be the creator of the parameters [of any relationship?], and I would want to fit into their … [tails off]. (Zak, sperm donor, identity-release and known donation)

> If somebody did get pregnant and somebody [a donor-conceived person] did want to speak to me than I'd be more than happy to talk to them, or if they wanted to get to know me a little bit I wouldn't mind, but obviously it's all on their terms. (Fran, egg donor, identity-release donation)

> It's got to be down to them … I think in any situation like that, if any child of any donation contacts you, you've got to take their lead. (Olive, egg donor, identity-release, donation)

These assertions that they would let donor-conceived people 'take the lead' in their relationship were typical of identity-release donors. This was the case for both those donors (like Becky, above) who said they were equally happy with the possibility of being contacted or not contacted in the future, and also for those (like Olive) who did express a preference (nearly always *for* contact and an ongoing relationship) but suggested that it would not be right to let their own preferences influence the relationship.

Those who had donated to someone they knew, also emphasised the importance of donors being responsive and letting others define the role they would take in relation to the recipient family. The key difference was that this group generally also included recipient parents, alongside their children, as people who would 'lead' this relationship. This was particularly the case for donors who were describing a situation in which their donor-conceived offspring were still very young (or not yet conceived). At this age, parents were framed as the best people to decide on how much, and what form of, involvement the donor would have in their child(ren)'s lives. Donors in this context tended to present themselves as available if and when their recipients wanted to introduce them to the children. Donors presented themselves as passive but highly responsive in such decision-making:

> I am going to always be around … I am happy with anything and if any of [the recipient parents], you know, in the future says can you pop round, I will be around. (Isaac, sperm donor, known, non-clinic donation)

> In terms of, you know … how much contact I want, I'm very much being led by the girls [the recipient couple]. So I will, if they want me there I will hear from them, if they don't … So yeah, I think that's the best way. (Gavin, sperm donor, known, non-clinic donation)

As Gavin suggests, donors who knew their recipients reported that they did not contact their recipients or suggest meeting up. Instead, they waited to be contacted or invited by their recipient parents. In some cases, this meant there had been no contact after conception or the birth, very occasional communication (e.g. a card at Christmas) or, in other cases, recipient families regularly met up with donors. For those who had donated to multiple known recipients, the relationships with each recipient family could vary widely between them.

When known donors talked about the future, they painted an ideal picture in which decision-making power shifted from recipient parents to their donor-conceived children:

> I mean, the agreement … with them is they will let the child know that I am the biological father and then it will be up to the child to decide if she wants to see me or not. (Enric, known, non-clinic sperm donor)

> Personally I'm hoping there will be more contact in the years ahead, but I won't be insisting on it or chasing it. I'll be leaving it for the [children] to decide. (Andy, sperm donor, known, non-clinic donation)

> Hopefully as and when any questions are raised by the children then they can be answered because certainly for the first few families [I donated to], they're in touch, you know, with me. (Beth, egg donor, known and identity-release donation)

Although donors frequently acknowledged that some recipient parents might not tell their children about their conception, nor their identity as the donor, most imagined that, in an ideal world, parents would disclose the donor conception at a young age and then they, the donor, would be on hand if and when the child wanted to know more about them or to develop a relationship.

Whether they were known or unknown, donors repeatedly emphasised the moral importance of assigning relational authority to recipient families, enabling them to decide what exactly their role as a donor would be. Donors often talked about 'playing things by ear' and expressing (or even having) preferences of their own about how things might play out was generally framed negatively. Donors used words like 'imposing 'or 'controlling' in relation to the idea that they might themselves have an agenda in terms of how these relationships unfolded, hence framing it as the 'wrong' approach.

8.4   Relationality and the Challenge of Assigning Relational Authority

We explore elsewhere the moral appeal of the idea that donors should let recipient families decide the nature of their connection, but note that it draws on cultural understandings of both what it means to be a parent and to give a gift (properly) and also culturally specific beliefs about the meaning of a person's 'origins' (Nordqvist and Gilman, 2022). However, our focus here is to explore the challenges that assigning relational authority creates for donors, because our data suggest that this is easier said than done.

One reason for these challenges is that donors are inevitably embedded in their relational networks; donors' lives and identities are fundamentally intertwined with those of others': their children, parents, siblings and wider family, but also friends, colleagues, acquaintances and so on. People develop a sense of self and experience their lives in and through these relationships (Mason, 2004; May, 2013; Smart, 2007). Furthermore, decisions and experiences in relation to any one particular relationship has to be understood in the context of the wider web of connections in which that relationship and both individuals are embedded (Nordqvist & Gilman, 2022).

In the following sections of this chapter, we share three composite case studies from our research: Lizzie, Jack and Kylie. In order to protect the anonymity of our participants, we have combined the stories of participants in each of these case studies. Lizzie, Jack and Kylie are composite characters whose experiences are based on two or more participants'

experiences. All three know that children have been born from their donations. Lizzie has donated eggs multiple times, including to people she had
got to know for the purposes of donation. Jack has also donated as a known
donor to a lesbian couple, friends of a friend, and Kylie has donated via an
identity-release pathway to an unknown recipient. Their stories illustrate
how attempts to 'let others lead' the relationships which follow from donation can throw up challenges in donors' own lives and relationships.

8.4.1 Lizzie

Lizzie has donated her eggs multiple times. Two cycles resulted in the
birth of a child, each to a different couple. In some ways the couples are
similar – both chose a 'known' donor and planned to be 'open' with any
child born, as per recommended 'best practice'. Both involved Lizzie in
various ways in their lives and Lizzie enjoyed getting to know them and
finding out their reasons for needing a donor. One couple, Gail and Tom,
were opposite sex and the other, Greg and Damon, same sex and also
needed the help of a surrogate (not Lizzie, in this case) to conceive. For
both donations, Lizzie enjoyed her sense of being part of a 'team', which
included not only her recipient couples but also the surrogate.

Both couples had told Lizzie that they planned to tell their child about
her role in their conception. Greg and Damon had taken photographs of
Lizzie with the intention of creating an 'our story' book for their child.
Lizzie had gone to great lengths to do her own research about donor conception and shared an understanding that this is best for children, so she
was very supportive of these decisions. However, disclosure was not a
condition of her donation. In fact, quite the opposite, because Lizzie had
concluded that for donation to work, she had to let her recipients 'call the
shots'. She explained that it would not be fair to hold her recipients to
something they might say when they were 'desperate' to have a baby.

Although both Greg and Damon and Gail and Tom had planned a similarly 'open' approach, things played out quite differently in each family,
after their children were born. Lizzie described Gail and Tom's approach
as 'extreme' transparency. She was invited to visit the family and was publicly celebrated as 'the egg donor' at family events (such as birthdays).
Gail made Lizzie, her daughter Nina's godmother. When Lizzie had her
own children, Gail referred to them as 'brothers and sisters' to Nina. This
was not quite the language Lizzie would have chosen herself but she went
along with it, because she felt it was right to let Gail and Tom define the
parameters of the relationship.

Lizzie also stayed in contact with Greg and Damon after the birth. However, by the age of six, Lizzie was aware they had not yet told Liam, their son, the full story of his conception nor her role as the donor. When the two families met up, Greg and Damon did not suggest there was any 'special' status to the relationships between them all, and so consequently the children knew one another as 'just friends'.

As time went on, Lizzie's intention to let each family decide how they wanted to frame the donation became increasingly difficult to maintain. Her own children were growing up and she started to feel uncomfortable about celebrating one donor sibling whilst keeping the other a secret. Her husband felt they were in a 'ridiculous situation' at the behest of these two families wishes but agreed to 'toe the line'.

'Letting others lead' also became increasingly difficult because over time, Gail became increasingly interested in Greg and Damon and their son, who she viewed as a sibling to Nina. Lizzie had told Gail a little bit about the family – including their names, roughly where they lived and a little bit about their lives – many of these details about her 'brother' had been passed on to Nina. However, Gail was keen to build these connections in person. Lizzie tried to put her off, knowing that Greg and Damon would not be interested and sensing that they might be quite threatened by Gail's enthusiasm for openness and her insistence on the importance of this sibling connection.

Lizzie and her family saw both the recipient couples separately, but because of these disparities between how each family wanted to manage the connections created by donation, challenges started to emerge. Lizzie was becoming increasingly aware and concerned that her own children (the eldest of whom was now of primary school age) might now be able to 'join the dots' and figure out that Liam was also their genetic half sibling. Even if Lizzie and her husband themselves kept the connection to Liam a secret, Nina had been told that she had a 'brother' in the town where Liam lived so there was the potential for Nina to pass this information, and its implications, to Lizzie's own children. If her children did indeed make this connection, then there was a risk they might 'out' Liam as donor-conceived and Lizzie as the donor. Going against her previous intention to stay out of such decisions, Lizzie decided she needed to check with Greg and Damon what exactly they had told their son. She sent the couple a carefully worded email to enquire 'where they were up to' in relation to such discussions and explaining her concerns about the information being passed between the children. Lizzie had been nervous about sending this email and indeed, Greg and Damon did not respond well. They stated that they would not be able to meet up again if there was 'any chance' that information about Liam's conception might be shared between the children. The two families had not been in touch for more than three years by the time of the interview.

8.4.2   Jack

Jack's story is less dramatic than Lizzie's but nevertheless it illustrates some of the same challenges donors encounter in their attempt to let others lead their relationship to recipient families.

Jack offered to donate sperm when he heard about some friends of a friend (a lesbian couple who we will call Jen and Melanie) who were looking for a donor. As a gay man, aware of other families through donor conception, the possibility of being a donor was not alien to him and he decided this was something he would like to do. His friend put forward his offer.

Jack, Jen and Melanie approached the donation in a calm and thoughtful manner. This was not something they thought anyone should rush into and they spent several months getting to know one another and making plans before deciding to go ahead with the donation. Jack agreed to the couple's suggestion that he would visit the family every so often and that he would not have any parental or financial responsibilities for the children born. They drew up a written agreement to that effect. They also discussed their plans for the future, including Jen and Melanie's hopes for a second child and Jack agreed that he would also be the donor for this and any future children they might want.

At the time of our interview, Jen and Melanie had one child from Jack's donations, still pre-school age. The careful plans the three adults had made prior to conception have played out. Jack was strongly committed to visiting the family regularly. He talked about the importance of being a reliable and stable (if occasional) presence in the child's life; someone who would 'be available' if they wanted to contact him or ask him anything. At the same time, he was very sensitive to the feelings of Jen and Melanie, particularly Melanie who he found more distant and suspected might have preferred to have used sperm from an anonymous donor. In order to ensure he is not perceived as 'intruding' or overstepping any boundaries, Jack has been careful to time his visits to avoid obvious 'family times' (e.g. birthdays or Christmas), delayed his first visit until at least a couple of months after the birth and has not offered to do any practical caring tasks (such as changing nappies or feeding). He told us that he hopes that he may play a bigger role in the child's life as they grow older but that this would only be at the request of them or their parents. Jack clearly enjoyed his visits to see the family.

However, he described the time spent together as somewhat 'intense', perhaps because of the emotional labour involved in ensuring sensitivity to everyone's expectations of him.

Jack has been very open about his donation with friends and ex-partners. However, with his family, he has been more selective about who he tells. Some siblings know but not others, and he has decided, with some sadness, not to tell his parents. He described his relationship with them as close but he expected they would struggle with the 'unconventionality' of the situation and might worry about the legal-financial implications for him. Jack's decision was also influenced by the importance he placed on not 'intruding' in the recipient's family. After they had gotten used to the idea, he suspected that, if his parents knew, they might want to meet the child, and that they might even see them as a grandchild.

This has indeed been the case with one of his sisters and her children (Jack's nieces and nephews) who he has told. Jack suspected that his sister would very much like to meet Jen and Melanie's child, seeing them as a cousin to her children and that his nieces and nephews would be excited about this too. But Jack sensed this is a sensitive situation which required careful management. He was aware that Jen and Melanie already have families of their own and that their family is already more 'complicated' than most, owing to his involvement. He is wary of, as he put it, 'swamping' their smaller extended families by introducing his. As he put it, he'd 'had no signals from the mums that they want that [meeting his family] to happen and it would be complicated for the child'. He hoped that in the future he might be able to ask Jen and Melanie if they would be willing to introduce his sister and his nieces and nephews, but he wanted to wait till the child was older so that they would remember the meeting as he expected it would be a one-off arrangement.

8.4.3   *Kylie and Charlotte*

Kylie was one of a small but significant sub-group of participants we interviewed, who were both donors and parents through donor conception. Having identified as a lesbian since her early teens, she described 'always knowing' that she would need the help of a sperm donor to have her own children. Consequently, when she and her wife Charlotte began thinking about starting a family, they decided to take part in an egg sharing programme whereby Kylie would undergo IVF using donor sperm, but she would share half of her eggs with an unknown recipient, in exchange for reduced cost treatment. Egg sharing meant treatment was much more attainable for the couple, from a financial perspective, but Kylie also saw it as a way to 'give something back', a form of 'fertility karma'.

At the time of her treatment, Kylie and Charlotte thought carefully about the responsibilities involved in both having a donor-conceived child and donating eggs. The couple saw the donation as part of their own process of becoming parents – a joint decision – and they felt that any future contact from the donor offspring concerned both of them. The couple were committed to the principle that donor-conceived people had what they understood as a human right to find out about and meet, if they wanted to, their donor. They said they would not have considered using an anonymous donor to conceive their own child nor would they have wanted Kylie to donate anonymously. In line with the principle of 'letting the [donor-conceived person] lead' the relationship, they thought that any person conceived from the donation should be able to make their own decision about whether and when to contact them, and any relation-ships which might develop from there. They understood that Kylie, as the donor, had no rights to make such decisions or to initiate contact but felt this was 'as it should be'. They emphasised that Kylie (and Charlotte) were making the choice for Kylie to donate eggs, whereas the donor-conceived person had no choice in being donor-conceived and hence should have more decision-making power in the future.

At the time of donation, the moral lines involved all seemed fairly clear cut and straightforward to them. It was only when their son was born that the right thing to do started to seem a bit less obvious and they started to question the dynamics of the identity-release system. Although he was still very young at the time, they had started to wonder about their son's future and whether he might decide one day to contact his donor or donor siblings. They had identified that, as both a donor-conceived person and the son of a donor, he was in a slightly discomfiting situation. Following UK identity-release policy, he had a right to trace his donor, and there was also a formal route, through the Donor Sibling Link (DSL), via which he could contact any donor-conceived siblings conceived from the same donor. However, there was no comparable route via which he could find his (equally genetically related) siblings from his Mum Kylie's donation. Alternatively, they speculated, he might feel strongly that he did not want to meet or know anything about any of his donor siblings but Kylie and Charlotte had already made a commitment to the recipient family and donor offspring that they would be available for contact and potentially a relationship of some kind.

The lack of decision-making power they had in their relationship to their donor offspring, and which they felt was 'absolutely as it should be', had the unintended effect of also disempowering their own son in how he might relate to any donor offspring from Kylie's donations. It made figuring out the 'right way' to behave somewhat more complicated than they had initially imagined. For example, they wondered how they ought to respond if their son wanted to search for his donor siblings (including those from her donated eggs) outside of official routes, for example via direct-to-consumer genetic testing and/or social media sites. They felt they would have to respect his wishes but should they encourage or actively help with such searches? What if the donor offspring did not want to be found or if they did not know they were donor conceived?

It would be wrong to present this shift in Kylie and Charlotte's thinking as a dramatic upheaval of their previous principles. After raising all of these issues, they ultimately reaffirmed their commitment to 'being available' to anyone conceived from their donation and hoped that they would raise their own son, particularly since he was donor-conceived himself, to understand and respect that commitment. However, the embeddedness of their connection to the donor offspring within their relationship to their son and their identities as mothers raised many ethical questions and somewhat undermined the simplicity of the idea that they could just 'let [others] lead'.

8.5 Conclusion: The Ethics of Openness and Its Ramifications

Our aim in this chapter has been to explore what the rise of an ethic of openness in donor conception means for egg and sperm donors, situating it in the context of their own lives and relationships. We have shown that this ethic, and particularly its focus on donor-conceived people's right to trace their donor, has redefined what it means to be one. Contemporary UK (identity-release and known) donors are not just required to 'know their place' as non-parents, but also to 'be available' to donor-conceived offspring. Interestingly, we found this to be the case in relation to both egg and sperm donors, although, in general, sperm donors placed more emphasis on their obligation to 'be available' to donor offspring and egg donors emphasised the importance of demonstrating their non-parental status (see Nordqvist and Gilman, 2022, for a full discussion). Donors resolve the paradox produced by these competing imperatives by seeking to hand over relational authority to the recipient family, and most specifically, the donor-conceived person. 'Letting them lead' relationships is understood as an integral part of what it means to be a 'good donor' in contemporary Britain.

Handing over relational authority in this way may sound easy enough in the abstract and a straightforwardly good way to behave. However, our case studies show that, when translated into practice, this approach throws up moral dilemmas and relational challenges in donors' own lives and relationships.

As with Lizzie's experience, challenges can emerge when relating to multiple recipient families. UK policy allows donors to donate to up to ten families (including for multiple births in each), and indeed, many of the donors in our study had donated to more than one family. Lizzie's set-up is therefore typical in that she has more than one recipient family to relate to. Her experience illustrates the difficulties that can emerge over time when donors take a moral position of 'letting others lead' relationships when there are multiple recipients families involved, all of whom may disagree on such matters, and it therefore becomes particularly unclear whose lead the donor should follow. People are embedded in relational frameworks, and people negotiate and understand connections differently, including how best to proceed. Not everyone agrees and opinions may diverge. This issue could, of course, also emerge in the context of a single family with donor-conceived children where, say, two siblings disagree on how to relate to their donor, or indeed, it may emerge in quite intense ways in cases where donors' gametes have been used to form large numbers of families.

Our cases also highlight that donors assigning relational authority to recipient families can produce tensions in their own personal relationships. Ironically, and as Cosson et al. (2021) and Dempsey et al. (2021) also demonstrate in relation to recipient family networks, we found that the ethic of openness could produce secrets in donors' own lives, with Lizzie and Jack both speaking of how their attempts at 'doing the right thing' – letting others lead – has created a situation where they feel compelled to keep secrets from their own family. Jack has decided not to tell his own mother and father, and has not introduced his sister and her children to the recipient family, although he knows it would mean a lot to them (and to him). Lizzie finds herself in a confusing situation, sandwiched between recipient families wanting different things, and, as a consequence, feels compelled to keep her role in Liam's conception a secret from her own children. It is with regards to their own children, that donors tend to experience these dilemmas as particularly problematic, as is illustrated in both Lizzie's case and Kylie and Charlotte's. The latter particularly illustrates how disempowered donors' own children are in terms of their own potential sense of connection to their parents' donor offspring. All case studies refer to pre-school children but it is likely that these kinds of dilemmas will become more acute as children get older, for example, what if Nina asks Lizzie directly to put her in touch with Liam?

We suggest that the difficulties donors experience in translating what is seen as both morally right and straightforward into practice can be explained by the relationally situated nature of donors' and recipients' lives and identities, and the way in which reproductive donation becomes embedded in complex networks of relationships. How someone came to be is also about who it brought into relation and how those relationships unfold over time. A child, when born, is connected not just to their parents, but also to extended family, friends and communities, and these processes of relating over time are an integral part of selves, lives and identities (Dempsey, Nordqvist, & Kelly, 2021; Mason, 2004). This is also true in the context of donation, and means that it would be erroneous to envision the connections that stem from donation as dyadic connections between, for example, a donor and their donor-offspring, and that they are better understood as messy, multiple and networked. Donors (and recipient families) often become deeply aware of this as is illustrated in all the case studies, perhaps most clearly in Lizzie's story. This means that the act of donating is not just a concern for donors, but also something that involves their children, siblings, parents and so on. Multiple actors across generations (including children, both *as children* and as they grow up) play an active part in defining parameters of relationships, and how they unfold. This relational complexity means it is often much harder to enact what may seem a morally straightforward principle (in this case, 'letting others lead' a relationship) in practice (see also Dempsey, Nordqvist & Kelly, 2021).

These findings raise important questions for current policy and practice formulation. As explored elsewhere (Nordqvist & Gilman, 2022), the ethic of openness in contemporary UK law and policy recognises only the 'donation triad' – the donor, the recipient family and the donor-conceived child – as having a stake in the connections that result from donor conception. This means that the relational understanding of donation giving rise to complex and networked connections is poorly reflected in current policy, and also in current moral understandings of what it means to be a 'good' donor. Hence our findings suggest a poor fit between current law and policy, and the multi-layered, messy and complex relational networks implicated in donation. Our argument here is not to suggest that the authority to define connections and relationships should swap hands from recipient families to donors, but it is to suggest a need to acknowledge the multi-layered, embedded and networked nature of connections that people experience in the context of reproductive donation and start a conversation about how this may be better accounted for in policy and practice.

References

Almeling, Rene. 2011. *Sex Cells: The Medical Market for Eggs and Sperm*. Berkeley: University of California Press.

Applegarth, Linda D., Nancy L. Kaufman, Mitasha Josephs-Sohan, Paul J. Christos, and Zev Rosenwaks. 2016. 'Parental Disclosure to Offspring Created with Oocyte Donation: Intentions versus Reality'. *Human Reproduction*, June. https://doi.org/10.1093/humrep/dew125.

Besson, S. 2007. 'Enforcing the Child's Right to Know Her Origins: Contrasting Approaches Under the Convention on the Rights of the Child and the European Convention on Human Rights'. *International Journal of Law, Policy and the Family* 21 (2): 137–59. https://doi.org/10.1093/lawfam/ebm003.

BICA. 2019. '*Guidelines for Good Practice in Fertility Counselling*'. York: BICA.

Blyth, Eric, and Abigail Farrand. 2004. 'Anonymity in Donor-Assisted Conception and the UN Convention on the Rights of the Child'. *The International Journal of Children's Rights* 12 (2): 89–104.

Carsten, Janet. 2000. '"Knowing Where You've Come from": Ruptures and Continuities of Time and Kinship in Narratives of Adoption Reunions'. *The Journal of the Royal Anthropological Institute* 6 (4): 687–703.

Cosson, Barbara, Deborah Dempsey, and Fiona Kelly. 2021. 'Secret Shame – Male Infertility and Donor Conception in the Wake of Retrospective Legislative Change'. *Men and Masculinities*, 25 (3): 497–515. https://doi.org/10.1177/1097184X211038329.

Crawshaw, Marilyn. 2008. 'Prospective Parents' Intentions Regarding Disclosure Following the Removal of Donor Anonymity'. *Human Fertility* 11 (2): 95–100.

Dempsey, Deborah. 2010. 'Conceiving and Negotiating Reproductive Relationships: Lesbians and Gay Men Forming Families with Children'. *Sociology* 44 (6): 1145–62.

Dempsey, Deborah, Petra Nordqvist, and Fiona Kelly. 2022. 'Beyond Secrecy and Openness: Telling a Relational Story about Children's Best Interests in Donor-Conceived Families'. *BioSocieties* 17: 527–48. https://doi.org/10.1057/s41292-021-00225-9.

Freeman, T., and S. Golombok. 2012. 'Donor Insemination: A Follow-up Study of Disclosure Decisions, Family Relationships and Child Adjustment at Adolescence'. *Reproductive Biomedicine Online* 25 (2): 193–203.

Frith, Lucy. 2001. 'Beneath the Rhetoric: The Role of Rights in the Practice of Non-Anonymous Gamete Donation'. *Bioethics* 15 (5–6): 473–84. https://doi.org/10.1111/1467-8519.00255.

Gilman, Leah, and Petra Nordqvist. 2018. 'Organizing Openness: How UK Policy Defines the Significance of Information and Information Sharing about Gamete Donation'. *International Journal of Law, Policy and the Family* 32 (3): 316–33. https://doi.org/10.1093/lawfam/eby014.

Grace, Victoria M., and Ken Daniels. 2007. 'The (Ir)Relevance of Genetics: Engendering Parallel Worlds of Procreation and Reproduction'. *Sociology of Health & Illness* 29 (5): 692–710.

Graham, Susanna, Sebastian Mohr, and Kate Bourne. 2016. 'Regulating the "Good" Donor: The Expectation and Experiences of Sperm Donors in Denmark and Victoria, Australia'. In *Regulating Reproductive Donation*, edited by Susan Golombok, Rosamund Scott, John B. Appleby, Martin Richards, and Stephen Wilkinson. Cambridge: Cambridge University Press.

Ilioi, Elena, Lucy Blake, Vasanti Jadva, Gabriela Roman, and Susan Golombok. 2017. 'The Role of Age of Disclosure of Biological Origins in the Psychological Wellbeing of Adolescents Conceived by Reproductive Donation: A Longitudinal Study from Age 1 to Age 14'. *Journal of Child Psychology and Psychiatry* 58 (3): 315–24. https://doi.org/10.1111/jcpp.12667.

Klotz, Maren. 2014. *(K) Information: Gamete Donation and Kinship Knowledge in Germany and Britain*. Vol. 32. Frankfurt: Campus Verlag.

Mason, Jennifer. 2004. 'Personal Narratives, Relational Selves: Residential Histories in the Living and Telling'. *The Sociological Review* 52 (2): 162–79.

May, Vanessa. 2013. *Connecting Self to Society: Belonging in a Changing World*. Basingstoke: Palgrave Macmillan.

Mohr, Sebastian. 2018. *Being a Sperm Donor: Masculinity, Sexuality, and Biosociality in Denmark*. New York: Berghahn Books.

Nachtigall, Robert D., Gay Becker, Seline Szkupinski Quiroga, and Jeanne M. Tschann. 1998. 'The Disclosure Decision: Concerns and Issues of Parents of Children Conceived through Donor Insemination'. *American Journal of Obstetrics and Gynecology* 178 (6): 1165–70. https://doi.org/10.1016/S0002-9378(98)70318-7.

Nachtigall, Robert D., Jeanne M. Tschann, Seline Szkupinski Quiroga, Linda Pitcher, and Gay Becker. 1997. 'Stigma, Disclosure, and Family Functioning among Parents of Children Conceived through Donor Insemination'. *Fertility and Sterility* 68 (1): 83–89.

Nordqvist, Petra. 2014. 'The Drive for Openness in Donor Conception: Disclosure and the Trouble with Real Life'. *International Journal of Law, Policy and the Family* 28 (3): 321–38.

Nordqvist, Petra, and Leah Gilman. 2022. *Donors: Curious Connections in Donor Conception*. London: Emerald Publishing.

Smart, Carol. 2007. *Personal Life: New Directions in Sociological Thinking*. Cambridge and Malden: Polity Press.

CHAPTER 9

On Familial Haunting
Donor-Conceived People's Experiences of Living with Anonymity and Absence

Giselle Newton

I've always known about the haunting. Yet the outline of my ghost for more than two decades was nebulous; no information to give him shape. Later, a faint sketch of the ghost was formed based on a three-page document, uncovered through four years of negotiation and waiting. At work in front of a bunch of students, I steal a glimpse at my screen to find (his?) cursive writing transported to another era, space, generation. Across the bright blasted photocopier white, hard to make out were the prescribed identity characteristics: "Occupation: security officer/part-time model. Interests: weights/cycling/ running/ sailing. Comment on donor personality by interviewer: friendly open manner". These records "become part of the contest between familiarity and strangeness, between hurting and healing, that the ghost is registering" (Gordon, 2008, p. 103). These scant details, a glimpse of the ghost, and each day since, his contours further inflated by my imagination.

Later, my peers and I learnt that all ghosts can be pinpointed through 'centiMorgans', soon experts in measuring via these units of genetic relatedness. I disembark a plane, streams of text flashing across the screen in quick succession, culminating in: "24 Oct 2020 9.11PM: Hi! I've solved it", my ghost almost certainly identified. His mother's funeral notice states his name alongside those of his two sisters. I examine their profiles as well as those of their children. Like wandering down a dark street looking into to see a family around a fire, the glow of the flames dancing across their faces. This phase, of looking in from the shadows uninvited, makes my stomach churn. I'm invisible to them, am I the ghost? I consider trespassing on private property, knocking on the door and confronting the haunting. No warrant to intrude. The prospect of denial and rejection tugging me away, keeping me out of sight. "Perhaps it's easier to co-exist with the figure of the ghost?" I wonder. I sit with the haunting.

As explored above in my personal account, the concept of 'haunting' offers significant utility for interpreting donor-conceived people's experiences of living with anonymity. By living with anonymity, I mean living with the knowledge that one was conceived using a gamete donor who was promised anonymity. As I explore in this chapter, the culture of anonymity and secrecy in donor conception has produced the conditions for ongoing haunting in the everyday lives of donor-conceived people. Haunting, according to Gordon, is a sociopolitical-psychological state in which repressed, unresolved or invisible past structures make themselves known and felt in the present (Gordon, 2008; Gordon et al., 2020). A focus on haunting invites us to listen carefully to donor-conceived people's accounts for experiences pushed to the peripheries, to unsettling, fleeting or illusive occurrences. As I articulate in this chapter, developing the concept of familial haunting, allows us to expand sociological conceptualisations of family by attending to accounts of absence, uncertainty and (unbe)longing.

9.1 Cultures of Anonymity and Secrecy: Ghostly Fathers

Donor conception has always been characterised by secrecy, omissions, partial knowledge and selective telling in relation to both the use of the practice and disclosure of the identities of gamete donors (Frith et al., 2018a). In the nineteenth century, as doctors began experimenting with artificial insemination by donor, the practice was met with suspicion, reflecting social attitudes towards masturbation and adultery (Allan, 2017; Swanson, 2012). Since the mid-1940s and for the best part of the remaining decades of the twentieth century, anonymity and secrecy were thought to protect the recipient couple and donor-conceived person from emotional harm and shame (Adams & Lorbach, 2012; Swanson, 2012). Doctors sought to create an illusion that the child was biologically related to the social father via matching techniques in which donors who had similar physical features were selected (Swanson, 2012). Other techniques such as sperm mixing and use of doctor sperm were also used during this period (Adams & Lorbach, 2012; Dingle, 2021; Rowland, 1985). Further, doctors encouraged couples to have sexual intercourse following insemination and to pretend that the insemination had not occurred (Allan, 2017; Swanson, 2012). As such, the issue of male infertility was rarely confronted within the family dynamics, rather it was "masked by a 'ghost father' who was ghostly because he never fully materialized, and was supposed to fade away as soon as conception occurred" (Swanson, 2012, p. 612; see also Newsweek, 1934).

Many doctors were also fearful of liability and the "binding" nature of anonymity agreements (Rowland, 1985) and kept inaccurate medical records or later modified or destroyed documentation (Adams & Lorbach, 2012; Dingle, 2021; Hewitt, 2002; Rowland, 1985). While donor conception has also been practised outside a clinical context, including in the context of queer and solo family arrangements (Dempsey, 2006; Kelly, 2010; Nordqvist, 2011; Power et al., 2010; Riggs, 2008), the era of anonymity continues to impact the lives of many – arguably most – donor-conceived adults today, restricting access to complete and accurate information about donors and donor siblings.

The last few decades have seen major shifts in social attitudes, professional perspectives and regulatory frameworks, which support openness in donor conception, underscoring donor-conceived people's "right to know" (Allan, 2017; Blyth et al., 2012; Nordqvist, 2014). However, in the Australian context, like other parts of the world, legislation is far from uniform and donor-conceived people's rights to access information about their conception and family are determined by year and jurisdiction of conception. This inconsistency creates tiers of donor-conceived "haves" and "have nots" in terms of formal avenues for accessing information and forging contact with family members.

An alternative route for searching and identifying donors and donor siblings has emerged through direct-to-consumer autosomal DNA testing platforms in which users are matched based on shared centiMorgans (units of genetic measurement). Scholars have argued that these technologies render donor anonymity and concealment of donor-conceived status "utopian" (Macpherson, 2019, p. 1847), with many donor-conceived people learning that they were conceived with donor gametes when they receive a high genetic match with a stranger (Darroch & Smith, 2021; Klotz, 2016; Newton et al., 2022). For people who are aware of their conception status, DNA testing often offers answers and/or hope for identifying unknown family members (Newton et al., 2022). However, success largely depends on the individual's genealogical knowledge, labour, and as I explore below, patience.

A rich field of scholarship has emerged which seeks to describe the experiences of those enmeshed in the practice of donor conception (Blyth et al., 2012). However, much of this research has focused on the perspectives of parents, with less capturing the experiences of donor-conceived people themselves (Jadva, 2021), who are arguably those most affected. Existing research has made it clear that the majority of donor-conceived people view any information about their donors as important (Rodino et al., 2011), and most desire contact with their donor and donor siblings (Beeson et al., 2011; Daniels, 2020; Dempsey et al., 2019; Macmillan et al.,

2021). For example, in a study of 69 Australian donor-conceived adults, Caitlin Macmillan and colleagues (2021) found that 88 per cent had been motivated to seek information about their donor and 71 per cent had been motivated to seek contact. Scholars have noted that many donor-conceived people have low expectations for the kind of relationships that could emerge, potentially as a coping strategy and/or for self-protection from rejection (Freeman et al., 2014; Scheib et al., 2017). Collectively, this scholarship raises interesting questions about how donor-conceived people decide whether to contact their donor and/or donor siblings and their everyday experiences and relationships to unknown family members. This chapter extends previous work by underscoring how framing anonymity as an issue of the past (re)produces ongoing haunting. Anonymity, secrecy and reform without concomitant processes of widespread truth-telling and equitable redress represent an injustice to those who continue to live with the lingering impacts of such past conditions.

9.2 On Haunting

In her book *Ghostly Matters*, Avery Gordon expands the scope of the empirical to include subjective experiences that are located at the edges of our consciousness (Gordon, 2008). Gordon proposes an attentiveness to the interrelationship between what she describes as the haunting and the ghost:

> If haunting describes how that which appears to be not there is often a seething presence, acting on and often meddling with taken-for granted realities, the ghost is just the sign, or the empirical evidence if you like, that tells you a haunting is taking place. (2008, p. 8)

Haunting, as a concept, accounts for the "tangible and tactile as well as ephemeral and imaginary" (Gordon, 2008, p. 201), and the aspects of individuals' experiences and identities which are "left in the shadows or on the margins" (Smart, 2007, p. 183). Indeed, Gordon's innovative approach to studying social reality aligns with Carol Smart's (2007) vision in *Personal Life* in which she articulated the need to "explore those families and relationships which exist in our imaginings and memories, since these are just as real ... [to understand] the realms of yearning, desires and inner emotion" (p. 4; see also Nordqvist, 2017).

Gordon explains how haunting is experienced when repressed social violence of the past makes itself known and felt in the present, sometimes explicitly, but often through murky traces or eery moments. In a similar vein, Ashley Barnwell (2019, p. 1116), drawing on Nixon's (2011) theory of slow violence, has mapped how, in the context of the family, slow violence can unfold through "shaming, silencing, ostracising, withholding recognition and effectively erasing memories and relationships". Critical, then, is a focus on how suppression, secrecy and silence have enduring impacts on family life and individuals' sense of familial (un)belonging across generations. The concept of haunting allows us to consider how social violence reshapes flows between past, present and future, altering personhood and relationality.

Below, I explore thematic analysis of accounts from donor-conceived people living with anonymity. Divided into three thematic domains, I chart (1) the complexities of living with the inner ghost, (2) how haunting reconfigures the passage of time including through the ongoing waiting and loss, and (3) relationality, ambivalence and the affective pull implicit in attempts to confront the ghost.

9.3   Methods

9.3.1   Data Collection

The accounts of donor-conceived adults that inform this chapter come from a multi-method study, exploring Australian donor-conceived people's experiences, conducted between 2019 and 2022. Ethics approval for the study was provided by the UNSW Sydney Human Research Ethics Committee (HC190998). This chapter draws on data collected in the form of semi-structured interviews ($N = 28$), conducted online between April and December 2020. Donor-conceived people who were Australian citizens or permanent residents, and who were members of Facebook groups for donor-conceived people and over 18 years old, were eligible to participate in interviews. Interviews lasted between one and three hours and all participants received an AU$30 voucher for their time. Interviews were audio recorded, transcribed in full, de-identified and all participants were assigned a pseudonym (used in excerpts below).

The sample included 23 women, 4 men and 1 non-binary person. Participants were conceived in six jurisdictions of Australia to heterosexual parents ($n = 25$), lesbian mothers ($n = 1$), and single mothers ($n = 2$). Participants ranged in age from 18 to 40 years old, and as such, were conceived during the era of anonymity. Participants reported learning of their donor-conceived status before turning 13 years old ($n = 10$), between 13 and 25 years old ($n = 9$), between 26 and 39 years old ($n = 9$). Participants learnt of their conception from different actors and processes including from a parent/s, grandparent or aunt, in instances of divorce, death, moving or following discussions about fertility; in a letter from a statutory authority; through or following direct-to-consumer DNA testing; or through a hunch or clash in information.

9.3.2   Data Analysis

Informed by the interpretive traditions within sociology, the interview data was coded following Braun and Clarke's (2020) approach to reflexive thematic analysis. This framework emphasises the importance of researcher reflexivity given researchers' subjectivity shapes analysis and findings (Braun & Clarke, 2020), and indeed, all participants were aware of the researcher's 'insider' status, as a donor-conceived person. Smart (2007), like Gordon (2008), has invited us to embrace alternative ways of knowing, shifting our style as well as our content to capture the interplay between researcher and researched via situated and reflexive analysis. To this end, it is important to reflect briefly on how the focus of the paper, living with anonymity, was shaped by my emic perspective (Lambert, 2020). My decision to share my own personal experiences in the form of opening and closing autoethnographic style vignettes, reflects the importance I place on making visible donor-conceived people's experiences and researcher reflexivity (see Newton, 2022; Newton & Southerton, 2023). Through my subjective engagement, grappling with my own and my peers' accounts of haunting, in this chapter I explore what it means to live with anonymity.

9.4   Findings

9.4.1   Complex Personhood: Accommodating the Ghost Within

Donor-conceived people's processes of identity (re)formation can be impacted by age of disclosure of conception status, conditions of disclosure and information about and contact with genetic family (Beeson et al., 2011; Frith et al., 2018a; Jadva et al., 2010; Macmillan et al., 2021). All participants in this study had been engaged in processes of searching for their donor and/or donor siblings using a variety of methods, such as accessing medical records, enrolment to state registries, media appearances, autosomal direct-to-consumer DNA testing, participation in social media and online forums, among other techniques. The first theme, derived from thematic analysis, encapsulates how participants felt about themselves during the period of living with anonymity.

Some participants described "not feeling like themselves". For example, Thomas explained the strangeness he felt upon learning he was donor-conceived in his mid-30s:

> ... a bit perplexed and a bit surreal. You know, that state of when you've been in an accident or something and you're kind of not quite yourself ... it's almost akin to a, a bereavement, a shock, where it's like you don't believe that they're dead or, and it's like, "That can't be," and, "How has that sort of been the case?" And it's just, it's hard to take in. (Thomas)

The above account, like others across the interviews, reveals the transformative period of coming to terms with the upheaval of the foundations of one's personhood. The haunting sets in as Thomas becomes aware that he has misrecognised himself, revealing a form of a complex personhood that must be grappled with. Similarly, Leah spoke of being startled by the new knowledge that she was donor conceived:

> By your mid-twenties, you feel like you've got a fair idea, to then like, to be a little bit blindsided by hearing that, especially because, you know, you've been told thing all your life ... I wonder a lot about, "Well, then who is this other person who has, you know, half of myself comes from?" Yeah. I guess it's hard to try to integrate that into who you thought you were and, yeah, I don't know. It just shakes you a bit. (Leah)

Leah recognises the difficulties she experiences in articulating the "seething presence" of the donor within herself (Gordon, 2008, p. 8). In this way, this new way of seeing – the haunting – accessed since participants learned they were donor conceived, was variously experienced, here as feeling 'blindsided' and 'shaken'.

For Fran, who learnt she was donor conceived at 31 years old, the ghost took over her face:

> I couldn't really look at myself in the mirror 'cause it kind of felt strange. It was like I'm not actually like half of who I thought I was. So that was really weird to me and I sort of grew up thinking, yeah, like I had my dad's nose ... But the donor must have looked very similar to my dad I guess. Trippy! (Fran)

Here we see how Fran is troubled by the contradiction of her personal narratives of familial resemblance. In this way, everyday encounters with one's own features were a persisting reminder of the unknown ghost. These dissociative symptoms had implications for how donor-conceived people felt about their bodies and about themselves (Daniels, 2020). Learning of donor-conceived status later in life required unpacking existing personal and relational narratives including those associated with resemblance, where features are read as continuities between past and present. Individuals also became aware of how the medical regime of anonymity sought to mask the donor through matching techniques to the social father, rendering him ghostly.

In contrast to the above accounts of late disclosure, another participant, Brooke, spoke of knowing that she was donor conceived since early childhood. Brooke's donor-conceived status began nagging at her after she had children in her 30s, she explained:

> I don't know, it just came. Like, all of a sudden, I had an overwhelming need to know where I came from, who my biological father was … I remember using that term "rollercoaster" a lot at that time. It was, probably I felt I was … I remember asking my husband if he thought I was crazy during that period of several months. (Brooke)

Living with anonymity unexpectedly gained prominence for Brooke, after having children (see also Indekeu & Hens, 2019, p. 25). The ghost emerged from the peripheries of the donor-conceived conscience to occupy the centre stage; the illusive vision and torment of the ghost seemingly irrational and indicative of craziness. While a break in the intergenerational chain of understanding biological heritage had previously not been significant to Brooke, now with children to consider, the lack of answers became a problem and she sought to resolve this uncertainty (for herself and her descendants).

Participants explained how donor-conceived status figured as a single aspect of individuals' intersectional identities and many donor-conceived people could, and would, live comfortably with anonymity their whole lives. However, the void in one's identity occupied by the anonymous donor could gain significance with diagnosis of a medical condition, when entering a new sexual relationship, in experiences of not recognising specific features or traits in their children, or other arbitrary encounters. The haunting could produce a something-to-be-done, a need for resolution or alleviation through searching for unknown family members. In this way, the donor's absence carried meaning and consequences; the nothing was something (Scott, 2018). Living with anonymity, then, represents a form of complex personhood characterised by this prevailing absent presence (Gordon, 2008; see also Broom et al., 2021). For donor-conceived people conceived during the era of anonymity, accommodating the ghost within formed part of their identity, sometimes temporarily and sometimes indefinitely, as I discuss in the next section.

9.4.2 *Temporal (Re)Configurations: Anticipation, Waiting, Loss*

Across the interviews, participants described how knowing they were donor conceived shaped experiences of temporality. Most participants had broad understandings of family, which included family members who were biologically related as well as family through social ties (see also Newton et al., 2023). Importantly, participants viewed their ghostly donor family – unknown biological family members – as part of their family. As such, while these relationships were framed as dormant, they could be activated with changes in circumstances, technologies and regulatory frameworks. The ghost could become known at any time. However, accessing and living these relationships depended on patience and waiting.

Several participants explored the temporal dimensions of searching and waiting, including the lengthy processes of interacting with medical institutions and authorities to secure information. While some participants felt they had agency and that hauntings could be (attempted to be) dealt with, others surrendered to the powerlessness of the "kinship blockage" (Carsten, 2007a, p. 85), recognising that hauntings would continue to figure in their experience of family:

> [It] can be quite painful, actually, and quite frustrating, and quite annoy-
> ing, knowing that it's just all out of our hands; we have to wait for our
> siblings to do a DNA test. (Mabel)

In the excerpt above, Mabel articulates the irritation, pain and helplessness she felt in relation to the non-relationships with her siblings. These negative feelings were coupled with a degree of suspense and anticipation towards the prospect that her siblings may participate in direct-to-consumer DNA testing. Across the interviews, it became clear that the culture of anonymity impinged on individuals' relational and agentive possibilities and for some this caused struggles and feelings of impotence. Participants revealed a normativity to waiting; the everyday haunting must be accepted, though forever mindful that the pace of social life could be accelerated at any time (see also Broom et al., 2018).

Some participants believed they had found all of their family members, yet a glimmer of uncertainty remained that could only be resolved over time:

> I was lucky. I was [conceived at hospital X] and they kept great records …
> I'm kind of, you know, five per cent thinking that we're gonna find out that
> there's more [siblings] out there because how much can you actually rely on
> what's been kept; you know, records. (Sharon)

Here Sharon foregrounded her distrust in the medical records (see also Newton et al., 2022), highlighting how gaining additional siblings was within the realm of possibility. It is perhaps in these circumstances – with the slightest tinge of uncertainty – where the haunting lingers. Indeed, it is highly unlikely that Sharon will ever be certain about exactly how many siblings she has, but will instead remain in a state of anticipation, wondering about the reach and boundaries of her family.

Several of the participants underscored how family is fostered over time and through shared experience and practices (Morgan, 2011), and new familial relationships would require a large investment of their time:

> That takes time, yeah. That's what a relationship is, requires experiences. Shared experiences. You have to show up and do things … I'm open to putting in the time to form those relationships and create them. But there is a big loss there 'cause you've lost that time. So those formative years. You can't go back and grow up together. (Ruth)

For Ruth, the absence of her donor and donor siblings symbolised lost time and as such, if/when a family member emerged, it would be necessary to compensate for time spent out-of-reach. Participants gestured to how meeting after childhood would markedly impact their experiences of siblinghood (see also Jadva et al., 2010). We see how haunting alters social experiences of linear time and life stages (Halberstam, 2005; Pearce, 2018), when "formative years" are experienced atypically during adulthood. Indeed, across the interviews there were indications of altered temporalities via the articulation of a form of ambiguous loss (and related missing and mourning) (Boss, 2007). Unknown family members could not be accounted for and, therefore, no resolution or closure could be achieved. In this way, time is frozen with limited means to make sense of (or even articulate) the importance/the affects of non-relationships.

Participants described having a sense that their donor or donor siblings were close, likely living in the same city, yet out-of-reach and unknowable. In this way, the culture of anonymity, and perhaps the doctors who promised such conditions, were responsible for 'stolen time' (and associated loss):

> When you do find these donor siblings that, you know, have been there the whole time and that you know you've missed out on 35 years of knowing that they even existed, and, you know, you've only got a certain amount of time to sit on this earth. (Jerome)

Jerome identified that living with anonymity required grieving the "what-could-have-been" (Gordon, 2008). While some participants invoked the loss of the past, Jerome's grief was future-facing, recognising time as a finite resource with imminent mortality. In this way, experiences of haunting reconfigured participants' experiences of their life courses and while relationships were not materialised, a ghostly presence was felt. As donor-conceived people lived with anonymity, their felt impressions of donors and donor siblings lingered, and so too did an ongoing sense of (unbe) longing and loss. These family members were neither alive nor dead, absent nor present, and could not be mourned during the state of in-between. Thus, the haunting represented unresolved grief (Boss, 2007; Lambert, 2020; Harrigan et al., 2014). More broadly, the sense of loss resulting from disrupted familial memory and continuity, and linear kinship (Carsten, 2007), gave rise to reconfigured temporality within and beyond lifetimes.

Participants described how donor conception also had impacts beyond their generation, haunting the bodies and selves of their children, grandchildren and future generations. For example, Simone expressed how living with anonymity produced guilt around the lack of information she could provide to her children:

> One of my greatest fears was: what am I passing down to them? What am I unaware of that I need to share with them? At what stage in their life do they ask someone they're dating for a DNA test to ensure they're not related to them? (Simone)

Without a family narrative to tell her children about their biological grandfather, Simone described how living anonymity is intergenerationally experienced; the sense of absence is passed on. As such, the haunting figures as a form of ongoing intergenerational social violence (Barnwell, 2019). While some families were better able to acknowledge, discuss and live with these absences, many people felt compelled to address the void, interrogate the ghost(s) and bring them to life.

9.4.3   Pull towards the Unknown: Relationality, Ambivalence and Affective Forces

The third thematic domain derived from analysis describes affective forces that pushed and pulled participants towards and away from making contact with their donor and donor siblings.

Participants underscored how non-relationships were highlighted in everyday encounters:

> I never knew when things would creep up. You know, it might be watching a movie where there would be, you know, the father unknown or, I don't

know, I can't even think of any of the movies but there's always something there, eh? Like that, that triggers. And then, all of a sudden, you know, I'd be days wondering, you know, having deep wonderings. (Henry)

Here, Henry underscores how he is unexpectedly reminded of his donor, leading to periods of heightened awareness of his donor-conceived status and associated lack of information about his donor's identity or whereabouts. We see here how feelings of (unbe)longing emerge in donor-conceived people's day-to-day lives; the spectre comes in to view as a reminder that one does not know oneself. Living with anonymity involves bracing for the moments that the ghost appears uninvited and finding ways to banish the ghost in such instances.

Some participants described yearning to know their family members, framing this desire as innate:

> It's such a deep longing. It's a natural kind of, even a, not a conscious feeling; it's a subconscious thing just to know who your person is, your identity, where you come from. (Fay)

Fay articulated the force compelling her to seek answers about the family history in which she was embedded. We see how anonymity can create a longing to belong. Participants living with anonymity were driven to better understand their identity and put an end to the haunting. Searching, then, offered hope: "horizons of being and becoming" (Eng, 2010, p. 184).

However, other participants expressed how they felt unable or unwilling to search for their donor because they were worried that it may upset their social father:

> If I were to meet the donor, I think it might offend my dad. So I don't want to meet the donor anyway 'cause my dad's my dad. It doesn't matter that the donor is my biological father. (Fran)

The above remark points to Fran's concerns about unresolved shame experienced by her social father in relation to infertility, giving rise to the need to protect her father's masculinity and pride (Cosson et al., 2021). While Fran is not coerced to keep the secret, her relational possibilities are still limited by her fear that her social father will not cope if she seeks out a relationship with her biological father. More broadly, here we see how disharmony and distress is delicately avoided within families (see Smith et al., 2021). For many donor-conceived people, the desire for a relationship with their donors must be carefully negotiated through forms of intensive emotional and relational labour to ensure non-biological parents do not feel threatened or replaced by ghostly donors. Searching, then, is not strictly an individual decision but a practice shaped by the attitudes of others within donor-conceived people's relational, and specifically familial, webs.

For other participants, concerns coalesced around regretting moving from the unknown to the known and regretting that trajectory:

> I'm scared to search. It must be maddening to hear, "Sorry, the dog ate your records," or a differently crushing, being rejected by your donor. I'm not strong enough to face that at the moment. (Shane)

In the above excerpt, Shane underscored the comfort felt within the unknown and their fear of familial rejection. In this sense, by searching for family as an adult, one becomes significantly vulnerable to the prospect of parental disapproval or rejection. Participants described having to construct a particular kind of personal narrative upon forging contact, framing themselves as successful, "well-adjusted", unthreatening, not needy, not looking for a "father", and not vying for inheritance. Engaging in searching involved inviting the familial stranger to evaluate their personal intentions, worth and potential to fit within their pre-established family structure. And fears prevailed about "not measuring up" (Freeman et al., 2014, p. 279).

In contrast to the above issue of fear of rejection, participants also discussed the likelihood that they might not like or approve of the person that they found. For example:

> I'm always terrified because I think, you know, "What if this person is open to meeting and I meet them, and I dislike them?," you know, "or I think they're awful?, Or they say something terrible?" Like I don't know if that's worse than the bubble of not knowing who they are (Dominique).

Here we can see what has been described as "a sense of the 'what ifness'" (Carsten, 2007, p. 86), that is, the uncertainty around what kind of person awaits and the vast array of possible outcomes. Like Dominique's questions above, participants described a range of "what ifs": What if the person is dead? What if they are a criminal? What if they do not respond? What if they donated thousands of times? What if they are my grandparents' age? The ambivalence described as part of these questions reflects the overwhelming uncertainty around forging familial relationships as an adult (see also Newton & Southerton, 2023). Like Shane, Dominique describes the comfort of the liminal "bubble", or the "fantasy" (Freeman et al., 2014, p. 278), in which the donor lingers neither absent nor present, dead or alive (Lambert, 2020).

In some instances, contact with a donor resulted in unsatisfactory or ambiguous answers. This was the case for Amira who called her donor after receiving no response to a letter sent via registered post:

> He goes, "I'm not exactly sure what you want from me." And I said to him, "Oh, well, let's start with a confirmation that you actually were a sperm donor in the 1980s." He goes, "This is nothing I can confirm or deny." ... and then I asked another question. "It's nothing I can confirm or deny." ... I said to him, "This just doesn't sound like it's gonna be a fruitful conversation. I'm just trying to establish my identity here. I'm 33 years old and I don't know anything about me." He's like, "I'm sorry, I can't help you". (Amira)

This excerpt reveals Amira's desperation and disappointment as she confronts the person she believes to be her donor. The pull towards making contact resulted in a sense of increased uncertainty; even direct contact with the presumed donor did not provide adequate evidence for Amira. While the haunting in some ways is alleviated as the ghost takes more shape, the emotional agony is often compounded by negative interactions between the donor-conceived person and the donor. Yet, the significance of the ghost becomes more pertinent as the hopes and desires for relational possibilities do not come to fruition (see also Scheib et al., 2017).

9.5   Conclusions

This chapter has revealed donor-conceived people's profoundly complex, emotional and dynamic experiences of living with anonymity. I have argued that donor-conceived people often experience non-relationships with donor family members as a haunting, an experience in which absence is more significant than presence. I have deployed the concept of haunting to make sense of how anonymity is experienced on a day-to-day basis; how anonymity *feels*. Through attentiveness to elements of familial connections that participants struggled to articulate, admit or understand, I have demonstrated how absence has a presence, through the figure of the ghostly father or siblings, or through distinct experiences of personhood, temporality and affective pull.

This chapter has conjured experiences of haunting in which familial non-relationships are lived and felt. I align with Ribbens McCarthy (2012), in emphasising the importance of engagement with the notion of "family", given its dominance in everyday social practices, representations and language in the English-speaking world. Indeed, it is often through normative assumptions around family that haunting is revealed or produced. It is critical that we continue to explore how individuals' dynamic positions within social webs, inflect their sense of identity, foregrounding "relational selves" (Mason, 2004, p. 177). Personhood and identity are always shaped by relationships to family, whether positive or negative, absent or present, alive or dead (or across these spectrums). Indeed, sociologists have tended to focus on tangible aspects of social life, neglecting the "no-things", such as non-relationships, non-identities, invisibilities, absences and void (Scott, 2018). Within the sociology of families and relationships there is significant scope to explore this terrain of non-relationships and their links to (unbe)longing. Here, I have attempted to contribute to this vision by exploring experiences of living with anonymity and absence.

As this chapter and previous scholarship has shown, many donor-conceived people view relationships with donors and donor siblings as important (Daniels, 2020; Rodino et al., 2011) and as something that they are entitled to (Allan, 2017; Newton et al., 2023). Exploring these emerging family forms offers important insights into social meanings ascribed to genetic relatedness and the role of family in individuals' sense of identity. Normative discourses of resemblance, relatedness and "genetic thinking" are a common feature in everyday life and contribute to individuals' ability to anchor familial belonging (Dempsey et al., 2019; Indekeu, 2015; Nordqvist, 2017). As I have demonstrated, in instances where genetic origins are unknown, (unbe)longing often lingers. Indeed, there is often ambivalence, fears and desires in relation to broaching the unknown, given the (dis)connection and (un)belonging that may be revealed (Ribbens McCarthy, 2012). More work is needed to further map familial (un)belonging across a range of family forms and social domains, to better understand how belonging as a social phenomenon can be situated, processual and negotiated (Newman et al., 2020).

With regulatory frameworks increasingly privileging donor-conceived people's rights and needs (Allan, 2017) and the growing uptake of social media and autosomal direct-to-consumer DNA testing (Darroch & Smith, 2021; Frith et al., 2018b; Klotz, 2016; Newton et al., 2022), a unique historical moment is unfolding. Donor-conceived people are challenging and reckoning with cultures of anonymity and secrecy, including where states are unwilling to console or acknowledge past wrongdoings. However, while donor-conceived people can maximise experiential knowledge from peers and digital technologies in creating agentive opportunities, there are limits to who can be found and whether expectations and visions will materialise. Framing anonymity as an issue of the past (re)produces haunting and represents an injustice to those who continue to live with the lingering impacts of such past conditions, including the descendants of donor-conceived people. Acknowledging and remembering past social wrongdoings is widely regarded as a positive approach in terms of collective identity and justice (Misztal, 2003). As such, across law, policy and practice it is essential that the history of donor conception practices is accurately documented, recognising that, while understandings and attitudes of the time were different, by today's standards and moralities those practices were harmful. Gordon argues that justice is "the social, economic, political and cultural changes required to eliminate the conditions that produce the organized or systemic violence in the first place" (Gordon et al., 2020, p. 341). Therefore, until there is a consistency and equity in the rights of donor-conceived people around the world, and a global commitment to processes of truth-telling and acknowledgement of past wrongdoings, there will be individual and collective, intergenerational haunting.

I have long lived with (coped with) anonymity. Yet I am still caught unprepared, I stutter and stammer when the ghost emerges. As I go about ordinary tasks on autopilot, I am jolted by the slap of the ghost's hand across my face, the sting of the presence of my donor's absence:

> As shampoo is being massaged into my scalp, my eyelids shut tightly so the suds don't burn my eyes. "Do both of your parents have your curly hair?" My mind darts, I think of him, "ha ha, no, just my mum".

As I glance down at the simian crease stamped upon my palm. A fleeting thought of him, a man I am determined has that same topographical map sprawled across his hand.

As they ask "Date of birth?" "any allergies?" "family history of blood clots?" I gulp, smile and shake my head, "I don't think so".

Haunting, for me, is part of being donor conceived; part of living with anonymity.

References

Adams, D., & Lorbach, C. (2012). Accessing donor conception information in Australia: A call for retrospective access. *Journal of Law and Medicine*, 19(4), 707–721.

Allan, S. (2017). *Donor Conception and the Search for Information: From Secrecy and Anonymity to Openness*. Abingdon: Routledge, Taylor and Francis Group.

Barnwell, A. (2019). Family secrets and the slow violence of social stigma. *Sociology*, 53(6), 1111–1126. https://doi.org/10.1177/0038038519846443

Beeson, D. R., Jennings, P. K., & Kramer, W. (2011). Offspring searching for their sperm donors: How family type shapes the process. *Human Reproduction*, 26(9), 2415–2424. https://doi.org/10.1093/humrep/der202

Blyth, E., Crawshaw, M., Frith, L., & Jones, C. (2012). Donor-conceived people's views and experiences of their genetic origins: A critical analysis of the research evidence. *Journal of Law and Medicine*, 19(4).

Boss, P. (2007). Ambiguous loss theory: Challenges for scholars and practitioners. *Family Relations*, 56(2), 105–110.

Braun, V., & Clarke, V. (2020). One size fits all? What counts as quality practice in (reflexive) thematic analysis? *Qualitative Research in Psychology*, 1–25. https://doi.org/10.1080/14780887.2020.1769238

Broom, A., Kenny, K., & Kirby, E. (2018). On waiting, hauntings and surviving: Chronicling life with cancer through solicited diaries. *The Sociological Review*, 66(3), 682–699. https://doi.org/10.1177/0038026117719216

Broom, A., Lewis, S., Parker, R., Williams Veazey, L., Kenny, K., Kirby, E., Kokanović, R., Lwin, Z., & Koh, E.-S. (2021). Personhood, belonging, affect and affliction. *The Sociological Review*, 69(5), 1051–1071. https://doi.org/10.1177/00380261211019266

Carsten, J. (2007). Connections and disconnections of memory and kinship in narratives of adoption reunions in Scotland. *Ghosts of Memory: Essays on Remembrance and Relatedness*, 83–103. https://doi.org/10.1002/9780470692301.ch4

Cosson, B., Dempsey, D., & Kelly, F. (2021). Secret shame – Male infertility and donor conception in the wake of retrospective legislative change. *Men and Masculinities*, 25(3), 497–515. https://doi.org/10.1177/1097184X211038329

Daniels, K. (2020). The perspective of adult donor conceived persons. In K. Beier, C. Brügge, P. Thorn, & C. Wiesemann (Eds.), *Assistierte Reproduktion mit Hilfe Dritter* (pp. 443–459). Springer Berlin Heidelberg. https://doi.org/10.1007/978-3-662-60298-0_29

Darroch, F., & Smith, I. (2021). Establishing identity: How direct-to-consumer genetic testing challenges the assumption of donor anonymity. *Family Court Review*, 59(1), 103–120. https://doi.org/10.1111/fcre.12553

Dempsey, D. (2006). Beyond choice: Family and kinship in the Australian lesbian and gay "baby boom" [PhD thesis]. La Trobe University.

Dempsey, D., Kelly, F., Horsfall, B., Hammarberg, K., Bourne, K., & Johnson, L. (2019). Applications to statutory donor registers in Victoria, Australia: Information sought and expectations of contact. *Reproductive Biomedicine & Society Online, 9*, 28–36. https://doi.org/10.1016/j.rbms.2019.08.002

Dingle, S. (2021). *Brave New Humans: The Dirty Reality of Donor Conception.* Hardie Grant Books.

Eng, D. L. (2010). *The Feeling of Kinship: Queer Liberalism and the Racialization of Intimacy.* Duke University Press.

Freeman, T., Bourne, K., Jadva, V., & Smith, V. (2014). Making connections: Contact between sperm donor relations. In *Relatedness in Assisted Reproduction: Families, Origins and Identities* (pp. 270–295). Cambridge University Press.

Frith, L., Blyth, E., Crawshaw, M., & van den Akker, O. (2018a). Secrets and disclosure in donor conception. *Sociology of Health & Illness, 40*(1), 188–203. https://doi.org/10.1111/1467-9566.12633

Frith, L., Blyth, E., Crawshaw, M., & van den Akker, O. (2018b). Searching for "relations" using a DNA linking register by adults conceived following sperm donation. *BioSocieties, 13*(1), 170–189. https://doi.org/10.1057/s41292-017-0063-2

Gordon, A. F. (2008). *Ghostly Matters: Haunting and the Sociological Imagination.* University of Minnesota Press.

Gordon, A. F., Hite, K., & Jara, D. (2020). Haunting and thinking from the Utopian margins: Conversation with Avery Gordon. *Memory Studies, 13*(3), 337–346. https://doi.org/10.1177/1750698020914017

Halberstam, J. J., & Halberstam, J. (2005). *In a Queer Time and Place: Transgender Bodies, Subcultural Lives.* New York University Press.

Harrigan, M. M., Dieter, S., Leinwohl, J., & Marrin, L. (2014). Redefining family: An analysis of adult donor-conceived offspring's discursive meaning-making. *Iowa Journal of Communication, 46*(1), 16–32.

Hewitt, G. (2002). Missing links: Identity issues of donor conceived people. *Journal of Fertility Counselling, 9*, 14–19.

Indekeu, A. (2015). Parent's expectations and experiences of resemblance through donor conception. *New Genetics and Society, 34*(4), 398–416. https://doi.org/10.1080/14636778.2015.1098525

Indekeu, A., & Hens, K. (2019). Part of my storyThe meaning and experiences of genes and genetics for sperm donor-conceived offspring. *New Genetics and Society, 38*(1), 18–37.

Jadva, V. (2021). Sibling relationships across families created through assisted reproduction. In *Brothers and Sisters* (pp. 171–184). Springer.

Jadva, V., Freeman, T., Kramer, W., & Golombok, S. (2010). Experiences of offspring searching for and contacting their donor siblings and donor. *Reproductive BioMedicine Online, 20*(4), 523–532. https://doi.org/10.1016/j.rbmo.2010.01.001

Kelly, F. (2010). An alternative conception: The legality of home insemination under Canada's Assisted Human Reproduction Act. *Canadian Journal of Family Law, 26*(1), 149–170.

Klotz, M. (2016). Wayward relations: Novel searches of the donor-conceived for genetic kinship. *Medical Anthropology, 35*(1), 45–57. https://doi.org/10.1080/01459740.2015.1012615

Lambert, C. (2020). The ambivalence of adoption: Adoptive families' stories. *Sociology*, 54(2), 363–379. https://doi.org/10.1177/0038038519880107

Macmillan, C. M., Allan, S., Johnstone, M., & Stokes, M. A. (2021). The motivations of donor-conceived adults for seeking information about, and contact with, sperm donors. *Reproductive BioMedicine Online*, 43(1), 149–158. https://doi.org/10.1016/j.rbmo.2021.04.005

Macpherson, I. (2019). Ethical reflections about the anonymity in gamete donation. *Human Reproduction*, 34(9), 1847–1848. https://doi.org/10.1093/humrep/dez142

Mason, J. (2004). Personal narratives, relational selves: Residential histories in the living and telling. *The Sociological Review*, 52(2), 162–179. https://doi.org/10.1111/j.1467-954X.2004.00463.x

Misztal, B. (2003). *Theories of Social Remembering*. McGraw-Hill Education (UK).

Morgan, D. (2011). *Rethinking Family Practices*. Springer.

Newman, C. E., Persson, A., Prankumar, S., Lea, T., & Aggleton, P. (2020). Experiences of family belonging among two generations of sexually diverse Australians. *Family Relations*, 69(2), 292–307. https://doi.org/10.1111/fare.12411

Newsweek. (1934, May 12). "Ghost" fathers: Children provided for the childless. *Newsweek*, 3(19), 16.

Newton, G. (2022). Doing reflexivity in research on donor conception: Examining moments of bonding and becoming. In R. M. Shaw (Ed.), *Reproductive Citizenship: Technologies, Rights and Relationships*. Palgrave Macmillan.

Newton, G., Drysdale, K., Zappavigna, M., & Newman, C. E. (2023) Truth, proof, sleuth: trust in direct-to-consumer DNA testing and other sources of identity information among Australian donor-conceived people. *Sociology*, 57(1). https://doi.org/10.1177/00380385221091184

Newton, G., & Southerton, C. (2023) Situated talk: A method for a reflexive encounter with #donorconceived on TikTok. *Media International Australia*, 186(1), 66–80. https://doi.org/10.1177/1329878X211064646

Newton, G., Zappavigna, M., Drysdale, K., & Newman, C. E. (2022) Memes as bonding icons for belonging in donor-conceived people. *Social Media and Society*, 8(1). https://doi.org/10.1177/20563051211069055.

Nixon, R. (2011). *Slow Violence and the Environmentalism of the Poor*. Harvard University Press. https://doi.org/10.4159/harvard.9780674061194

Nordqvist, P. (2011). "Dealing with sperm": Comparing lesbians' clinical and non-clinical donor conception processes. *Sociology of Health & Illness*, 33(1), 114–129. https://doi.org/10.1111/j.1467-9566.2010.01279.x

Nordqvist, P. (2014). The drive for openness in donor conception: Disclosure and the trouble with real life. *International Journal of Law, Policy and the Family*, 28(3), 321–338. https://doi.org/10.1093/lawfam/ebu010

Nordqvist, P. (2017). Genetic thinking and everyday living: On family practices and family imaginaries. *The Sociological Review*, 65(4), 865–881. https://doi.org/10.1177/0038026117711645

Pearce, R. (2018). Trans temporalities and non-linear ageing. In A. King, K. Almack, Y.-T. Suen, & S. Westwood (Eds.), *Older Lesbian, Gay, Bisexual and Trans People: Minding the Knowledge Gaps* (1st ed.). Routledge.

Power, J., Perlesz, A., Brown, R., Schofield, M., Pitts, M., McNair, R., & Bickerdike, A. (2010). Diversity, tradition and family: Australian same-sex attracted parents and their families. *Gay and Lesbian Issues and Psychology Review*, 6(2), 66.

Ribbens McCarthy, J. (2012). The powerful relational language of "family": Togetherness, belonging and personhood. *The Sociological Review*, 60(1), 68–90. https://doi.org/10.1111/j.1467-954X.2011.02045.x

Riggs, D. W. (2008). Lesbian mothers, gay sperm donors, and community: Ensuring the well-being of children and families. *Health Sociology Review*, 17(3), 226–234.

Rodino, I. S., Burton, P. J., & Sanders, K. A. (2011). Donor information considered important to donors, recipients and offspring: An Australian perspective. *Reproductive BioMedicine Online*, 22(3), 303–311. https://doi.org/10.1016/j.rbmo.2010.11.007

Rowland, R. (1985). The social and psychological consequences of secrecy in artificial insemination by donor (AID) programmes. *Social Science & Medicine*, 21(4), 391–396. https://doi.org/10.1016/0277-9536(85)90219-9

Scheib, J. E., Ruby, A., & Benward, J. (2017). Who requests their sperm donor's identity? The first ten years of information releases to adults with open-identity donors. *Fertility and Sterility*, 107(2), 483–493. https://doi.org/10.1016/j.fertnstert.2016.10.023

Scott, S. (2018). A sociology of nothing: Understanding the unmarked. *Sociology*, 52(1), 3–19. https://doi.org/10.1177/0038038517690681

Smart, C. (2007). *Personal Life: New Directions in Sociological Thinking*. Polity.

Smith, A. K., Persson, A., Drysdale, K., Bryant, J., Valentine, K., Wallace, J., Hamilton, M., Gray, R. M., & Newman, C. E. (2021). Family imaginaries in the disclosure of a blood-borne virus. *Sociology of Health & Illness*. https://doi.org/10.1111/1467-9566.13316

Swanson, K. W. (2012). Adultery by doctor: Artificial insemination, 1890–1945. *Chicago-Kent Law Review*, 87(2), 44.

CHAPTER 10

Assisted Reproduction and Making Kin Connections between Māori and Pākehā in Aotearoa New Zealand

Rhonda M. Shaw

10.1 Introduction

Assisted reproductive technologies (ARTs) do not enter cultural voids or vacuums, but are shaped by local moralities, religious and spiritual beliefs, and different social and regulatory contexts. Aotearoa New Zealand (Aotearoa) is no exception to this. While there is a limited body of empirical research documenting Māori (the Indigenous people of Aotearoa) views and experiences of ARTs in Aotearoa, what literature exists shows Māori who experience fertility issues are less likely than Pākehā (European settlers) to seek fertility clinic assistance (Reynolds & Smith, 2012; Righarts et al., 2021). A combination of factors are involved: lack of awareness of ARTs; the ethnocentric nature of fertility services; financial barriers; the perceived incompatibility of ARTs with notions of whānau (extended family groups) and whakapapa (genealogy); a preference for whāngai (explained later) as a cultural response to infertility within whānau, hapū (sub-tribe), or iwi (ancestral group) (Glover, 2008, 2009; Glover & Rousseau, 2007; Reynolds & Smith, 2012); and the lack of identity-release donors who are Māori (MacManus, 2017).

Of particular significance to Māori, as opposed to other cultural and ethnic groups in Aotearoa, is both the importance of whāngai as a reproductive option and the tracing of genealogy and exchange of information about genetic origins within whānau. In this chapter, I investigate the view that the transfer of reproductive materials and services for Māori between known and unknown donors and recipients has implications for social identity in ways that may not be deemed as significant for Pākehā. The aim of the chapter is to critically examine assumptions about the differences between Māori and Pākehā kinship affinities in the process of accessing assisted reproduction to create families. As such, the chapter pays particular attention to Māori insights into meanings of whānau to understand how ARTs interact with notions of whanaungatanga (relationships, kinship, sense of family connection) and whakapapa (genealogy).

For Māori, whānau is inherently intergenerational and includes grand-parents, parents, aunties, uncles, cousins, and children (Durie-Hall & Metge, 1992). These individuals belong to an ancestral line (whakapapa) that connects them to their hapū and iwi. Whānau is popularly under-stood to include what Pākehā refer to as the nuclear family, in addition to extended family, and ancestors. Knowledge of whakapapa is an important principle of Māori culture as it ensures people know their ancestral lineage. This knowledge not only affords a sense of identity and psychosocial well-being, but also connects Māori to their reproductive past and future. As an aspect of Te Ao Māori (the Māori worldview), the notion of whaka-papa captures the generational temporality of 'deep time' (Waldby, 2019), which connects born and unborn children to past generations through genetic kinship. According to Waldby (2019, p. 26), this generational time 'encompasses the succession of life-times and the possible ways in which generations are created and coexist'.

Te Ao Māori has implications for tikanga (cultural protocols and practices) around assisted reproduction. As Lovelock (2010, pp. 136–137) explains, for Māori, decisions relating to the donation of genetic mate-rial are made by whānau, and Māori who donate genetic material must continue to be socially responsible for the use of that material. "Mixing" gametes without whānau consent is therefore traditionally unacceptable. This understanding of kinship connection, which goes beyond the idea of gamete provision as an unconditional, unidirectional gift, has been theo-rised in relation to the concept of gift-exchange, and draws on Mauss's view that the giver's identity, essence, or spirit is inserted or invested in the gift or donative act. Because gift-exchange involves giving, receiving, *and* reciprocating, donative acts establish social bonds (Shaw, 2007). For Māori, gift-exchange is a complex relational ontology; sharing biological matter such as body parts and substances not only creates relationship responsibilities between donors and recipients but it implicates entire kin networks (Salmond, 2012). Where gift-exchange exists, donors do not construe bodily gifts, such as the provision of gametes, tissue, or reproduc-tive services as alienable, and may not see themselves as ever relinquishing control over that which is given. For those who subscribe to Te Ao Māori, the transfer of reproductive matter between known and unknown donors and recipients has implications for Māori social identity, in ways that may not be as significant for Pākehā (Shaw, 2020).

10.2   Information Sharing in Aotearoa

Māori views regarding whakapapa are recognised in legislation, policy, and practice surrounding ARTs in Aotearoa. The sacredness of whakapapa to Māori is also noted in the local media, so contemporary Pākehā are informed to an extent about the topic of information sharing in relation to Te Ao Māori. Since the late 1980s and early 1990s, fertility clinics have operated with a policy of openness and transparency regarding donor information for offspring conceived by third-party reproductive assistance (Adair & Rogan, 1998; Daniels & Lewis, 1996; Ellis & Irwin, 2002). One influence for this policy stems from the move towards open adoption, with the Adult Adoption Information Act 1985, which recognises the interests of children, their right to kinship knowledge and ability to access their genetic heritage (Coney & Else, 1999). A second influence comes from fertility clinic counsellors and consumer-led groups in the early 1990s who maintained the importance of a culture of information sharing for the psychological and emotional well-being of donor-conceived offspring (Daniels & Lewis, 1996; Hargreaves & Daniels, 2007). Additionally, as stated above, access to genetic knowledge was recognised as significant to Māori, for whom genealogy is key to locating individuals within broader networks of kin relations and belonging (whanaungatanga) (Daniels & Douglass, 2008; Shaw, 2015; Webber, n.d.).

This openness policy was made law by the Human Assisted Reproductive Technology Act 2004 (HART Act) and was subsequently followed by the introduction of a legal register for records of gamete donations resulting in births after 20 August 2005 (Daniels & Douglass, 2008). Prior to 2005, no official records were kept for clinic-recruited donors in Aotearoa, and they typically remained anonymous. Nowadays, while open-identity donors are not legally liable for any children produced by their donative acts, their details are recorded on the HART register and made available to donor offspring when they reach the age of 18, or earlier upon application by parent(s) (Daniels & Douglass, 2008). Contact between donors, offspring, and recipients is facilitated through the Department of Internal Affairs (Te Tari Taiwhenua), which holds records for births, deaths, and marriages in Aotearoa, or alternatively through fertility clinic providers. As of February 2022, fertility service providers must comply with the new Ngā Paerewa standard, which requires them to 'encourage and support people to inform offspring of their genetic and gestational origins' and 'store information to enable access' (Te Aka Matua o te Ture, 2021, p. 140).

Use of known donors in fertility clinics is encouraged due to the long wait list for identity-release donors, which, at the present time, is currently between 18 and 24 months. Identity-release donors are unknown to parents at the time of donation but may become known to recipients and offspring under the provisions of the HART Act. Although studies in Aotearoa have documented gamete provision and relationships between known donors, surrogates, and intended parents outside the clinic context (see Gibson, 2021; Glover, 2009; Surtees, 2017), there is no legal obligation to hold information about known donors in the case of self-arranged donor insemination or for non-clinic assisted traditional surrogacy arrangements. While these individuals are familiar to intended parents as acquaintances, friends, relatives, or people met on social media platforms, and are often open to future contact with offspring (Daniels et al., 2012; Gibson, 2021), they may hold different ideas about the limits and boundaries of donor-recipient and offspring contact (see Hertz et al., 2015). As discussed below, establishing relatedness requires working out how to manage who is part of one's family and kinship network and who is not.

10.3   Conceptual Framing

In this chapter, I discuss how policies, practices, and ideas about donor-recipient contact in the context of Aotearoa affect people's perceptions and experiences of kinship connectedness. Where previously I have examined first-person accounts from egg donors and surrogate mothers (Shaw, 2007, 2015), this chapter includes original data from a study with recipients accessing assisted reproduction. To facilitate the discussion, I draw on the sociological notion of kinship affinities developed by Mason (2008), and extended by Nordqvist (2014, 2019, 2019a; Nordqvist and Smart, 2014), to illuminate the different ways people who use assisted reproduction for family building imagine and practise relatedness as part of their personal lives.

Mason discusses four dimensions of kinship affinity, which may or may not resonate with people's perceptions of familial relatedness: fixed affinities, negotiated and created affinities, ethereal affinities, and sensory affinities. In Mason's framework, the idea that kinship connections are fixed comes closest to the view of kinship as an essential biogenetic relation between people who form families. This is because fixed affinities, as Mason (2008, p. 33) describes them, are 'in no sense chosen' and cannot be undone. Nevertheless, while people in some cultures place primary importance on familial duties and obligations based on genealogical ties and consanguineous relationships, Mason (2008, p. 33) proposes that fixity in terms of kinship responsibilities tend to be 'negotiated commitments' rather than assumed. In fact, Mason emphasises that kinship should not be conflated with scientific understandings of genetics but is 'layered with creative interpretations' (Nordqvist, 2019, p. 53). We see this, Mason argues, with respect to children's imaginings of particular individuals as family members but with whom they have no biogenetic or affinal link. Rather, the kinship connection is imagined and secured due to the strength and longevity of their parent's biographical relationship to these people. In this way, Mason suggests that people choreograph their kinship fixity to one another by constructing accounts of familiarity or a 'shared life trajectory' (Nordqvist, 2014) as non-negotiable.

Kinship affinity that comes into being through negotiation and creativity is the second salient aspect of familial connectedness Mason refers to. This kind of connection may be implicated by genetics, but the emphasis here has less to do with the idea of family as an institution or thing-like structure and more to do with how people practise family; that is, what matters is the way family is defined, communicated, and displayed through people's interpersonal relationships. Instead of assuming familial responsibilities stem from a person's genealogical positioning in a family tree, the kind of affinity that comes into play with this form of kin-making is an open-ended process and must be worked out cumulatively.

The third kind of kinship affinity, which Mason (2008, p. 37) states is less comprehensively covered in the sociological literature, refers to 'mysterious, magical, psychic, metaphysical, spiritual, and above all, ethereal – matters that are considered beyond (rational) explanation'. Rather than reflecting scientific notions of kinship as substantially fixed in blood or genes or individualistic notions of family as fictive, elective, or chosen, Mason (2008, p. 39) avers that the significance of ethereal affinities has 'differential resonance across varying socio-cultural contexts'. Nordqvist and Smart (2014, p. 107) allude to an ethereal affinity of sorts with reference to 'enigmatic relationships' that are imagined by families using unknown donors who acquire a mystical 'absent presence' in their lives but whom they never meet. Mason's idea also resonates with the Māori cosmological story of creation, wherein the kinship network is interrelated with the natural environment and spiritual domains (Salmond, 2012), thus having an ethereal dimension that is ontologically linked to wider understandings of whānau, ancestry, and belonging.

The final form of kinship affinity Mason identifies is materially embedded in memories of sensory experiences people have had with biogenetic and imagined kin. These affinities reference the senses – smell, taste, touch, vision, and sound – and are associated with particular persons who are regarded as part of people's family. These kinds of connections are embodied, relational, and inter-physical, depending on affective temporalities rooted in everyday life. Mason regards these kinship affinities as tangible (vivid, real, palpable) ways people make sense of and understand kinship ties. In the following discussion, Mason's framework of tangible affinities is linked to data from a qualitative study undertaken in Aotearoa documenting the cultural, ethical, and spiritual meanings individuals attach to building families in the process of utilising assisted reproduction.

10.4 Methods and Ethical Guidelines

The study is based on in-depth semi-structured interviews with participants who have experienced fertility issues for social or medical reasons and have sought reproductive assistance, using a range of procedures and treatments, to create families. The interviews explored participants' views and experiences of their reproductive journeys, meanings around family, the significance of genetics for family building, participants' experiences of fertility clinics where relevant, barriers to accessing treatment, and guidance and support for views relating to culture and spirituality when seeking assisted reproduction. The 30 interviews for the study were narrative focused, lasted between 60 and 120 minutes, and were conducted in person or over the video-communication platform Zoom during 2020 to 2021. The ethical framework for the study draws on *Te Ara Tika* (Pūtaiora Writing Group, 2010) guidelines, which are underpinned by culturally appropriate and sensitive research practices. Accordingly, the interviews for the study were conducted by the author, who is Pākehā, and Danielle Webb, a Māori research assistant. The study received institutional research ethics approval from Te Herenga Waka–Victoria University of Wellington.

There are very few published studies to date with Māori about infertility and accessing assisted reproduction. In the following discussion, data is included from three Māori participants (Awhina, Ngaio, Pania) and two Pākehā participants (Brooke, Jade) who expressed commitment to Te Ao Māori, honouring the principles of the Treaty of Waitangi (the founding document of Aotearoa) and had respective connections to Māori communities. In this dataset, one Māori participant saw a fertility specialist to discuss *in vitro* fertilisation (IVF) and four participants used donated sperm. Two participants relied on identity-release clinic donors and two participants used known donors outside the clinic context. All five participants identified as cisgender women, two were married, three were single, two identified as heterosexual, one identified as lesbian, and two identified as queer. The ages of the participants at the time of interview ranged from 28 to 47 years.

While five interviews do not represent Māori or Pākehā perspectives on accessing ARTs in Aotearoa generally, Braun and Clarke (2013) point out that a small sample size can be desirable in experience-focused qualitative research. The sample of five interviews in this discussion reflects some of the challenges of recruiting a small and hard-to-reach Indigenous population and the sensitive and personal nature of researching infertility in Aotearoa, particularly with Māori and Pasifika groups (Baker, 2005; Foaese, 2017). As such, a purposive sampling method was used to recruit the participants through social media platforms, networks, recruitment flyers, and snowballing. The interviews were audio-recorded, transcribed verbatim, and sent to participants who requested their transcript for checking. Data were analysed manually using thematic analysis as outlined by Braun and Clarke's (2013) six-phase method. Theoretical concepts informed by new kinship thinking in sociology, as discussed in the previous section, were used to assist the coding process. In this chapter, the data are organised around the themes 'Knowing where you come from' and 'Making up kin'. To protect confidentiality, participants have been given pseudonyms.

10.5   Knowing Where You Come From

Mason takes the view that genes and blood are not determining markers of kinship and belonging. Yet for some individuals and cultural groups, being able to trace genealogical information in cases of assisted reproduction is crucial and coincides with broader social trends in popular culture such as searching through ancestry websites, which emphasise the place of genetics as a key determinant of identity formation (Shaw, 2015). The idea that kinship is fixed by biological relatedness is not only a powerful motivation for people within whānau to assist one another's reproductive journeys, it impacts information sharing. In this study, the matter of biogenetic substance was pivotal for several Māori participants. Pania, a single mother, commented that for her 'the Māori side of our family and where we come from and what not … the idea that I might have a child who doesn't know half of where he comes from is just out of the question'. Similarly, Jade, who identified as Pākehā and queer, agreed both she and the biological father of her child should be named as parents on the birth certificate. This was imperative, Jade explained, as '[*donor friend's*] concern was whakapapa for [*child*]; if he wasn't named on her birth certificate, then her whakapapa to [*iwi*] would not be solidified, so we had to name, you know, name him, and he is her dad'.

Likewise, Ngaio explained that she and her same-gender partner wanted their two children to have contact with their sperm donor to 'keep the whakapapa ties open so they know their genealogy'. Ngaio added that she wanted her eldest child to 'be empowered' so that 'she's got all the information there and it's up to her now how she ends up choosing to use it. She knows who he [*donor*] is, so she knows her whakapapa.' Ngaio's motivation to empower her daughter not only reflected customary norms; she wanted both siblings to have a shared life trajectory via the same donor, as well as protect her children from being teased at school for not having a 'dad'. For Ngaio, it was important that her children were aware of their genetic origins for developmental and social reasons.

These obligations and responsibilities regarding whakapapa as fixed kinship affinities are documented in two earlier studies with Māori on their views and experiences of infertility (Glover, 2008; Reynolds & Smith, 2012). In Glover's study, participants questioned locating identity outside ties of genetic inheritance, due to the importance placed on whakapapa as an essential component of personhood. For one interviewee in this study, donor anonymity and non-relatedness left a host of unresolved questions, such as: 'Whose tapu? Whose mana? Whose mauri? Whose wairua? Whose hau? All these ingredients make up that tinana. That's the Māori notion of life – all those things together' (Glover & Rousseau, 2007, p. 122). Likewise, another informant commented that the use of donated gametes connected respective families, saying, 'I think you'd be quite hard pressed to find a Māori who didn't think that was then a link' (Glover, 2008, p. 88).

From the perspective of these informants, not knowing the origin and genetic legacy of donative material is concerning and stems from the belief that incorporating reproductive tissue intertwines physiology, psychology, spirit, and affect, thereby communicating the passage of flesh and blood that materialises in a new aspect of identity. What is given in the process of third-party reproduction is not simply the generous gift of shared body tissue, but, as I have intimated elsewhere, a different kind of futurity for those concerned and the groups to which they belong (Shaw, 2015, 2020). It is not just bodily matter that gets transferred between donors, recipients, and the larger group, but also rights and responsibilities, and with that, the importance of information sharing about donor conception.

Knowledge of whakapapa also has practical significance for Māori who seek to gain access to entitlements under state law in Aotearoa. To access collective resources, Māori must prove legitimate membership of an iwi, which involves registration of members on centralised databases. As a Māori fertility counsellor in Shaw's (2020, p. 24) *Expert Views on Assisted Reproduction* study commented:

> For some Māori who are, you know into their culture, or immersed in their culture, it's a difficult thing because it's like well, okay, so if you go down blunt lines, this baby then whakapapa's to these people, but if you're talking socially well, then they whakapapa to these people, and then you know, the strange things that you end up talking about, like well, what if they want a scholarship? … You've got to have at least, I guess, two generations, you've got to know your parents, and you've got to know your grandparents to be able to do it, and then it's like, oh well, what about … you know, what about land claims?

This is not a one-off statement. In Glover's research, for example, an informant explains that children without whakapapa knowledge, 'could run into difficulties when it comes to getting education grants … Because in our corporate office … all the beneficiaries have to know their whakapapa back to a certain person' (Glover & Rousseau, 2007, p. 126). For Brooke, a Pākehā participant in my study, facilitating contact with her identity-release donor, who identified as Māori, was complicated and fraught. Brooke did not want to deny her child whakapapa links that could be important to him later in life but establishing contact with the donor was proving more difficult than she envisaged – though she was not interested in resorting to sleuthing practices to make connection. Initially the donor agreed to contact with Brooke's son 'when he's ready', but there was no interaction beyond that. Reflecting on the process, Brooke commented:

> So, I want to be true to that with [*child*]. I identify as Pākehā and don't have any Māori whakapapa in my whānau, but I want to support [*child*] in his identity and stuff, and part of doing that is knowing more. But in the context of where I come from with my family, you know, I understand that family dynamics can be difficult. That's why I actually sent the email to [*fertility counsellor*] to check for me. It wasn't her job, but she offered [*to forward it*] which was really kind, and said, 'Have you shared with your family or your whānau? The reason I ask is because I know it's very important in Māori culture to know your hapū and iwi ties and your marae and stuff and I want to support [*child*] in that, but I don't want to go blundering in if that's not okay with you,' or something like that. And I didn't hear back from him and that really ****** me off.

For some Pākehā, it may be assumed that Māori donors will want to contact recipients and form connections with biological offspring for ontological and spiritual reasons to do with whakapapa. The burden of this
projected expectation, however, may not align with the views of every
Māori individual and could be a contributing factor to low donation rates
by Māori at fertility clinics.

In some iwi, knowledge of whakapapa and mana whenua (land) rights
apply beyond whānau of origin, extending to children who are whāngai,
adopted or donor conceived. Described as a common practice among
Māori for consolidating relationships (Smith, 2012), there are many reasons
to whāngai a child. Aside from strengthening one's whakapapa or providing better educational and material opportunities for the child, whāngai is
also regarded as 'a cultural alternative to undertaking fertility treatment'
(Pihama, 2012, p. 234). It represents a traditional system of assisted reproduction that provides long-term care for those who are raised by non-
biological guardians, usually by close relatives but sometimes by different
iwi (McRae & Nikora, 2006). The practice of whāngai assumes openness
and knowledge of one's whakapapa, so unlike the history of adoption in
Aotearoa, there are no closed relationships. There may be cultural pressure
for anyone considering ART to whāngai children who need care rather
than seek clinic-assisted fertility treatment in the first instance (Pihama,
2012). This reflects both the prohibitive costs of fertility treatment, which
exclude many Māori who, on average, experience lower socioeconomic
status than non-Māori (Marriott & Sim, 2015), and strong cultural reasons
for valorising whāngai over assisted reproduction.

In my study, Awhina, who was in a heterosexual marital relationship
trying to access public funding for IVF, spoke positively about whāngai as
a potential family building option, should efforts to access IVF fail. She
commented:

> I think with like our family bond as well, like, even though I can't have kids,
> I'm still young … But like, my sister has said that if I still haven't had a
> kid by [*age x*], if her and her husband are actually willing to at that stage in
> life, that they'll have a baby for me. Just go whāngai or something, which I
> reckon is real nice. And my brother said the same thing too.

While Awhina was comfortable to 'go whāngai', as she put it, she had not
considered the prospect of egg donation when the interviewer raised this
option with her, nor had it been suggested by the specialist. Aside from
precluding the promise of genetic continuity and a biological relationship
with her future child, this may have to do with Aotearoa's Clinical Priority

Access Criteria that determine eligibility for publicly funded fertility pro-vision. These criteria are based on a range of specifications, including the Body Mass Index (BMI) of the person seeking treatment. To be eligible for government assistance women's BMI must be inside the range of 18–32 kg/m², or medical practitioners will decline referrals for public funding (National Women's Health, 2021). This phenomenon disproportionately affects Māori and Pasifika women who do not conform to Western ideals around BMI, as was the case for Awhina, who disclosed a BMI higher than 32 kg/m². Awhina was told she would be declined referrals until she lost weight, on the grounds that a lower BMI would increase the effectiveness of fertility treatment (see Shaw & Fehoko, 2022, for a critique of BMI as a criterion for fertility treatment access).

10.6   Making Up Kin

In traditional Māori society, iwi survival is regarded as paramount and those of childbearing age are expected to reproduce (Glover & Rousseau, 2007). The fulfilment of this cultural preference has not diminished over time: because children are considered taonga (highly prized), reproduc-tivity elevates a person's status within the whānau and community (Cram & Pitama, 1998). Awhina, for instance, took for granted that 'Māori whānau are really big and you want that for your family too'. This think-ing confirms Glover's research, whose participants linked fertility to cul-tural and gendered responsibilities within iwi, stating: 'we are here to propagate the next generation, your whakapapa'; 'women are produced to have children ... to keep the whakapapa going'; 'we're put on this earth for a reason and it's to carry on whakapapa, and a lot of us take it very, very seriously' (Glover & Rousseau, 2007, pp. 121–122). Many Māori are therefore sympathetic to those seeking assisted reproduction for the purposes of whānau building. Additionally, because expectations to reproduce exist regardless of sexuality, social pressure to have children also impacts takatāpui (Māori with diverse genders, sexualities, and sex characteristics) (Kerekere, 2017; Pihama, 2012).

Advances in ARTs and changes to social attitudes and legislation in Aotearoa over the last 30 years have opened up new possibilities for fam-ily building; enabling people to think more creatively about fixed kinship affinities in relation to ways of doing family. We can recognise these inter-secting factors in participants' talk about the technologies they sought to utilise to construct their families. For instance, in contrast to the view that ARTs 'are sometimes seen as antithetical to Māori custom because they offend the "principles of nature"' (Durie, 2008, p. 11), Awhina took the view that tikanga around assisted reproduction was dynamic and adaptable to new social situations and conditions. In a conversation thread with the interviewer Awhina shared her perspective:

> I've just always wanted a baby. So, however it happens, I don't mind. Like, I know, like, a lot of people get scared of doing IVF as well, because, you know, it's like you're taking parts of your body out and you know, in the Māori worldview, body parts just stay with you, you shouldn't be mucking around with it. But for me, I don't know. I think I'm just kind of modernised and I don't mind.
>
> Interviewer: And do you think that even within Te Ao Māori, do you think that is changing as well?
>
> I definitely reckon it is. It's definitely modernising, and because infertility is … like when we first started, go for it, it was an open conversation.

In addition to technological nous, researchers in Aotearoa studying two-mother families have drawn attention to how the process of defining, communicating, and displaying families built by ARTs also entails creative strategies, careful deliberation, and conscious effort (O'Neill et al., 2012; Surtees, 2017). This was the case with Ngaio and her wife, for example, where decisions were made about whether one woman gives birth to all the children or both women give birth. Jade likewise spoke about the imaginative effort and decision-making that went into thinking about the process of family building. She contributed:

> As queers we have to be so conscious in how we do this … it's not like, oops, I'm pregnant, it's such an emotionally exhausting process and we have to, conjure up this, you know all very consciously and it's so, there's so much talking and decision-making, and intentionality to create a family. And all these people were having these opinions that it wasn't great, I was like 'do you not realise like, this is not just like, oops, I'm going to get pregnant by accident, and not know the person, this is so intentional.' Yeah, so those were some hard discussions to have to make.

Ngaio and her wife had more involvement with their sperm donor's mother than they initially planned. At first Ngaio was not sure about the extent to which she wanted to encourage the relationship, but grew accustomed to the idea, commenting:

> It's another tie of being good friends with someone, and then my wife had a closer relationship with his mother before I knew her. So, when the mother did find out [*about the birth*] she was kind of like, 'Oh, yous [*sic*] are my daughters now'. She is from [*Pacific Island*], so very family-orientated, very

similar to Māori. It wasn't a question of, is it okay? So, when my daughter was born, it was like, 'Oh, baby is born.' We let our friend know. And then, of course, it was like, 'Oh, mum and dad want to come over.' I was like, 'oh, this is annoying'. But at the same time, we're like, well, don't really want to say 'no' and 'what does it hurt?' So ... we did go and visit her quite a bit.

Jade also had a strong relationship with her donor, a long-standing friend with whom she had discussed self-arranged donor conception on several occasions. Their relationship was not romantic, but they shared a mutual conception of co-parenting which ended up spanning numerous whānau across several households. Jade describes the reproductive relationship with her donor friend in the following account.

> For me, the idea was wanting it to be a very whānau-centred approach. I always wanted my baby to have a dad, it was never this, "I want to be a lesbian single mum" with only a donor, that was not my plan ever. I just, you know, have grown up and worked a lot in Māori communities, the concept of whānau was really, really important to me. I did a lot of ... work in an organisation that had heavy [iwi] influence, heavy [iwi] whānau influence, and [donor friend] is [iwi], and that organisation were very much a whānau. So, to know that my baby would be [iwi], and in that wider whānau was really important to me. Yeah, so [donor friend] and I went to a restaurant for dinner, and we talked about being parents together, what that might look like. It was all very informal ... I wanted to create a whānau with zero state involvement, I didn't want legalities, I didn't want lawyers, I didn't want the state to have any control in how a family looked. So, that was really important to me, that we self-defined this whānau creation, and yeah, and that it was just based on a friendship, not any weird legal structures or whatever. Yeah, so we just decided that we would go forth and try and conceive, by at home insemination.

Expressing her resistance to state interference in the process of family building with her donor, Jade illustrates Mason's conception of kinship affinity as a negotiated and creative achievement. While Jade attains a measure of relational reproductive autonomy to create her non-normative family by sidestepping the clinic and regulatory context, Brooke has less agency negotiating contact with her identity-release donor. For Brooke, the desire to interact with her donor was not reciprocated as she had imagined it would be, making the donor's 'absent presence' a constant theme throughout the interview. Although Brooke and her child had met a dibling (donor-conceived sibling) and their family, it was the donor who Brooke envisaged as part of her child's everyday life, saying:

> The reason I chose that donor was because he'd said he was open to contact. I was quite excited by that. And to clarify, I wasn't looking for a romantic relationship; I was looking for a distant uncle, I guess, if you are thinking

of it, or whānau relationship, something. Not a father relationship. Not a romantic relationship. But a 'hey, you helped make this family and you're really welcome here'.

Brooke's expectations around contact with the donor, which were tied to her understanding of whakapapa, did not match his. For the sake of her child, Brooke refused to abandon contacting the donor, resulting in subsequent conversations with the interviewer and a fertility counsellor post-interview. Contrastingly, the key issue for Pania – who also relied on an identity-release donor – in terms of family was around connectedness rather than heritability. So, although Pania valued her Māori heritage and could,

> [*Whakapapa*] back five generations and then find all the extended family from those ancestors … I have sufficient relationships to not feel the need to go looking for extra family, particularly people who I maybe haven't grown up with … So, I guess in that respect I chose a clinic-based donor.

Unlike Brooke, the information Pania retained about her donor's profile did not weigh on her mind, as she was not affectively invested in the 'nitty gritty details' about what the clinic donor did in their life, their background, or where they came from. Pania went on to say that when she looked at her child and saw certain features, she thought 'oh, you must have got those from your donor, because those aren't my toes, so there's a certain element of wonder there, but that's kind of where it ends'.

10.7 Conclusions

This chapter examines the dataset of five research participants who expressed explicit commitment to Te Ao Māori in the process of accessing assisted reproduction for family building purposes. The data indicate the importance for all five participants of whakapapa and the ability to trace genealogical knowledge for their offspring. At the same time, findings show differences in kinship affinity between participants' views around heritability and connectedness depending on their relationships with prospective or actual donors. In line with the view that children are part of wider whakapapa relationships, the prospect of whāngai, which was suggested by Awhina's siblings as a reproductive option should her IVF journey be unsuccessful, was received enthusiastically. Ngaio and Jade, who both had extended family relationships with known donors and their respective whānau, likewise managed their reproductive relationships with openness and flexibility. The creative engagement of extended kin responsibilities experienced by Ngaio and Jade, was not replicated in the family building projects of Pania and Brooke. While lack of connectedness between Pania and her identity-release donor did not negatively impact her equanimity, this was not entirely so for Brooke, whose own donor sought to limit kinship connections with his donor-conceived offspring until 'he's ready'. Finally, given the paucity of research in this area, further study comparing the motivations and experiences of identity-release and previously known donors and their relationships with recipients and donor-conceived offspring – particularly those who identify as Māori or rely on Māori donors – is warranted.

Acknowledgements

Many thanks to Danielle Webb (Ngāpuhi) for her research assistance and the participants who contributed their stories to this study.

References

Adair, V., & Rogan, C. (1998). Infertility and parenting: The story so far. In V. Adair & R. Dixon (Eds.), *The Family in Aotearoa/New Zealand* (pp. 260–283). Auckland: Addison Wesley Longman.

Baker, M. (2005). Medically assisted conception: Revolutionizing family or perpetuating a nuclear and gendered model? *Journal of Comparative Family Studies, 36*(4), 521–543. https://doi.org/10.3138/jcfs.36.4.521

Braun, V., & Clarke, V. (2013). *Successful Qualitative Research: A Practical Guide for Beginners*. Los Angeles: Sage.

Coney, S., & Else, A. (1999). *Protecting Our Future: The Case for Greater Regulation of Assisted Reproductive Technology*. Auckland: Women's Health Action Trust.

Cram, F., & Pitama, S. (1998). Ko tōku whānau, ko tōku mana. In V. Adair & R. Dixon (Eds.), *The Family in Aotearoa/New Zealand* (pp. 130–157). Auckland: Addison Wesley Longman.

Daniels, K. (2007). Donor gametes: Anonymous or identified? *Best Practice & Research Clinical Obstetrics and Gynaecology, 21*(1), 113–128. https://doi.org/10.1016/j.bpobgyn.2006.09.010

Daniels, K., & Douglass, A. (2008). Access to genetic information by donor offspring and donors: Medicine, policy and law in New Zealand. *Medicine and Law, 27,* 131–146.

Daniels, K., & Lewis, G. M. (1996). Openness of information in the use of donor gametes: Developments in New Zealand. *Journal of Reproductive and Infant Psychology, 14*(1), 57–68. https://doi.org/10.1080/02646839608405859

Daniels, K. R., Kramer, W., & Perez-y-Perez, M. V. (2012). Semen donors who are open to contact with their offspring: Issues and implications for them and their families. *Reproductive BioMedicine Online, 25,* 670–677. https://doi.org/10.1016/j.rbmo.2012.09.009

Durie, M. (2008). Bioethics in research: The ethics of indigeneity. Paper presented at the Ninth Global Forum on Bioethics in Research. http://gfbr9.hrc.govt.nz/article

Durie-Hall, D., & Metge, J. (1992). Kua Tutū Te Puehu, Kia Mau: Maori aspirations and family law. In M. Heneghan & B. Atkin (Eds.), *Family Law Policy in New Zealand* (pp. 54–82). Auckland: Oxford University Press.

Ellis, J., & Irwin, R. (2002). *Oocyte Recipients and Donors: Choosing a Relationship*, Auckland, New Zealand: Fertility Associates. Unpublished paper.

Foaese, A. (2017). *Pasifika Women's Experiences of Infertility in Canterbury and Wellington* [Unpublished master's thesis]. University of Otago.

Gibson, H. (2021). *Kin-making in the Reproductive Penumbra: Surrogacy in Aotearoa New Zealand* [Unpublished doctoral thesis]. Te Herenga Waka/Victoria University of Wellington.

Glover, M., & Rousseau, B. (2007). 'Your child is your whakapapa': Māori considerations of assisted human reproduction and relatedness. *SITES: New Series*, 4(2), 117–136. https://doi.org/10.11157/sites-vol4iss2id76

Glover, M. (2008). *Māori Attitudes to Assisted Human Reproduction: An Exploratory Study*. Auckland: University of Auckland, Department of Social & Community Health.

Glover, M., McKree, A., & Dyall, L. (2009). Assisted reproduction: Issues for Takatāpui (New Zealand Indigenous non-heterosexuals). *Journal of GLBT Family Studies*, 5(4), 295–311. https://doi.org/10.1080/15504280903263702

Hargreaves, K., & Daniels, K. (2007). Parents' dilemmas in sharing donor insemination conception stories with their children. *Children & Society*, 21, 420–431. https://doi.org/10.1111/j.1099-0860.2006.00079.x

Hertz, R., Nelson, M. K., & Kramer, W. (2015). Sperm donors describe the experience of contact with their donor-conceived offspring. *Facts, Views & Vision in ObGyn*, 7(2), 91–100.

Kerekere, E. (2017). *Part of the Whānau: The Emergence of Takatāpui Identity – He Whāriki Takatāpui* [Unpublished doctoral thesis]. Victoria University of Wellington.

Lovelock, K. (2010). Conceiving reproduction: New reproductive technologies and the redefinition of kinship narrative in New Zealand society. *Anthropological Forum*, 20(2), 125–146. https://doi.org/10.1080/00664677.2010.487296

MacManus, J. (2017). Meet the couple who tried to get sperm on Reddit. https://thespinoff.co.nz/parenting/17-10-2017/meet-the-couple-who-tried-to-get-sperm-on-reddit/ (accessed 20 September 2021).

Marriot, L., & Sim, D. (2015). Indicators of inequality for Māori and Pacific people. *Journal of New Zealand Studies*, 20, 24–50.

Mason, J. (2008). Tangible affinities and real-life fascination of kinship. *Sociology*, 42(1), 29–45. https://doi.org/10.1177/0038038507084824

McRae, K. O., & Nikora, L. W. (2006) Whāngai: Remembering, understanding and experiencing. *MAI Review*, 1, 1–18.

National Women's Health. (2021). *Public funding*. National Women's Health https://nationalwomenshealth.adhb.govt.nz/our-services/fertility/public-funding/ (accessed 19 October 2021).

Nordqvist, P. (2014). Bringing kinship into being: Connectedness, donor conception and lesbian parenthood. *Sociology, 48*(2), 268–283. https://doi.org/10.1177/0038038513477936

Nordqvist, P. (2019). Kinship: How being related matters in personal life. In V. May, V. & P. Nordqvist (Eds.), *Sociology of Personal Life* (2nd ed., pp 46–59). London: Red Globe Press.

Nordqvist, P. (2019a). Un/familiar connections: On the relevance of a sociology of personal life for exploring egg and sperm donation. *Sociology of Health & Illness, 41*(3), 601–615. https://doi.org/10.1111/1467-9566.12862

Nordqvist, P., & Smart, C. (2014). *Relative Strangers: Family Life, Genes and Donor Conception.* Basingstoke: Palgrave Macmillan.

O'Neill, K., Hamer, H. P., & Dixon, R. (2012). 'A lesbian family in a straight world': The impact of the transition to parenthood on couple relationships in planned lesbian families. *Women's Studies Journal, 26*(2), 39–53.

Pihama, L. (2012). Experiences of Whānau Māori within fertility clinics. In P. Reynolds & C. Smith (Eds.), *The Gift of Children: Māori and Infertility* (pp. 203–234). Wellington: Huia Publishers.

Pūtaiora Writing Group. (2010). *Te Ara Tika: Guidelines for Māori Research Ethics: A Framework for Researchers and Ethics Committee Members.* Auckland: Health Research Council of New Zealand.

Reynolds, P., & Smith, C. (2012). Introduction: He Kākano: Māori and assisted reproductive technologies. In P. Reynolds & C. Smith (Eds.), *The Gift of Children: Māori and Infertility* (pp. xiii–xix). Wellington: Huia Publishers.

Righarts, A., Dickson, N. P., Ekeroma, A., Gray, A. R., Parkin, L., & Gillett, W. R. (2021). The burden of infertility in New Zealand: A baseline survey of prevalence and service use. *Australian and New Zealand Journal of Obstetrics and Gynaecology, 61*, 439–447. https://doi.org/10.1111/ajo.13323

Salmond, A. (2012). Ontological quarrels: Indigeneity, exclusion and citizenship in a relational world. *Anthropological Theory, 12*(2), 115–41. https://doi.org/10.1177/1463499612454119

Shaw, R. M. (2020). Should surrogate pregnancy arrangements be enforceable in Aotearoa New Zealand? *Policy Quarterly, 16*(1), 18–25. https://doi.org/10.26686/pq.v16i1.6351

Shaw, R. M. (2015). *Ethics, Moral Life and the Body.* Basingstoke: Palgrave Macmillan.

Shaw, R. (2007). The gift-exchange and reciprocity of women in donor-assisted conception. *The Sociological Review, 55*(2), 293–310. https://doi.org/10.1111/j.1467-954X.2007.00706.x

Shaw, R. M., & Fehoko, E. (2022). Epistemic injustice and Body Mass Index: Examining Māori and Pacific women's access to fertility treatment in Aotearoa New Zealand. *Fat Studies.* Online first. https://doi:10.1080/21604851.2022.2063507

Smith, C. (2012). Tamaiti Whāngai and fertility. In P. Reynolds & C. Smith (Eds.), *The Gift of Children: Māori and Infertility* (pp. 143–202). Wellington: Huia Publishers.

Surtees, N. (2017). Narrating Connections and Boundaries: Constructing Relatedness in Lesbian Known Donor Familial Configurations [Unpublished doctoral thesis]. University of Canterbury.

Te Aka Matua o te Ture/Law Commission (2021). *Te Kōpū Whāngai: He Arotake: Review of Surrogacy*. Wellington: NZLC.

Waldby, C. (2019). *The Oocyte Economy; The Changing Meaning of Human Eggs*. Durham, NC: Duke University Press.

CHAPTER II

'Spunkles', Donors, and Fathers

Men, Trans/Masculine, and Non-Binary People's Accounts of Sperm Donors and Their Relationships to Children

Damien W. Riggs, Sally Hines, Ruth Pearce,
Carla A. Pfeffer, and Francis Ray White

II.I   Introduction

It might be premature to say that, as we enter the third decade of the twenty-first century, pregnant men are 'everywhere', but their cultural presence in the Westernised world over the past decade has undeniably accelerated. Trans, intersex, non-binary, and gender-nonconforming individuals have, of course, been experiencing conception, pregnancy, and childbirth through-out human history. For example, Fausto-Sterling (2000) describes reports of Austrian soldier and blacksmith Daniel Burghammer giving birth in 1601, and Lothstein (1988) provides several clinical case studies from the mid–late twentieth century. What has changed is that men's pregnancies in particular have achieved spectacular media prominence in recent years, fuelled by sensationalist headlines and growth of trans liberation movements.

However, the apparent visibility of pregnant men masks a deeper sense in which their possibility, their realness, is continuously denied. Either men who experience pregnancy are framed as not 'really' men; or they are seen as having temporarily suspended their masculine status or are legally defined as 'mothers'. It is as if the spectacle of the 'pregnant man' is presented only to reaffirm its impossibility. The debate this produces has tended to focus on whether or not a man can be pregnant, should be pregnant, or why they would want to be pregnant in the first place. Not only does this discourse reproduce the assumption that pregnancy is a quintes-sentially female experience and one equated only with cisgender women's bodies, but it directs the focus onto the person's gender, often ignoring the experience of getting and being pregnant.

While the primacy of the body for cisgender women's everyday lives, identities, and social practices has a long history in feminist work, the sig-nificance of the body in the construction of masculinity is more of a recent development, emerging from media studies and cultural sociology in the 1990s. Early empirical studies on the embodied nature of masculinity were diverse, encompassing topics such as the economy and the workplace, consumption, health, the media, education, sport, and interpersonal violence, as sites of the construction of hegemonic masculinity (Connell, 1995). As Gill, Henwood, and McLean suggest, uniting this work was a consensus amongst masculinity scholars that 'a significant change has occurred, in which men's bodies as bodies have gone from near invisibility to hypervisibility in the course of a decade' (2005, p. 44). However, work on masculinity and embodiment has largely concerned the experiences and practices of cisgender men, leaving the bodies of trans/masculine and non-binary people largely unaccounted for.

In this chapter we draw on our international study of 51 men, trans/masculine, or non-binary people's experiences with pregnancy. Specifically, we draw on a subsample of nine participants who conceived using a known donor. Most of our participants conceived with a cisgender male partner (and for most this occurred after they had transitioned), and a small number used anonymous donor sperm from a fertility clinic. Our interest in this chapter, however, is on how those who conceived specifically via a known donor navigated social scripts about disclosure and relationships with donors. As Nordqvist (2021) argues, while telling children about their conception is increasingly seen as important, cultural scripts for doing so are lacking. Drawing on social scripting theory (Gagnon & Smith, 1973), Nordqvist argues that 'scripts operate as a kind of grammar for how people make sense of themselves and the relationships in which they are embedded' (p. 680). Social scripting occurs on three levels: (1) broader cultural narratives, (2) interpersonal interactions, and (3) intrapsychically within individuals as they take up broader cultural narratives that potentially guide their decisions and actions. In the context of donor conception, and in the absence of widely available social scripts circulating as cultural narratives, individual families may find it difficult to navigate talking about donor conception.

If the above is true for cisgender heterosexual, lesbian, and/or single parents of donor-conceived children, then it is likely especially so for men, trans/masculine, and non-binary people. As we explore below, gestational parenthood for this diverse group of people is framed by social scripting at all three levels described above, yet is largely lacking a positive focus on scripts about men, trans/masculine, and non-binary people and conception, including in regard to disclosure of donor conception to children. Our argument in this chapter is that the lack of such scripting likely has implications for the decisions that men, trans/masculine, and non-binary people make about the disclosure of donor conception to their children, and how relationships are formed with donors after the child's birth.

To provide a framework for our data, we first briefly explore the three levels of social scripting outlined above as they specifically apply to pregnant men, trans/masculine, and non-binary people, before then outlining our study and describing our findings. The chapter concludes by considering the types of information and support that might benefit men, trans/masculine, and non-binary people sharing information about conception with their children.

11.2   Social Scripting and Trans Reproduction

As previously noted, there are three levels at which social scripting operates: the broader social context, the interpersonal, and the intrapsychic. In terms of the broader social context, it is arguably the media through which scripts about trans people and reproduction are most obviously disseminated. In their analysis of media scripting about trans reproduction, Lampe et al. (2019) argue that a repeated theme in media accounts of trans men and pregnancy is the idea that each account constructs such pregnancies as something 'new' or as the 'first'. As Pearce and White (2019) note, such framing involves the active production of ignorance about the long histories of trans reproduction. Further, we suggest that for men, trans/masculine, and non-binary people specifically, narratives of 'newness' may prevent people from connecting to existing narratives of trans reproduction (such as Califia's, 2000, first-person account of Matt Rice's pregnancy), thus cutting them off from information that may help them navigate conception and ways of disclosing and talking about donor conception to children.

Lampe et al. (2019) further note that media representations function by centring cisgenderist accounts of trans reproduction, such that men, trans/masculine, and non-binary people who experience pregnancy are made intelligible only through recourse to cisgender women's pregnancies. This ignores the unique differences at both the level of biology (i.e., those in receipt of testosterone prior to conception are likely to have markedly different experiences of conceiving) and the social (i.e., men, trans/masculine, and non-binary pregnancies are 'read' in markedly different ways to pregnancies by cisgender women). In this chapter, we refrain from using literature on cisgender lesbian women and donor conception as a counterpoint, as we believe it would only serve to perpetuate assumptions of commensurability, and indeed foster the idea that cisgender women's pregnancies are the normative point of comparison for men, trans/masculine, and non-binary people.

Indeed, Riggs (2014) has examined how this incommensurability is routinely resisted and denied by some trans men. For example, Riggs (2014) notes that in Oprah Winfrey's interview with Thomas Beatie and his then wife, Winfrey repeatedly pressured Beatie to explain to the audience how it was that he could be a pregnant man. This included asking Beatie to share his experiences around the death of his mother (with Winfrey suggesting that the death of Beatie's mother meant he had 'no feminine images'), Winfrey repeatedly contradicting Beatie's account of his masculinity (which he framed as a lifelong feeling, and Winfrey countered this with a focus on Beatie taking part in Miss Teen Hawaii), and Winfrey insisting on a prurient focus on Beatie's genitalia. Throughout the interview, Winfrey drew on highly normative cisgenderist ideologies to suggest that pregnancy is the same for people of all genders, that there are only two genders, and reinforced a normative account of Beatie's reproductive and sexed body. Throughout the interview, Beatie effectively countered Winfrey's line of argument, yet in so doing was repeatedly forced to adopt a relatively normative account of his gender as masculine.

Such negotiations with masculinity are replete across the literature on men, trans/masculine, and non-binary people and pregnancy. Riggs (2013), for example, explored how trans men, in their public self-representations, account for masculinity as part of their pregnancy journeys. For some men, their masculinity is positioned as tenuous in the face of highly feminised narratives of pregnancy. More specifically, their masculinity is positioned as tenuous by *other people*: by people who misgender them in hospitals, strangers who refuse to view them as pregnant men, and broader discourses that position all pregnancies as, by default, undertaken by women. Other men may feel that pregnancy compromises their masculinity, particularly in regard to inhabiting a pregnant body they struggle to view as masculine. Yet other men may refuse the feminisation of pregnancy, instead seeing their pregnant or lactating bodies as serving a purpose, one that does not inherently undermine their experience of masculinity. Indeed, in an account of their own pregnancy, Wallace (2010) discusses the 'manly art of pregnancy', noting that a

> pregnant person is at once a biologist, a mechanic, a weight lifter, and someone providing for hir family. Women can do those things, of course, but our culture still views them as masculine things, and in this way pregnancy made me more of a man, not less of one … Pregnancy helped me look, feel and act more like an archetype of Man, and eventually lifted me to its pinnacle by making me a dad. (p. 133)

Finally at the social level of scripting, Lampe et al. (2019) note that both sensationalist (i.e., 'first', 'new') and cisgenderist media accounts serve to marginalise experiences of discrimination among men, trans/masculine, and non-binary people in the context of reproduction. This occurs because acting as though each pregnant man is a 'first' ignores the experiences of the considerable number of pregnant men who have come before, each documenting and resisting the marginalisation they experience. While recognising and celebrating the joys of reproduction for growing numbers of men, trans/masculine, and non-binary people is important, this should not come at the expense of recognising the significant challenges that many men, trans/masculine, and non-binary people experience in seeking to conceive.

This brings us to the level of interpersonal and social scripting. The small body of literature on men, trans/masculine, and non-binary people, and conception suggests that fertility clinics often enact cisgenderism, including in terms of misgendering people's genders and bodies, failing to understand the specificities of trans people's reproductive needs, and outright hostility (e.g., Charter et al., 2018; James-Abra et al., 2015). For some of our participants, seeking known donor sperm was a product of previous negative experiences with fertility clinics (Riggs et al., 2021). Further, at the interpersonal level of social scripting about trans reproduction, family members may also be a source of negative messaging about trans reproduction. In our study, we found that some men, trans/masculine, and non-binary people were reticent to tell family members about trying to conceive, out of concern about negative responses (Riggs et al., 2021). Feeling cut off from family members at such a crucial time can mean that some men, trans/masculine, and non-binary people are prevented from opportunities to practise or discuss available social scripts for talking about donor conception.

Finally, at the individual or intrapsychic level, known donor conception is framed in the few studies that focus on this for men, trans/masculine, and non-binary people, as 'easier' than conception through fertility clinics, but not without challenges. Charter et al. (2018) found that participants experienced known donor conception as 'easier' and 'less confronting' compared to experiences with fertility clinics. Riggs et al. (2021) similarly found that negotiations with known donors in terms of receipt of sperm were often framed through the use of jocular language, making light of the situation. Yet at the same time, some participants spoke of challenges in negotiating receipt of donor sperm, particularly when known donors sought to conceive through intercourse. Again, we would propose that the considerable emotion work undertaken by many men, trans/masculine, and non-binary people seeking to conceive via known donor sperm may reduce opportunities for attention to what comes next, namely disclosing donor conception to children.

While it is certainly the case that similar accounts of engaging with known donors are evident in research with cisgender women, our argument in this chapter is that this is not commensurate to the experiences of men, trans/masculine, and non-binary people. This is for at least two reasons. First, while accounts may seem similar, they are provided by people with different genders. As the long history of so-called 'sex difference' research has demonstrated, people of different genders may have similar experiences, but the social meanings of those experiences are particular. In other words, men, trans/masculine, and non-binary people's experiences of conception are distinct from those of cisgender women due to their positionality and the web of historical and ongoing social relations in which they are embedded. Second, these differing social locations and relationships fundamentally shape how men, trans/masculine, and non-binary people are 'read' by others. When it comes to known donors specifically, how men, trans/masculine, and non-binary people are 'read' by donors is likely different to how cisgender women are 'read' again due to normative gender and sexuality assumptions.

At every level of social scripting, there are barriers to men, trans/masculine, and non-binary people thinking ahead to the matter of disclosure. These barriers encompass negative media scripting that both ignores continuities in community knowledge about conception and emphasises comparisons to cisgender women. This is at the expense of considering the specificities of men, trans/masculine, and non-binary people's experiences. For example, negative clinic experiences for men, trans/masculine, and non-binary people might keep them from benefiting from what might otherwise serve as a useful resource for disclosure scripting; transphobic experiences with family might prevent access to safe discussions with them about disclosure scripting; and challenges for this particular population in the context of known donor conception might steer focus away from looking further into the future to consider scripting about disclosure. These gaps in social scripting about disclosure are especially salient given Bonan et al. (2021) found that almost all trans men in their study who conceived using donor sperm intended to disclose information about the donor to their children in the future. In other words, there is a potential gap between intending to disclose and having the available social scripts and scripting resources through which to do so.

11.3   The Study

The broader international study reported in this chapter was funded by the Economic and Social Research Council (ES/N019067/1). Inclusion criteria for participants were: (i) identifying as a man, trans/masculine, or non-binary; (ii) having experienced at least one pregnancy; (iii) living in Australia, the European Union (including the United Kingdom), the United States, or Canada; (iv) being at least 18 years of age; and (v) having conceived after coming out or beginning a social and/or medical transition. Ethics approval was granted by each of the authors' universities. A purposive sampling technique was employed to obtain participants using social media and social network recruitment, including targeted recruitment distributed to groups comprised of men, trans/masculine, and non-binary people of colour. Research information and recruitment flyers were posted to social media accounts (e.g., private Facebook groups), shared at community conferences and events, and circulated via researcher and participant networks.

Semi-structured interviews were conducted either in person or via tele- and/or videoconference facilitated by Skype, Whereby, or Zoom, by a research associate of the first author (for Australian interviews), by the third author (for interviews in the European Union), or by the fourth author (for interviews in the United States and Canada). Interviews were conducted between June 2018 and October 2019. In terms of interview questions specific to the present chapter, a general question was asked about experiences of pregnancy, with a specific follow-up probe asking: 'How did you become pregnant?' Interviews ranged from less than 60 minutes to over 3 hours, with an average length of 100 minutes. Interviews were transcribed by a professional service and participants either chose their own pseudonym or were allocated a pseudonym if they did not opt to choose their own. Participants were also asked about pronouns, with most using either he/him or they/them.

Given the relatively small subsample included in this chapter, we only provide limited demographic information and we present it collectively, rather than by individual, so as to ensure anonymity (information about the broader sample is available in Riggs et al., 2021). In the subsample included in this chapter, the average age was 34 years (range 24–49 years). Participants described their gender as non-binary, trans male, trans man, transmasculine, or genderqueer. Participants described their sexuality as queer, pansexual, or undefined. Most participants had one child (range 1–3). Of the subsample participants, three were single, two were in relationships with women, and four were in relationships with men. Participants lived in Australia, Germany, Canada, the United Kingdom, or the United States. However, almost half of participants included in the subsample were from Australia. All participants included in the subsample conceived using sperm from a known donor who was either a friend or an acquaintance.

11.4 Thematic Analysis of Interviews

For the purposes of this chapter, responses to the probe question, 'How did you become pregnant?', were extracted for analysis. Importantly, while this question was included in the interview schedule and purposively selected for analysis in the present chapter, the analysis itself was inductive. Having extracted interview responses in relation to becoming pregnant, the first author coded the data according to the approach to thematic analysis outlined by Braun and Clarke (2006). The first author read all transcripts three times, looking for repeated topics or codes. The first author then developed themes based on the codes. While codes encompass broad salient topics repeated across the data set, themes by comparison organise codes into logical and coherent sets of information. Themes developed are indicative of topics seen as salient by researchers, rather than being exhaustive of all possible readings of the dataset. Further, codes and themes were not mutually exclusive across participants; some gave interview responses located within more than one code or theme. The first author then identified and collated representative quotations for each theme. As such, the quotations included in the results are indicative but not exhaustive of each theme. Having identified representative quotations for each theme, the first author then compiled the thematic groupings and developed the results reported below.

11.4.1 Theme 1: Navigating the Donor's Role

In this first theme, participants spoke about the role of donors, primarily in regard to their potential involvement in the child's life. Most participants spoke about being clear from the outset what they wanted from a donor and used this to guide their search for a donor. Most participants clearly stated they did not want a co-parent, but at the same time wanted someone who could be known by the child. As Benjamin suggests:

> I know other people for them it's less of a thing, but it felt, I don't know, this whole question of finding a sperm donor who is agreeing to be an open donor but who doesn't want to be a father, like for me it was like,

I don't know, an act of rebellion but also solidarity, of queer solidarity. I always wanted to have an open donor, I find it very important for the kid to be afterwards able to at least see a face and reach out. I don't want any responsibility for the other biologically involved person, but I find it's very important for the kid to be able to at least get an impression of you.

To be an 'open donor' but not a father is, for Benjamin, an act of queer solidarity and rebellion. This, we would suggest, references the separation of genetics from identity, such that providing sperm does not by default make one a parent. In the context of societies where the two are presumed to be one and the same (Moore, 2008), seeing sperm donation as just that is indeed an act of rebellion. In some respects, Benjamin's account creates a possible space for scripting disclosure: that a child could be told that their parent(s) and donor engaged in an act of solidarity and rebellion in conceiving them, acts that at the same time allow a space for the child to at least have 'an impression' of the donor.

Finn, by comparison, was more blunt about what he wanted from a donor, without the same focus on what a child might want:

So I was like, okay, from among friends I had asked one person who was at the time a lover of mine. But who was not interested in co-parenting. And I was not interested in having a co-parent. It was like, will you please be my sperm donor and not be a co-parent?

In some respects, Finn's account may be seen as instrumentalising the role of the donor. Yet we suggest that accounts such as Finn's highlight that, for some men, trans/masculine, and non-binary people, when it comes to negotiating receipt of donor sperm, what is most salient is finding a donor who will respect their decisions about parenting. Given the donor was a lover, it would appear important to Finn that there was a separation between their role as kin-adjacent in terms of Finn, and their role as a sperm donor. By contrast, a small number of participants were open to donors playing more of a role:

Denver: For me, I had ... he was a donor, but he was also involved. I wanted to know the donor, and I wanted to know that I could trust them, and things like that. And I trusted him as a dad, he's a great father, and all of that, I just didn't trust him with me [in terms of how] he viewed me [as a trans person].

Denver narrated a complex series of shifts, from the donor being sim-ply a donor, to being someone involved in their children's lives, to being a father. The complexities, for Denver, related to their own relationship with, and trust of, the donor, though at the forefront for them was a focus on allowing the children to determine their relationship with the donor, as we will explore in the final theme later on.

11.4.2   Theme 2: Kinship in the Context of Donor Conception

In contrast to some of the more instrumentalist accounts included in the first theme above, or Denver's account which recognised the donor's relationship to the children without necessarily signifying a relationship between Denver and the donor, participants included in this second theme spoke about creating kinship with donors. Echoing Weston's (1997) account of families of choice, participants such as Dee developed their own language for talking about the role of both the donor and their extended family:

> We spent time contracting together and figuring out what it is that felt important to us. And so, he's the kid's Spunkle, and in their lives as extended family. His parents are GrandSpunkle and GrandSparkle, and know the kids, and the kids know them. And that's actually been a very rich and lovely process ...

INTERVIEWER: If you think about your children and their grandparents. How many sets of grandparents do you consider your children to have?

DEE: I mean they would only count [partner]'s parents and my parents as their grandparents. Grandspunkle and Grandsparkle are a different deal. They're not grandparents. I don't know. They're grandparent-adjacent.

Here, Dee makes an interesting set of claims. First, the process of 'contracting' was reciprocal, a process of negotiation, resulting in kinship terms for the donor and his parents. At the same time, when asked about the child's grandparents, a line is drawn between Dee and their partner's parents as grandparents, and the role of the donor's parents as 'grandparent-adjacent'. The language of 'spunkle', 'grandspunkle', and 'grandsparkle' brings the donor and his family into relationship with the recipients and their child, but it is a mediated relationship. It is a relationship that is 'rich and lovely', but at the same time it is a relationship wrought primarily by the fact of conception, rather than by a claim to kinship in the first instance. Other participants noted more traditional kinship claims between donor and child, such that genetic relationships were equated with kinship:

INTERVIEWER: Is he ever going to be involved in her life?

CHARLIE: He is involved. He's uncle Michael. We made it clear from when we started that he would always be uncle and that we'd involve his family if they're interested. So she sees her Irish nana as she's called, as often as she can. So she's still gonna know where she's come from, she's gonna have all the links to any cousins and stuff. And obviously we're gonna meet her cousins. Because I don't see pretty much any of my family. [Michael has been] one of my best mates for years, so his family is kinda like my family anyway. So it was nice and it was effortless.

Here, Charlie notes that he and his partner were the ones directing the relationship ('we made it clear'), designating an uncle role from the outset. Importantly, while this is a kinship designation, it is nonetheless a chosen kinship designation (i.e., uncle rather than father). This represents an interesting reworking of traditional kinship relations: the donor is genetically related to the child but is not their father, arguably because the donor is a 'best mate' and 'pretty much part of the family' to Charlie, perhaps akin to his brother. Emphasised here is the relationship between Charlie and Michael first and foremost, even if by extension that grants a relationship to the child.

11.4.3   Theme 3: Children's Agency in Directing Relationships

In this final theme we explore how a number of participants oriented to the idea that relationships with donors should be determined by children, albeit with this requiring that parents create a space for this possibility:

SAM: There were sometimes people asking around who I was with or making assumptions of whether I was in a relationship or not, so I was quite conscious of kind of explaining that I was doing it as single person with a donor. And at that stage, I guess I wasn't explicitly including the donor in the family structure that would unfold, so it wasn't till [child] was a toddler, and donor was kind of visible in his life, that we started talking about donor dad, or Dad, or the distinctions of those things.

For participants such as Sam, openness to the role of the donor as determined by the child was somewhat unintentional. Sam was clear they were conceiving as a 'single person with a donor', with no role for the donor in the 'family structure'. But as Sam notes, the unfolding of life after the arrival of the child meant that the identity of the donor shifted as the child grew. By contrast, for participants such as Denver, there was a sense of purposiveness in ensuring from the onset that a relationship between donor and children was possible, even if the relationship was to be determined by the two in conjunction:

DENVER: For me, I wanted to have him involved, because I felt that, because he was ... or, if he wanted to, I felt like his relationship with his potential children was his business, not really mine. That's how I felt about it. And I didn't feel like, for the kids, I wanted to step in the way of what they wanted either, so I just sort of left it to him if he wanted to be involved or not, and for them to be able to establish their own relationships.

Despite some of the challenges that Denver experienced in their relationship with the donor, as indicated in the first theme, Denver was willing to step back and leave space for the donor and children to determine their relationships. This required that the donor be visible in their lives from the onset, while at the same time not predetermining what they all might decide about the nature of the relationship.

11.5 Conclusion

In this chapter, we have explored how a subsample of men, trans/masculine, and non-binary people talk about known donor conception, and the relationship of children to donors. Alongside our review of the literature on social scripting for men, trans/masculine, and non-binary people in regard to conception, we identified potential barriers to social scripting that require attention. The first of these are analogies made between cisgender women and men, trans/masculine, and non-binary people in terms of reproduction. As we have argued elsewhere, a more productive analogy is between cisgender men and gestational parents who are men, trans/masculine, and non-binary (e.g., Riggs et al., 2020). While we would not wish to suggest that all men, trans/masculine. and non-binary people subscribe to masculinist norms, we do wish to reiterate that men, trans/masculine, and non-binary people navigate donor conception in a way that is not commensurate to the experiences of cisgender women. Going forward, then, it will be important for research to examine how men, trans/masculine, and non-binary people who are gestational parents navigate masculinist norms in regard to donor conception, and how challenging such norms may help to address barriers to developing scripts about disclosing donor conception (e.g., see Barnes, 2014).

A second barrier relates to competencies among fertility clinic staff to meet the needs of men, trans/masculine, and non-binary people. While not all people may choose or be able to access donor sperm via clinics, even if such clinics are trans inclusive, it is vital that this is a possibility. This is important given that fertility clinics, as part of fertility counselling offered, are typically likely to address the topic of scripting for disclosure (Goedeke & Payne, 2010). Research has identified barriers to trans inclusion in fertility clinics (e.g., see Bartholomaeus & Riggs, 2020; Epstein, 2018), outlining clear steps that clinics can take to ensure the inclusion of trans people seeking to access reproductive services.

Another barrier pertains to family support and its role in scripting about donor conception. While families can certainly be holders of secrets about donor conception, family relationships can also be a key context through which people navigate decisions about disclosure (Dempsey et al., 2021). Research on therapy aiming to support trans families suggests a number of key avenues for undertaking this work, including focus on how best to support pregnant trans people (e.g., Blumer et al., 2013; von Doussa et al., 2021).

Among our participants, many spoke about purposive contracting with donors, specifically focusing on their role, legal requirements, and financial responsibilities to the child. Yet, despite this clear focus on contracting, often missing was a focus on scripting for disclosure to children, and how relationships between the donor and child would be navigated. In addition to addressing the barriers outlined above, then, additional forms of social scripting disclosure, that are specific to men, trans/masculine, and non-binary people who conceive using known donor sperm, are needed. Since the experiences of men, trans/masculine, and non-binary people who conceive using known donor sperm are not commensurate to the experiences of cisgender women, existing social scripts may be inadequate. For example, while cisgender women are likely to need to script ways to tell their children that donor sperm was used in their conception, they are unlikely to need to script that, as women, they gave birth. By contrast, for men, trans/masculine, and non-binary people, there is likely the need to script both donor conception *and* gestational parenthood in a world where it is presumed that only women give birth.

Drawing on our findings, our first suggestion in terms of scripting for men, trans/masculine, and non-binary people would be the importance of honouring and sharing the long histories of conception and gestation by men, trans/masculine, and non-binary people. As Lampe et al. (2019) discuss, too often Thomas Beatie is heralded as the 'first pregnant man'. Yet, men, trans/masculine, and non-binary people have spoken about being gestational parents in the media, to researchers, and in medical settings for decades (e.g., see Califia, 2000; Lothstein, 1988). Ensuring that long-standing histories of men, trans/masculine, and non-binary people navigating conception are made available, including considerations of how they script disclosure, is an important aspect of ensuring that future individuals navigating conception do not feel like they are reinventing the wheel. Indeed, documenting these histories and making them available publicly is an important task that lies ahead for those working in the space of trans reproduction.

Second, the idea of donor conception being an act of rebellion and solidarity offers an important opportunity for scripting about disclosure, an opportunity that both celebrates the joys of conception for men, trans/

masculine, and non-binary people, as well as recognising the marginalisation that men, trans/masculine, and non-binary people too often face in conceiving. Talking about the *need* for rebellion and solidarity offers men, trans/masculine, and non-binary gestational parents opportunities to talk about cisgenderism with their children, and to frame their conception and the role of the donor as an act of resistance to cisgenderism. This offers a unique trans-specific form of social scripting that introduces children not just to their conception and donor, but to the broader social contexts in which their conception occurred.

Finally, in terms of trans-specific social scripting for disclosure, our findings suggest the importance of exploring which kinship or kinship-adjacent relationships are made salient among men, trans/masculine, and non-binary people. Part of acknowledging the formative role of cisgenderism in the conception experiences of men, trans/masculine, and non-binary people involves acknowledging that decisions about kinship and the role of donors are likely shaped by what is intelligible, what is expected, and how gender plays a role in this. Particularly when it comes to cisgender men as donors, how social expectations about such men as donors shape openness to disclosure is a topic that warrants closer attention in social scripting. While research suggests that trans men, in particular, are very open to disclosure about conception to children (e.g., Bonan et al., 2021), whether this actually occurs in practice will likely be shaped by views on how donors relate to or impact upon cisgenderist assumptions. Exploring ways to script for known donors in ways that do not overwrite the role of men, trans/masculine, and non-binary people in their children's lives is thus an important avenue for future research.

Beyond trans-specific social scripts for disclosure, ongoing attention is needed to what is required to ensure children can determine the nature of their relationship to their donor. While some of our participants spoke about making donors salient in terms of racial matching between donors and recipients, and others spoke about a purposive desire to create a space for relationships between donors and children, we must wonder what this means for the agency of children in determining relationships. At the very least, mechanisms that protect the needs of children are needed, which would include mechanisms for recording information about donor conception that is enduring and not dependent on the parent(s) as the sole holders of the information. As explored above, there are a number of barriers and potential facilitators of donor linking in the lives of men, trans/masculine, and non-binary people who are gestational parents. But beyond parents themselves, it is important that future avenues are created and formalised for the children of men, trans/masculine, and non-binary people to make agentic decisions about accessing information.

Donor registers are one obvious avenue but, as we would argue, accessing donor registers are in a sense an end point to a journey that starts well before that. Given that known donor conception often occurs in the shadow of the law, existing donor registers may be insufficient. Talking about donor conception by creating trans-specific social scripts is one part of that journey. Having children's picture books about donor conception that are trans-inclusive are another. Having public stories that celebrate trans conception and recognise its long histories are another part of that journey. Creating spaces where a diversity of kinship relationships with donors are possible, and indeed intelligible, are yet another part of that journey. In other words, what is needed to ensure children's agency in the context of donor-linking are a diversity of trans-specific and trans-inclusive approaches to scripting donor conception that challenge cisgenderism and create possibilities for futures where children are able to create their own scripts about their families and all those involved in their conception.

References

Barnes, L. W. (2014). *Conceiving Masculinity: Male Infertility, Medicine, and Identity*. Temple University Press.

Bartholomaeus, C., & Riggs, D. W. (2020). Transgender and non-binary Australians' experiences with healthcare professionals in relation to fertility preservation. *Culture, Health & Sexuality*, 22(2), 129–145. https://doi.org/10.1080/13691058.2019.1580388

Blumer, M. L., Ansara, Y. G., & Watson, C. M. (2013). Cisgenderism in family therapy: How everyday clinical practices can delegitimize people's gender self-designations. *Journal of Family Psychotherapy*, 24(4), 267–285. https://doi.org/10.1080/08975353.2013.849551

Bonan, S., Chapel-Lardic, E., Rosenblum, O., Dudkiewicz-Sibony, C., Chamouard, L., Wolf, J. P., ... & Drouineaud, V. (2021). Characteristics and intentions of heterosexual couples comprising a transgender man awaiting sperm donation to conceive a child. *Andrology*, 9(6), 1799–1807. https://doi-org/10.1111/andr.13103

Califia, P. (2000, 20 June). Family values. *The Village Voice*. Retrieved from www.villagevoice.com/2000/06/20/family-values/

Charter, R., Ussher, J. M., Perz, J., & Robinson, K. (2018). The transgender parent: Experiences and constructions of pregnancy and parenthood for transgender men in Australia. *International Journal of Transgenderism*, 19(1), 64–77. https://doi.org/10.1080/15532739.2017.1399496

Connell, R. (1995). *Masculinities*. Polity Press.

Dempsey, D., Nordqvist, P., & Kelly, F. (2021). Beyond secrecy and openness: Telling a relational story about children's best interests in donor-conceived families. *BioSocieties, 17*(1), 527–548. https://doi.org/10.1057/s41292-021-00225-9

Epstein, R. (2018). Space invaders: Queer and trans bodies in fertility clinics. *Sexualities, 21*(7), 1039–1058. https://doi.org/10.1177/1363460717720365

Fausto-Sterling, A. (2000). *Sexing the Body*. Basic Books.

Gagnon, J. & Simon, W. (1973). *Sexual Conduct*. Hutchinson.

Gill, R., Henwood, K., & McLean, C. (2005). Body projects and the regulation of normative masculinity. *Body & Society, 11*(1), 37–62. https://doi.org/10.1177/1357034X05049849

Goedeke, S., & Payne, D. (2010). A qualitative study of New Zealand fertility counsellors' roles and practices regarding embryo donation. *Human Reproduction, 25*(11), 2821–2828. https://doi.org/10.1093/humrep/deq233

James-Abra, S., Tarasoff, L. A., Green, D., Epstein, R., Anderson, S., Marvel, S., ... & Ross, L. E. (2015). Trans people's experiences with assisted reproduction services: A qualitative study. *Human Reproduction, 30*(6), 1365–1374. https://doi.org/10.1093/humrep/dev087

Lampe, N. M., Carter, S. K., & Sumerau, J. E. (2019). Continuity and change in gender frames: The case of transgender reproduction. *Gender & Society, 33*(6), 865–887. https://doi.org/10.1177/0891243219857979

Lothstein, L. M. (1988). Female-to-male transsexuals who have delivered and reared their children. *Annals of Sex Research*, 1(1), 151–166.

Moore, L. J. (2008). *Sperm Counts: Overcome by Man's Most Precious Fluid*. New York University Press.

Nordqvist, P. (2021). Telling reproductive stories: Social scripts, relationality and donor conception. *Sociology, 55*(4), 677–695. https://doi.org/10.1177/0038038520981860

Pearce, R., & White, F. R. (2019). Beyond the pregnant man: Representing trans pregnancy in A Deal With The Universe. *Feminist Media Studies, 19*(5), 764–767. https://doi.org/10.1080/14680777.2019.1630925

Riggs, D.W. (2013). Transgender men's self-representations of bearing children post-transition. In F. Green & M. Friedman (Eds.), *Chasing Rainbows: Exploring Gender Fluid Parenting Practices* (pp. 62–71). Demeter Press.

Riggs, D.W. (2014). What makes a man? Thomas Beattie, embodiment, and 'mundane transphobia'. *Feminism and Psychology*, 24, 157–171. https://doi.org/10.1177/0959353514526221

Riggs, D.W., Pearce, R., Pfeffer, C.A., Hines, S., Ray White, F., & Ruspini, E. (2020). Men, trans/masculine, and non-binary people's experiences of pregnancy loss: An international qualitative study. *BMC Pregnancy and Childbirth*. https://doi.org/10.1186/s12884-020-03166-6

Riggs, D. W., Pfeffer, C. A., Pearce, R., Hines, S., & White, F. R. (2021). Men, trans/masculine, and non-binary people negotiating conception: normative resistance and inventive pragmatism. *International Journal of Transgender Health, 22*(1–2), 6–17. https://doi.org/10.1080/15532739.2020.1808554

Von Doussa, H., Beauchamp, J., Goldner, S., & Zipper, B. (2021). Reflections and (un) learnings on supporting transgender and gender diverse people and their families in a mental health family service new to this work. *Psychotherapy and Counselling Journal of Australia, 8*(2). https://pacja.org.au/2020/12/reflections-and-unlearnings-on-supporting-transgender-and-gender-diverse-people-and-their-families-in-a-mental-health-family-service-new-to-this-work-2/

Wallace, J. (2010). The manly art of pregnancy. In K. Bornstein & S. Bear Bergman (Eds.), *Gender Outlaws: The Next Generation* (pp. 188–94). Seal Press.

Weston, K. (1997). *Families We Choose: Lesbians, Gays, Kinship*. Columbia University Press.

PART III

Institutionalised Resistance to Openness

CHAPTER 12

Knowing Origins

Naomi Cahn

12.1 Introduction

While assisted reproductive technology and the use of donor gametes have required new ways of defining parenthood, in the United States they have not yet fostered law reform on the identity rights of a child in these new families. Substantively, when it comes to the anonymity of donors and siblings' ability to find one another, there has been minimal legal movement compared, for example, to similar jurisdictions such as the United Kingdom and Australia.[1] The US Supreme Court has held that parents deserve "special weight" and deference with respect to decisions about their children, and those decisions include choices concerning the identity of donors (*Elk Grove Unified School District* v. *Newdow*, 2004; *Troxel* v. *Granville*, 2000). Cases that have considered the rights of genetically related donor-conceived offspring to learn about one another with one another have rejected any such rights. And no state yet gives donor-conceived offspring the absolute right to know the identity of their donors. Instead, when donor-conceived offspring and their families have formed relationships with one another, or learned the identity of their donors, it has been through voluntary and nongovernmental means.

Both the legal and the pragmatic contexts for nondisclosure are changing globally and having a significant impact in the United States. A variety of developments call into question the ethics of anonymity – indeed, the very ability to "promise" anonymity itself may border on the fraudulent. First, as the number of donor-conceived people grows, and as more adults learn they were donor-conceived, they are increasingly advocating for additional information about their donors, leading to more awareness of, and engagement, with these issues. Second, growing numbers of

---

[1] See Appleton (2015, p. 114), who asks "how would we analyze known-donor controversies if we shifted the focus to children?" For further argument on the need to respect children's rights in assisted reproductive technology, see Wilson (2003).

single-parent and same-sex families mean that the use of donor gametes is coming into the open and subject to more public discussion. Moreover, surrogates and the families they have helped create are forming bonds that ensure the surrogate is known to the child. Third, advances in technology, ranging from genetic testing to internet expansion, enable offspring to find siblings and the donor – and, for those who did not previously know, to find out that they themselves are donor conceived. Moreover, technology is facilitating the use of the intending parents' own gametes (through, for example, *in vitro* gametogenesis), potentially rendering the use of donor gametes obsolete. Finally, recent legislation and proposed laws (e.g., provisions in the Uniform Parentage Act 2017 and pending legislation) directly address identity disclosure, providing the donor with a veto over disclosure in the weaker form of such proposals and mandating disclosure, in the stronger form. There are some in the United States, however, that oppose additional regulation, raising questions not just about the pragmatic issues of compliance but also about constitutional issues, such as privacy (Trachman, 2022a).

This chapter traces the development of the regulation of donor conception in the United States, addressing laws concerning both anonymity, as well as those that enable legal recognition of genetic ties, such as through designations of surrogate decisionmakers and recognition of sibling relationships. It also shows that the feasibility of promising anonymity to donors is no longer viable. Finally, it notes the development, and ethical questions, about new technologies that may render "third party reproduction" itself irrelevant; for example, *in vitro* gametogenesis and other advances allow individuals to self-reproduce, without the need for donor gametes.

12.2   The US Approach to Donor Conception

In the past, parents were told to keep secret the very fact of donor conception, and there was even some legal uncertainty about the legitimacy of offspring. Much has changed, but there remain multiple levels of secrecy and disclosure in the donor world in the United States, in contrast to countries such as the United Kingdom, New Zealand, or Australia.

12.2.1   Secrecy

First, many donor-conceived offspring simply do not know that they are donor conceived. Journalist Dani Shapiro, on a whim, took a DNA test, and found – at the age of 54 – that she had been conceived through a process of "confused donor sperm," in which the sperm of her mother's husband (the man Shapiro knew as her father) was mixed with an anonymous donor (Glazer, 2019). A second level concerns the layers of secrecy between offspring, donors, and parents who have used donor gametes. This secrecy is the product of cultural norms and contracts, not US constitutional principles or legislation. While donors and parents each typically sign agreements pertaining to anonymity, very few court opinions have interpreted the validity, and applicability, of these documents (Cahn, 2012, p. 737; Entrikin, 2020, p. 833).

The first level of secrecy – failure to disclose donor conception – is beginning to dissolve (Samuels, 2018). The Ethics Committee of the American Society for Reproductive Medicine (ASRM), a US-based international fertility organization that provides ethical and practice-oriented guidelines for its members as well as legislative advocacy on fertility, recommended in 2013 (and reiterated in 2018) that it "strongly" encourages parents to disclose their use of donor gametes to their offspring.[2] There is no monitoring of disclosure, and no information is available to offspring about their donor conception, even on birth certificates. Nonetheless, there is a growing rate of disclosure in most jurisdictions, although children of heterosexual couples typically learn later than do those of single women or lesbians (Zadeh, 2018). The second level of disclosure, concerning the identity of donors, however, has proven far more resistant to change. This section discusses the US approach to regulation of donor conception as context for explaining the current inconsistent ad hoc approach to disclosure.

12.2.2 Existing Regulation

The donor gamete industry in the United States is lightly regulated by both the federal government and individual states.[3] At the federal level, there are two different sets of minimal oversight. First, the US Congress mandates the collection of certain types of information about the success of fertility cycles, and the Centers for Disease Control and Prevention (CDC) publishes an annual compilation of said data (2021). The CDC data includes self-reported clinic data on when an egg or embryo is used;

---

[2] At both times, it noted that disclosure is "ultimately the choice of recipient parents" (Ethics Committee of the American Society for Reproductive Medicine, 2013, p. 45; see also ASRM, 2018, p. 601).

[3] Some states do address aspects of the gamete-provision process and may require additional record-keeping or screening (Cahn, 2012, p. 386). Close to 40 per cent of states require insurance coverage of fertility, although not all cover *in vitro* fertilization (Resolve, n.d.).

it does not track the use of third-party sperm. Moreover, the purpose of the data is to measure success and safety. It includes which "cycles" – that is, which single attempts at IVF – use a donated egg rather than the patient's egg, but it does not include whether the patient recipient is the intended mother or a gestational surrogate, nor whether the sperm used is the intended father's or a donor's (Samuels, 2018). Approximately 24,000 cycles involved donated eggs or donated embryos, and more than 40 percent of those cycles resulted in live births, that is, "singleton" or multiple births (CDC, 2021, p. 24). Using CDC data, researchers have compiled information about surrogacy usage. But there are no data about sperm usage (Bionews, n.d.).

Second, the Food and Drug Administration (FDA) treats donor gametes like other human tissue and has adopted regulations that require testing for a variety of communicable and sexually transmitted diseases, and then the quarantining of donor gametes for six months before they can be used.[4] Genetic testing is not required. The records must be kept for ten years (21 CFR, 2021), but there is no system for tracking the children born through the use of any particular donor's gametes; that is, gamete purchasers are not required to report results to anyone. Nor are donors required to report any subsequent medical conditions. Consequently, there is no mandatory mechanism that enables the sharing of health information, much less any records. And there is no oversight of the people who become donors. For example, when James Aggeles applied to Xytex, an Atlanta based sperm bank, he claimed that he had graduated from college, had a master's degree, and was pursuing "his Ph.D. in artificial intelligence. None of this was true, however, as Aggeles had actually dropped out of school at that time ... had also been hospitalized and diagnosed with psychotic schizophrenia, narcissistic personality disorder, and significant grandiose delusions," and yet, Xytex approved Aggeles within two weeks. (*Doe 1* v. *Xytex Corp.*, 2017). Private law, in the form of tort suits, does provide some minimal check, and states have begun enacting fertility fraud laws; such actions, however, do not address anonymity.

For the past few decades, advocates for the donor-conceived community, scholars, and ethicists have called for additional oversight of the donor gamete industry on issues ranging from limits on the number of

---

[4] Required testing for all HCT/P donors extends to HIV, HBV (Hepatitis), HCV, Syphilis, West Nile Virus, CMV, HTLV, Chlamydia and Gonorrhea, as well as sepsis and smallpox (FDA, 2019; see also 21 CFR, 2021).

offspring born from an individual's gametes, genetic testing of gametes, improved record-keeping and disclosure, and limitations on the number of offspring, but federal regulation has not resulted (Elston, 2020, p. 47; see also Kramer & Cahn, 2013).

The private market has stepped in, and (as discussed below, states are beginning to enact their own legislation. First, an increasing number of sperm banks offer genetic testing and identity disclosure. For example, The Sperm Bank of California (n.d.) stopped providing anonymous sperm in 2016. California Cryobank, which claims to be one of the largest banks, offers Anonymous, Open, and ID Disclosure donors (California Cryobank, n.d.). RMACT allows for open identity and anonymous egg donors, and it also warns, ominously, that "both parties … must agree not to seek information concerning the other" (Reproductive Medicine Associates of Connecticut, n.d.). There are, however, problems with implementation, including companies' attempts to control any contact efforts (US Donor Conceived Council, 2022).

Restrictions on contact between recipients and donors, and the difficulty of maintaining anonymity, rose to national attention following a case involving a parent who made contact with her donor's relatives. Danielle Teuscher had purchased sperm from Northwest Cryobank, whose customer agreement for donor sperm precluded the purchaser from attempting to obtain any information about her donor (other than through the seller).[5] However, Teuscher used a commercially available DNA test on her donor-conceived daughter and found a close relative who indicated on the DNA site that she was "open to contact." After reaching out to that individual, Teuscher received the following in reply, "I don't understand," and did not pursue any further contact. Northwest Cryobank then sent her a letter, demanding that she stop all attempts to contact the donor or any of the donor's relatives, threatening to seek liquidated damages of $20,000, and informing her that the Cryobank was denying her permission to use the remaining four vials of the donor's sperm – vials that Teuscher had already purchased (Mroz, 2019; Trachman, 2019). Anonymity is serious business.

Mutual consent registries, most prominently the Donor Sibling Registry, provide an option for donor-conceived families to find one another. A growing number of US-based sperm banks have even developed their own registries (e.g., Seattle Sperm Bank).

---

[5] The agreement also required her to agree "never" to contact or try to contact the donor (Declaration in Support of a Motion for a Preliminary Injunction; see also Cahn, 2020, p. 30; Gan-Or, 2020, p. 793).

12.3   Legal Challenges to Anonymity

While there is no federal legislation on donor identity disclosure, individual states and the Uniform Law Commission (a national organization that seeks to develop model or uniform laws for state adoption) have
taken some steps forward on the issues. This section provides an overview
of cases and statutes in the area, and also includes issues with respect to
donor-conceived siblings.

12.3.1   Caselaw

i. *Donor disclosure*: State courts have considered requests to disclose
   a donor's identity but that has not yet occurred in the context of
   offsprings' US constitutional claims; so far, no court has ordered
   disclosure.[6] In perhaps the most famous case, *Johnson* v. *Superior
   Court*, the disclosure of the genetic parent's identity was incidental
   to the tort claims being brought against the clinic that had provided
   the allegedly defective sperm (2000).[7] The court held that, under
   certain circumstances, records relating to insemination, "including
   a sperm donor's identity and related information contained in those
   records" could be subject to disclosure. Because the case concerned
   the parents' tort claims, the court was not required to decide whether
   offspring could sue for disclosure. Nonetheless, by recognizing that
   disclosure might be permitted under certain conditions, the court left
   open that possibility (Cahn, 2009, p. 211).

ii. *Half-siblings*: When it comes to half-siblings, there is little law
    on the right to identifying information or to remain in contact.
    In the United States, even for full-blooded siblings, the Supreme
    Court has never held there is an associational right that must be
    protected, although states may have their own laws to preserve such
    relationships (Cahn, 2012; Hasday, 2012). While numerous minors
    who are half-siblings (because they share a donor) have established
    close relationships, this occurs through mutual consent registries and
    generally involves parents who are supportive of such relationships
    (Kramer & Cahn, 2013).

---

[6] For example, in *Johnson* v. *Superior Court*, the court recognized that the state's interests outweighed
those of the donor (2000, pp. 878–79; see also Cahn, 2014a, p. 1124; *Doe* v. *XYZ Co.*, 2009,
pp. 123–24). Other countries have chosen different approaches to anonymity (Allan, 2016).

[7] The relevant law allows for "inspection" of records relating to the insemination "only upon an order
of the court for good cause shown" (*Johnson* v. *Superior Court*, 2000).

Only a few cases have considered the rights of donor-conceived half-siblings, and those cases concerned familial-type claims (visitation), rather than information disclosure.

12.3.1.1   Perry-Rogers *v.* Fasano *(2000)*

Perhaps the first case to consider the potential of sibling rights in the ART context was *Perry-Rogers*, though it is notable that the two children were not biologically related. Two couples, one white (Donna and Richard Fasano) and one black (Deborah Perry-Rogers and Robert Rogers), were patients at the same fertility facility. Embryos from both couples were transferred to Donna Fasano and, as a result of the fertility clinic's mistake, Fasano effectively became the gestational carrier for the Perry-Rogers' baby. When Fasano subsequently gave birth to two children, one was her biological child and the other was the biological child of the Perry-Rogers. Approximately four months after the babies were born, the Fasanos agreed to relinquish custody of the black child to his biological parents, conditioned upon visitation. Although the Perry-Rogers subsequently opposed the visitation provision, the lower court granted visitation. On appeal, the court interpreted New York law, which entitles "siblings related by whole or half-blood" to petition for visitation, not to include the Fasano child, who was related only through gestation to the Perry-Rogers child (*Perry-Rogers* v. *Fasano*, 2000, p. 25).

12.3.1.2   *Bobbie Jo R. v. Traci W.*[8]

In perhaps the first case to consider donor-conceived half-sibling rights explicitly, a West Virginia court rejected a mother's claim of associational rights between her child and the child of another woman born through the same donor.[9] In that case, Bobbie Jo sought visitation rights on behalf of her donor-conceived son with a half-sibling. Bobbie Jo had been in a relationship with the birth mothers of each child and also claimed custody rights for herself. (One suspects that she helped choose the same donor for each child.) The court noted that it might have been more hospitable to a claim had the siblings been close at any point in their lives; there was no such claim in the case (Cahn, 2014b).

---

[8] Professor Courtney Joslin, the Reporter for the Uniform Parentage Act (UPA), sent an email in 2013 asking if I had seen this West Virginia case. While there may be additional cases raising these issues, they are not reported.

[9] The court in *Bobbie Jo R.* v. *Traci W.* stated: "it is noteworthy that [the two half-siblings] never lived together, and likely never met. Our jurisprudence on matters of sibling visitation emphasizes the continuation of established, beneficial relationships." (2013, p. 3 n. 4).

12.3.1.3   Pasik *v.* Russell *(2015)*

Susan Russell and Elizabeth Pasik, who entered into a relationship in 1998, decided to start a family together. Pasik purchased donor sperm and, using that sperm, Pasik and Russell each gave birth to two children. The four children share the same sperm donor and the women raised the four children together. When the mothers' relationship ended in April 2011, each woman assumed custody of the two children to whom she had given birth. For the next two years, Pasik continued to be involved with the two children living with Russell and provided financial support.

After Russell cut off contact, Pasik petitioned the court for time-sharing with the children as the de facto or psychological parent. I became involved in an amicus brief that focused on sibling rights and the significant harm that separating siblings and severing the relationship between them has on the children.[10] When the Florida Appellate Court issued its decision, finding that Pasik did not have standing, the court failed to address the issue of sibling rights.

12.3.1.4   *Section Summary*

Federal legislation recognizes siblings' associational claims in foster care (Mandelbaum, 2011, p. 14; Post et al., 2015, p. 329), but it is rarely recognized in other contexts (Hasday, 2012; Jones, 1993, p. 1195; Scharf, 2015, p. 125). Consequently, the rights of donor-conceived offspring to maintain contact with one another is one part of this larger (non)recognition of sibling rights and shows the importance of state law (Nejaime, 2017).

12.3.2   *Statutes*

An increasing number of American states have begun to address issues involving donor disclosure, and, as of 2023, momentum is growing to bring US state laws in line with other countries. In the first domestic law in the United States to do so, a 2011 State of Washington statute required disclosure of donor-identifying information and medical history when a child turns 18, but the law also permitted the donor to sign an affidavit of nondisclosure at the time of donation, thereby precluding disclosure.[11]

---

[10] Elliot H. Scherker of Greenberg Traurig was the primary author.

[11] Wash Rev Code § 26.26.750 (2017) was repealed (by Laws 2018 c 6, § 907(75), effective January 1, 2019) when Washington adopted the newest UPA and incorporated the Article 9 provisions for donor identifying information and medical history into § 805; see also S.B. 6037 (2017) on the Uniform Parentage Act.

In 2015, similar legislation was introduced in the state of Utah. Like the Washington statute, it would have permitted a donor-conceived individual who was at least 18 years old to access identifying information about the donor, unless the donor had submitted an affidavit denying such disclosure (Cahn, 2018, p. 1448). Shortly after its introduction, the original bill was replaced by a proposal to permit donor-conceived offspring to obtain access only to nonidentifying medical information. The more limited substitute bill was enacted.

A more promising development is the 2017 Uniform Parentage Act, which is modeled on the Washington state law, and provides a template for states (Cahn & Suter, 2022b). It does not mandate disclosure, but it does require that fertility clinics collect identifying information from the donor and that the donor signs a "declaration" on whether the donor agrees to disclosure. Even if the donor has not consented to disclosure, the clinic must make a "good faith" effort to provide any donor-conceived child who requests it with nonidentifying information and also to notify the donor of any request for information, allowing the donor to reconsider the disclosure declaration (UPA, 2017e). A donor who consented to disclosure at the time of donation is not permitted to withdraw consent, based on the theory that the parents may have chosen the gametes – at least in part – because of the agreement to disclose identity, and "the equities weigh in favor of holding the donor to his or her original position permitting identity disclosure" (UPA, 2017d; see also Davies, 2020). Regardless of the content of the declaration, the donor continues to have no parental rights or obligations (UPA, 2017b).[12]

It remains to be seen whether, and how quickly, states will adopt legislation based on the revised Uniform Parentage Act. In the first few years after its promulgation, six states enacted it. (Uniform Law Commission), with most including the provisions relating to donor conception (Cahn & Suter, 2022b). Regardless of how many more states adopt it, the proposals relating to donor identity disclosure are a significant step that would also change clinics' record-keeping requirements.

On the other hand, as the Reporter for the Act acknowledged in explaining the provisions on donor identity disclosure and rights to access information:

> Article 9 [which contains the relevant provisions] stakes out a middle ground with respect to information disclosure. Article 9 does not require disclosure of the identity of any third-party gamete providers. It does, however, require sperm banks and fertility clinics to collect identifying and medical

---

[12] The Act precludes a donor from using genetic testing to establish parentage (UPA, 2017c).

history information from all gamete providers and to obtain a declaration from all gamete providers addressing whether they would like their identity disclosed upon request once the child turns age eighteen [and] requires covered facilities to make a good faith effort to disclose nonidentifying medical history information regarding the gamete provider upon request. (Joslin, 2018, pp. 467–68)

Thus, the new Act does not *mandate* identity disclosure, and, of course, offspring who do not know they are donor conceived may not even know to ask about the nonidentifying medical history information. There are also calls to amend the Act to end the possibility of a donor opting out of disclosure.

The final crack in protecting anonymity is a Colorado bill that was enacted in 2022 that requires identity release donation, beginning in 2025, sets limits on the number of families per donor, and provides additional regulation (Cahn & Suter, 2022b). Other states may follow suit.

12.3.3   Industry Guidance

The primary organization for the fertility industry is the American Society for Reproductive Medicine. It issues ethical guidelines that, while not legally binding, are highly influential for its members. It has evolved in its recognition of pragmatic aspects of identity disclosure.

In its 2009 ethical guidance concerning donor gametes, the ASRM stated:

Programs should fully inform donors of the clinic's policies about information sharing and contact, but they should caution that policies cannot be guaranteed if laws or individual circumstances change.

6. Although data are sparse about the outcomes of contact between donor and offspring, programs and agencies should inform donors *that the possibility of contact from offspring in the future cannot be foreclosed.* (ASRM, 2009, p. 22)

In 2014, the comparable provision became:

Programs should fully inform donors and recipients of donor gametes of their clinic's policies about information sharing and contact, but they should caution that policies cannot be guaranteed if laws or individual circumstances change *and that the possibility exists of contact from offspring in the future.* (ASRM, 2014, p. 675)

By 2019, this language suggested:

Programs should caution participants that policies related to information sharing are not guaranteed since laws or individual circumstances change and *that there is a possibility they may be contacted by offspring in the future.*

> Similarly, maintaining anonymity of parties cannot be guaranteed since commercially available genetic testing and agencies that allow dissemination of identifying information through social media increases the risk of inadvertent disclosure of participants. (ASRM, 2019, p. 664)[13]

Although not yet advocating disclosure, the ASRM has moved from noting that possible contact cannot be foreclosed to a positive statement about the possibility of contact; that is, it has moved towards recognizing that anonymity can no longer be guaranteed and that donors should be aware that they may be contacted by offspring. Even the titles of the guidance documents – in 2009, the document was titled *Interests, Obligations, and Rights of the Donor*, but by 2014 "of the Donor" had been dropped – shows evolution towards acknowledgment that donor conception is not simply about the rights of the donor.

According to a survey of the 41 sperm banks that operate in the United States, only 50 per cent actually conduct the ASRM-recommended psychological evaluations of donors, and only two banks require that donors undergo psychoeducational counselling before they donate (US Donor Conceived Council, 2022).

12.4   Opposition to Ending Anonymity

So why isn't there more regulation? There are a variety of factors that explain this regulatory vacuum. First is the market-oriented outlook on reproduction that wants as little governmental control as possible. Unlike other countries, there is no federal health care system, and each of the many states can regulate on its own.

Moreover, the multibillion-dollar fertility industry claims the industry is highly regulated, and it opposes further regulation. But little of that regulation is mandatory; for example, there is no federal requirement to verify information submitted by donors or to track their medical issues (Cahn & Suter, 2022a). Those defending the industry point to self-regulation as the key to any further guidelines (Suter & Cahn, 2022a).

Second are concerns about supply. In an effort to test how ending anonymity in the United States would affect men's willingness to donate sperm, Glenn Cohen and his colleagues conducted a study with actual donors (2016). The study provides important data on both the cost and

---

[13] In addition, the ASRM notes that based on potential legal developments and because it is becoming "increasingly easy to conduct searches for individuals on the Internet or through social media, programs should make it clear to donors that they cannot guarantee immunity from future contact by recipients or offspring" (2019, p. 666).

willingness of these anonymous donors to become known: approximately 29 per cent of the active donors would choose not to donate under a disclosure system, and, among those who would, the average increase in payment to donate was $60 (Cohen et al., 2016, pp. 470, 482).

The author's conclusions are, necessarily, somewhat speculative. Yet without knowing the size of the current donor supply – and the US keeps no records on donor sperm, apart from those related to medical testing (Kramer & Cahn, 2013) – there is no way of estimating these "arguable" financial implications. Moreover, concerns about supply assume no new recruitment efforts may be developed and banks may be able to recruit donors less concerned about money and more concerned about helping create families. Indeed, in Australia, the supply of donor sperm increased after anonymity was removed (Adams et al., 2016).

Third are the politics. There is a risk that anti-abortion legislation – particularly after the US Supreme Court's 2022 opinion finding no constitutional right to an abortion[14] – could be deemed to apply to assisted reproductive technology, and the potential of regulating this form of families might, it is feared, result in further regulation of issues such as just who can form families. A related problem concerns US conceptions of privacy and autonomy (Suter & Cahn, 2022a) if donors must consent to the prospective release of information. These issues can, of course, be handled through appropriate counselling and understanding of the process. The requirement of consent ensures that privacy is protected.

12.5 New Technologies and Donor Disclosure

Two technological developments provide context – and impetus – for the movement towards donor disclosure. The first is the virtual end of anonymity. The second is the future of reproduction and the questions it raises about the potential need for gamete donation at all.

12.5.1 Genetic Testing

Advances in DNA testing, including direct-to-consumer kits, mean the ability to maintain secrecy about involvement in donor conception is questionable. Offspring, regardless of whether they were told they were donor conceived, are, if they engage in such testing, likely to find out their genetic origins (Glazer, 2019), and offspring who want more information about

---

[14] *Dobbs* v. *Jackson Women's Health Organization*, 597 U.S. ___ (2022).

their donor can obtain access to the identity of potential relatives, including that of their donor. The two leading DNA test companies, Ancestry.com and 23andMe, have more than 30 million members looking for information about their ancestry, in their combined databases (Mendoza & Diallo, 2020; see also Harper et al., 2016). The ubiquity of this technology challenges the maintenance of anonymity; even if banks promise confidentiality to donors,[15] genetic testing could easily lead to learning the identity of the donor, an issue that parents and donors need to consider when they "choose" anonymity (e.g., Harper et al., 2016; Johnston, 2016; Ishii et al., 2022). Indeed, people who were not even aware of their donor conception have used this "direct-to-consumer" testing to learn that they are donor conceived, even though they did not have cause to question their origins (Copeland, 2017; Crawshaw, 2017). While parents are under no obligation to tell their children that they are donor conceived, such secrets may damage relationships – and may not even continue to be secrets (Kramer & Cahn, 2013).

Thus, although sperm banks and egg agencies may continue to guarantee that they will not release records, they cannot guarantee that offspring will not be able to discover the identity of the donor. They may, consequently, have a duty to counsel gamete donors (Borry et al., 2013).

12.5.2   Will We Still Need Donors?

There are a number of potential technologies on the horizon that will largely, although not completely, eliminate the need for donor gametes. Consider that, with the development of intracytoplasmic sperm injection (ICSI), which allows for the injection of sperm into an egg, many heterosexual couples no longer need sperm donation. However, in the United States, it appears that the majority of those seeking sperm donors are now single women and lesbian couples, though accurate records do not exist. This is in line with statistics from the Australian state of Victoria, in which the largest groups of donor sperm users were women who were single (53 per cent of users) or in same-sex relationships (34 per cent) (VARTA, 2021, p. 33). In addition, single men and gay male couples still need eggs (and a woman to carry the child), although the costs of surrogacy inhibit demand. The use of mitochondrial replacement, which does require a donor egg, is now possible, but it involves a technologically complex procedure that will not require a significant number of donors.

---

[15] E.g., as one bank explains, "becoming a Non-Id Release sperm donor means your information will always be confidential and Cryos will never release your identity" (Cryos, n.d.).

Furthermore, the development of *in vitro* gametogenesis, which allows for the creation of sperm or egg cells through the use of adult cells, may foster the production of an unlimited supply of sperm and eggs genetically related to the intended parents, largely eliminating the need for donor gametes altogether as a response to infertility.

Finally, as increasing numbers of those seeking donors become single individuals or those in same-sex relationships who need donor gametes to procreate whatever their fertility status, the role of anonymity in these relationships may change the dynamic underlying gamete donation.

The future of sperm and egg donation is thus under pressure from a variety of technologies, both internal from new technologies and external from the demands of donor-conceived people to the reproductive market.

12.6   Moving Forward

The trajectory in the United States is towards donor identity disclosure. As sperm and egg banks increasingly offer the possibility of open ID donors, genetic testing becomes more widespread, and other countries end anonymity, anonymity remains unlikely to continue as a pragmatic matter in the United States. New legal approaches are developing; the law is beginning to catch up to the technology and to respond to the interests of donor-conceived people. The questions will then become how best to counsel donors, the intending parent(s), and donor-conceived offspring about their options (Cahn, 2017, pp. 379–80).

Acknowledgments

Thanks to Max Larson and Megan Lee for research assistance.

References

11 Siblings Met in Orlando. (2017, January 21). The donor sibling registry. https://donorsiblingregistry.com/success_stories/253

21 CFR § 1271 (2021)

Adams, D. H., Ullah, S., & de Lacey, S. (2016). Does the removal of anonymity reduce sperm donors in Australia? *Journal of Law and Medicine, 23*(3), 628–636.

Allan, S. (2016). Donor identification: Victorian legislation gives rights to all donor-conceived people. *Family Matters, 98,* 43–55. https://papers.ssrn.com/sol3/papers.cfm?abstract_id=3010387

Appleton, S. F. (2015). Between the binaries: Exploring the legal boundaries of nonanonymous sperm donation. *Family Law Quarterly, 49*(1), 93–115. www.jstor.org/stable/24577604

BioNews comment articles written by Wendy Kramer. (n.d.). BioNews. Retrieved June 29, 2021, from www.bionews.org.uk/page_5695

Bobbie Jo R. v. Traci W., No. 11–1753, 2013 WL 2462173 (W. Va. June 7, 2013)

Borry, P., Rusu, O., & Howard, H. (2013). Genetic testing: Anonymity of sperm donors under threat. *Nature, 469*, 169. https://doi.org/10.1038/496169e

Cahn, N. R. (2009). Necessary subjects: The need for a mandatory national donor gamete databank. *DePaul Journal of Health Care Law, 12*, 203–228.

Cahn, N. R. (2012). The new kinship. *Georgetown Law Journal, 100*(2), 367–429. https://papers.ssrn.com/sol3/papers.cfm?abstract_id=2018969

Cahn, N. R. (2014a). Do tell! The rights of donor-conceived offspring. *Hofstra Law Review, 42*(4), 1077–1124. https://scholarlycommons.law.hofstra.edu/hlr/vol42/iss4/3

Cahn, N. R. (2014b). The uncertain legal basis for the new kinship. *Journal of Family Issues, 36*(4), 501–518. https://doi.org/10.1177/0192513X14563797

Cahn, N. R. (2017). What's right about knowing? *Journal of Law & Biosciences, 4*, 377–83. http://dx.doi.org/10.2139/ssrn.3011639

Cahn, N. R. (2018). The new "art" of family: Connecting assisted reproductive technologies & identity rights. *University of Illinois Law Review, 2018*, 1443–1471.

Cahn, N. R. (2020). Crispr parents and informed consent. *Southern Methodist University Science and Technology Law Review, 23*(1), 3–30. https://scholar.smu.edu/scitech/vol23/iss1/2

Cahn, N. & Suter, S. (2022a). The art of regulating ART. *Chicago-Kent Law Review* (96), 29–86.

Cahn, N. & Suter, S. (2022b). Generations later, the rights of donor-conceived people are becoming law. *The Hill*, https://thehill.com/opinion/healthcare/3460149-generations-later-the-rights-of-donor-conceived-people-are-becoming-law/?rl=1

California Cryobank. (n.d.). *Donor types.* www.cryobank.com/how-it-works/donor-types/

Centers for Disease Control and Prevention. (2021, April 20). *ART Success Rates.* www.cdc.gov/art/artdata/index.html

Cohen, I. G., Coan, T., Ottey, M., & Boyd, C. (2016). Sperm donor anonymity and compensation: An experiment with American sperm donors. *Journal of Law & the Biosciences, 3*(3), 468–488. https://doi.org/10.1093/jlb/lsw052

Copeland, L. (2017, July 27). Who was she? A DNA test only opened new mysteries. *Washington Post.* www.washingtonpost.com/graphics/2017/lifestyle/she-thought-she-was-irish-until-a-dna-test-opened-a-100-year-old-mystery/

Crawshaw, M. (2017). Direct-to-consumer DNA testing: The fallout for individuals and their families unexpectedly learning of their donor conception origins. *Human Fertility, 21*(4), 225–228. https://doi.org/10.1080/14647273.2017.1339127

Cryos. (n.d.). *ID release or non-ID release sperm donor?* www.cryosinternational.com/en-us/us-shop/become-a-donor/become-a-sperm-donor/how-to-become-a-sperm-donor/id-release-or-non-id-release-sperm-donor/

Davies, S. (2020). Queering America's heteronormative family law through "well-conceived" legislation (or, genetic parents exist and sometimes your kid might want to know them). *American Journal of Law & Medicine, 46*(1), 89–110. https://doi.org/10.1177/0098858820919554

Declaration in Support of a Motion for a Preliminary Injunction (2019) Teuscher v. CCB-NWB, Att. A. para.VIII, E. Wash., No. 19-CV-00204.

Doe v. *XYZ Co.*, 914 N.E.2d 117 (Mass. App. Ct. 2009)

Doe 1 v. *Xytex Corp.*, No. 1:16-CV-1453-TWT, 2017 WL 1036484 (N.D. Ga. Mar. 17, 2017).

Donor Sibling Registry. (n.d.). https://donorsiblingregistry.com/

Elk Grove Unified School District v. *Newdow,* 542 US 1 (2004)

Elston, S. W. (2020). Swipe right for daddy: Modern marketing of sperm and the need for honesty and transparency in advertising. *Journal of Health & Life Sciences Law, 13,* 28–56.

Entrikin, J. L. (2020). Family secrets and relational privacy: Protecting not-so-personal, sensitive information from public disclosure. *University of Miami Law Review, 74*(3), 781–897. https://repository.law.miami.edu/umlr/vol74/iss3/5

Ethics Committee of the American Society for Reproductive Medicine. (2009). Interests, obligations, and rights of the donor in gamete donation. *Fertility and Sterility, 91*(1), 22–27. https://doi.org/10.1016/j.fertnstert.2008.09.062

Ethics Committee of the American Society for Reproductive Medicine. (2013). Informing offspring of their conception by gamete or embryo donation: A committee opinion. *Fertility and Sterility, 100*(1), 45–49. https://doi.org/10.1016/j.fertnstert.2013.02.028

Ethics Committee of the American Society for Reproductive Medicine. (2014). Interests, obligations, and rights in gamete donation: a committee opinion. *Fertility and Sterility, 102*(3), 675–81. https://doi.org/10.1016/j.fertnstert.2014.06.001

Ethics Committee of the American Society for Reproductive Medicine. (2018). Informing offspring of their conception by gamete or embryo donation: An Ethics Committee opinion. *Fertility and Sterility, 109*(4), 601–605. https://doi.org/10.1016/j.fertnstert.2018.01.001

Ethics Committee of the American Society for Reproductive Medicine. (2019). Interests, obligations, and rights in gamete and embryo donation: An Ethics Committee opinion. *Fertility and Sterility, 111*(4), 664–670. https://doi.org/10.1016/j.fertnstert.2019.01.018

Food and Drug Administration. (2019, May 3). *Testing donors of human cells, tissues, and cellular and tissue-based products (HCT/P): Specific requirements.* www.fda.gov/vaccines-blood-biologics/safety-availability-biologics/testing-donors-human-cells-tissues-and-cellular-and-tissue-based-products-hctp-specific-requirements

Gan-Or, N. Y. (2020). Reproductive dreams and nightmares: Sperm donation in the age of at-home genetic testing. *Loyola University Chicago Law Journal, 51*(3), 791–833. https://lawecommons.luc.edu/luclj/vol51/iss3/5

Glazer, E. (2019, July 23). *DNA testing forever changed donor conception.* Harvard Health publishing. www.health.harvard.edu/blog/dna-testing-forever-changed-donor-conception-2019072317394

Harper, J. C., Kennett, D., & Reisel, D. (2016). The end of donor anonymity: How genetic testing is likely to drive anonymous gamete donation out of business. *Human Reproduction, 31*(6), 1135–1140. https://doi.org/10.1093/humrep/dew065

Hasday, J. E. (2012). Siblings in law. *Vanderbilt Law Review, 65*(3), 897–931. https://scholarship.law.vanderbilt.edu/vlr/vol65/iss3/4

Ishii, T., & de Miguel Beriain, I. (2022). Shifting to a model of donor conception that entails a communication agreement among the parents, donor, and offspring. *BMC Medical Ethics, 23*(1), 1–11. https://doi.org/10.1186/s12910-022-00756-1

Johnson v. *Superior Court,* 95 Cal. Rptr. 2d 864 (Cal. App. 2d Dist. 2000).

Johnston, L. (2016, July 3). Sperm donors fear "hi dad" showdown as DNA testing becomes more accessible. *Express.* www.express.co.uk/life-style/health/685599/Sperm-donors-DNA-testing-biological-father-offspring-anonymity

Jones, B. (1993). Do siblings possess constitutional rights? *Cornell Law Review, 78*(6), 1187–1220. http://scholarship.law.cornell.edu/clr/vol78/iss6/4

Joslin, C. G. (2018). Preface to the UPA (2017). *Family Law Quarterly, 52,* 437–69.

Kramer, W., & Cahn, N. R. (2013). *Finding Our Families: A First-of-Its-Kind Book for Donor-Conceived People and Their Families.* Avery Publishing Group.

Mandelbaum, R. (2011). Delicate balances: Assessing the needs and rights of siblings in foster care to maintain their relationships post-adoption. *New Mexico Law Review, 41*(1), 1–67. https://digitalrepository.unm.edu/nmlr/vol41/iss1/3

Mendoza, B., & Diallo, A. (2020, October 26). *The best DNA testing kit.* Wirecutter. www.nytimes.com/wirecutter/reviews/best-dna-test/

Mroz, J. (2019, February 16). A mother learns the identity of her child's grandmother. A sperm bank threatens to sue. *NY Times.* www.nytimes.com/2019/02/16/health/sperm-donation-dna-testing.html

Nejaime, D. (2017). The family's constitution. *Constitutional Commentary, 32,* 413–448. https://scholarship.law.umn.edu/concomm/280

Perry-Rogers v. *Fasano,* 715 N.Y.S.2d 19 (N.Y. App. Div. 1st Dept. 2000)

Post, D. J., McCarthy, S., Sherman, R., & Bayimli, S. (2015). Are you still my family? Post-adoption sibling visitation. *Capital University Law Review, 43*(2), 307–372.

Reproductive Medicine Associates of Connecticut. (n.d.). *Anonymous Egg Donation.* www.rmact.com/anonymous-egg-donation

Resolve. (n.d.). Infertility coverage by state. https://resolve.org/what-are-my-options/insurance-coverage/infertility-coverage-state/

Rhode Island Title 15, Chapter 8.1, Sections 901 et seq. (2021)

Russell v. *Pasik,* 178 So. 3d 55 (Fla. 2d Dist. App. 2015)

Samuels, E. J. (2018). An immodest proposal for birth registration in donor-assisted reproduction, in the interest of science and human rights. *New Mexico Law Review, 48*(3), 416–451. https://scholarworks.law.ubalt.edu/fac_articles/5

S.B. 6037, 2017–2018 Regular Session (Wash. 2017).

Scharf, R. L. (2015). Separated at adoption: Addressing the challenges of maintaining sibling-of-origin bonds in post-adoption families. *UC Davis Journal of Juvenile Law & Policy, 19*(1), 84–125. https://scholars.law.unlv.edu/facpub/928

Seattle Sperm Bank. (n.d.). *SSB connects.* www.seattlespermbank.com/services/ssb-connects/

Sperm Bank of California, The. (n.d.). *Identity release program.* www.thespermbankofca
.org/content/identity-release-program

Trachman, E. (2019, February 6). Beware of the home DNA kit! You may find
yourself being sued by a sperm bank. Above the Law. https://abovethelaw
.com/2019/02/beware-of-the-home-dna-kit-you-may-find-yourself-being-
sued-by-a-sperm-bank/

Trachman, E. (2022a). Colorado is poised to pass a groundbreaking Donor-
Conceived Person Protection Act. *Above the Law.* https://abovethelaw.com/2022/
05/colorado-is-poised-to-pass-a-groundbreaking-donor-conceived-person-
protection-act

Trachman, E. (2022b). New York proposes Donor-Conceived Person
Protection Act. Above the Law. https://abovethelaw.com/2022/01/new-york-
proposes-donor-conceived-person-protection-act/

Troxel v. *Granville*, 530 US 57 (2000)

Uniform Law Commission. (n.d.). *Parentage Act.* www.uniformlaws.org/committees/
community-home?CommunityKey=c4f37d2d-4d20-4be0-8256-22dd73af068f

Uniform Parentage Act § 9 (2017a)

Uniform Parentage Act § 102(3) (2017b)

Uniform Parentage Act § 502(b)(2) (2017c)

Uniform Parentage Act § 904 cmt (2017d)

Uniform Parentage Act § 905(b) (2017e)

US Donor Conceived Council. (2022). 2022 Survey of U.S. sperm banks. www
.usdcc.org/2022/04/19/2022-survey-of-us-sperm-banks/

VARTA. (2021). 2021 Annual Report. www.varta.org.au/sites/default/files/2021-
12/varta-annual-report-2021.pdf

Wash. Rev. Code § 26.26.750 (2017)

Wash. Rev. Code § 26.26A.815 (2019)

Wilson, R. F. (2003). Uncovering the rationale for requiring infertility in surrogacy arrangements. *American Journal of Law & Medicine, 29*(2–3), 337–362.

Zadeh, S., Ilioi, E.g., Jadva, V., & Golombok, S. (2018). The perspectives of adolescents conceived using surrogacy, egg or sperm donation, *Human Reproduction,*
33(6), 1099–1106, https://doi.org/10.1093/humrep/dey088

CHAPTER 13

Donor Anonymity and the Rights of Donor-Conceived People in Japan

Yukari Semba

13.1 Introduction: Donor Anonymity in Japan

In Japan, Dr. Kakuich Ando of Keio University Hospital began practicing donor insemination (DI) in 1948, wherein the first Japanese DI baby was born in 1949. Since then, scholars have estimated that more than 15,000 donor-conceived individuals have been born through DI (Hibino & Allan, 2020). In Japan, the majority of cases of DI were practiced as an option for couples experiencing male infertility by obstetrician–gynecologists (ob-gyns) at medical institutions registered with the Japan Society of Obstetrics Gynecology (JSOG) as the implementation facilities for DI. In 1999, JSOG began compiling and publishing DI-related records and reported that approximately 100 children are born per year via DI. Recently, however, fertility clinics that offer DI are facing a severe shortage in sperm donors. As of 2021, Japan has 12 registered medical institutions for DI. A newspaper reported that only 5 out of the 12 institutions offer DI as a service in 2018 (Yomiuri Shimbun Online, 2021). More than half of the DI procedures performed in Japan every year were conducted at Keio University Hospital Tokyo: approximately 1,500 procedures were performed annually after the first successful attempt by Dr. Ando (*Mainichi Shimbun Online*, 2020). However, the hospital stopped taking appointments from new infertility clients for DI in the summer of 2018 due to a decrease in anonymous sperm donors. Previously, the hospital had secured approximately 10 new anonymous sperm donors every year. When the importance of the "right to know donor offspring's biological origins" began to be emphasized, and Keio University Hospital began explaining in June 2017 that it might be forced to disclose donor information if a donor-conceived person files a lawsuit demanding to know, the number of new donors reduced to zero, and several donors demanded from the hospital that their donated sperm should no longer be used (Nomura, 2018). As a result, infertile couples are required to wait for a long time to receive DI, such that a few seeking donated sperm opt to access overseas sperm banks or online sperm donation services without the involvement of medical professionals (Osaki, 2020). In addition, medical institutions provide DI only to legally married heterosexual couples. Lesbian couples and single women who wish to reproduce via donated sperm must recruit donors by themselves (Higashi, 2017). Against this background, assuming that more children are born via DI in Japan per year than that reported by JSOG is reasonable.

During the early 2000s, several DI-conceived adults in Japan publicly called for donor information. In response, several Japanese researchers have highlighted the issues of donor anonymity and the right of donor offspring to know donor information. Since the 2000s, scholars increasingly examined the situation surrounding donor conception in Japan from various perspectives. For example, Kusaka et al. (2006) explored the psychological aspects of DI offspring; Ninomiya (2010) examined the relationship among DI offspring, birth mother, social father, and the donor from legal aspects. Moreover, Semba et al. (2006) engaged in studies on issues regarding the right of donor offspring to obtain donor information from the ethical aspect, whereas Saimura (2008) asserted the right of donor offspring to know as an important human right through social work experiences. Miyajima (2017) conducted a comparative study on DI in Japan and New Zealand; Shimizu et al. (2020) examined the psychological aspect of Japanese parents who conceived children via DI; and Kuji et al. (2000, 2005) conducted questionnaire surveys on men who conceived a child through DI about disclosure to the child and sperm donors about the right of donor offspring.

Since the late 1990s, Japan recognized the need for legislation on assisted reproductive technologies (ARTs), including donor conception and the right of donor offspring to obtain donor information based on the results of these studies and the wishes of donor-conceived individuals, parents who had donor-conceived children, and intended parents. However, the legislative progress has been extremely slow. In the past two decades, several special governmental committees were appointed to discuss the legal regulations including gamete donor anonymity. However, despite lengthy discussions between numerous researchers and professionals, the legislative progress remained inactive for decades. The first law addressing donor conception was enacted in December 2020. The law states that a woman who gave birth to a child is the mother, and the mother's husband is irrefutably the father if he agreed to the use of the sperm. However, the status and responsibilities of donors in relation to donor-conceived children are unclear. In addition, the law omits the right of donor-conceived individuals to access information on their biological origins. Instead, additional clauses in the law state that "necessary legal measures will be taken within a target of roughly two years," regarding children's right to know the donor. The reason is that lawmakers are struggling to reach a conclusion on many issues regarding the right of donor offspring to obtain information about their donor and surrogacy. For example, Toshiharu Furukawa proposed that policymakers say that only donor genetic and kinship information should be disclosed to donor offspring given their health issues and consanguinity (Yokota & Watanabe, 2020).

This chapter first introduces the historical and cultural background of how sperm donor anonymity and the right of donor-conceived individuals to know their biological origin have been socially perceived in Japan. Second, it reviews the position of various governmental committees since the late 1990s on issues related to the anonymity of gamete donors and the right of donor-conceived individuals to know their biological origins. Third, it provides an overview of how donor-conceived individuals, parents, and intended parents with donor-conceived children, have faced the issues. Finally, this chapter examines the reasons why the development of legislation regarding donor conception is slow and why the Japanese Government seems to have placed the rights of donor-conceived individuals to obtain donor information in the "too hard" basket. Data and research materials are drawn from official government documents, official announcements, reports from support groups for donor offspring and parents of DI-conceived children, intended parents and parliamentary debates, and information from Japanese news media.

13.2 Historical and Cultural Backgrounds of Donor Anonymity in Japan

After World War II, Dr. Kakuichi Ando with his colleagues at the Department of Obstetrics and Gynecology, Keio University School of Medicine, formed a birth control unit at the hospital in July 1947 because the high birthrate was a serious problem at the time in Japan (Yui, 2015). However, he found that many women who visited the unit were experiencing infertility problems instead of seeking contraceptive advice (Yui, 2021). Dr. Ando practiced the first DI in 1948. Dr. Rihachi Iizuka initially implemented DI as an assistant professor under Dr. Ando and mentioned in an interview that many Japanese men became infertile during World War II when they were sent overseas as soldiers and contracted malaria or other sicknesses. Therefore, these men should be regarded as victims of war (Sakai and Kasuga, 2004). Despite arguments against the claim that infertile men were victims of war immediately after the war (Yui, 2012), a sympathetic view of male infertility certainly existed at the time due to the cultural background of Japan.

In Japanese culture, the eldest son traditionally carries on the household and family line (Wakabayashi and Horioka, 2006). Hence, a couple whose husband was the eldest son of the family was expected to bear children. Although this idea has been disregarded in recent years, couples experiencing infertility problems may have faced additional social pressure during the 1940s (Castro-Vàzquez, 2017). This emphasis on paternal duty underlined DI in Japan.

Ando stated that, "although AID (DI) may be a curious method, it is superior to adoption because a child is related by blood to the wife, and it does not hurt purity because the wife only receives gametes without coitus" (1960). Based on these points, the blood relationship between parents and children was seemingly important for infertile couples at the time. In addition, many people opposed DI on the grounds that it was considered blasphemous or involved the creation of an artificial human. Beliefs also existed that DI could exert a negative impact on the parent–child relationship (Asahi Home & Welfare Weekly [Katei Asahi], 1949). Therefore, infertile couples worried about social prejudice toward them and their children.

Dr. Ando cited the following conditions for performing DI when the first DI baby was born:[1]

> (1) The aspiration of the infertile couple is of the utmost importance. Consent should be obtained from both husband and wife.
> (2) The donor should have no genetic defects, and all phenotypical traits must be most similar to the infertile husband's and superior to the husband's.
> (3) The donor should not be told who the recipient couple is nor should the couple know who the donor is. Also, the recipient couples should not tell their children that they were conceived through DI.

When the first successful DI was made public in September 1949, the legal status of the donor-conceived child, the recognition of the obligations of the intended father to support the child, and inheritance issues became questions of concern for researchers in the legal and social fields. In Japan,

---

[1] Yui (2021) translated Dr. Ando's statement in Ando (1949) into English.

Article 772 (1) under the Civil Code stipulates the father–child relationship as follows: "A child conceived by a wife during marriage shall be presumed a child of her husband." Thus, the husband who consents to his wife giving birth via donated sperm is legally regarded as the father of the donor-conceived child.

In 1997, when the JSOG established guidelines for DI, they endorsed the ideas of Dr. Ando and stipulated that sperm donors must be anonymous volunteers. Although the guidelines were revised in 2006, donor anonymity was retained.

13.3 Public Attitudes toward Donor Conception in Japan

An important and ongoing debate about gamete donation is whether donor-conceived individuals should be informed about the facts of their conception and, if so, to what extent should information be revealed (Ethics Committee of the American Society for Reproductive Medicine, 2013). The United Nations Convention on the Rights of the Child argues that a child has rights to a name, nationality, knowledge of his/her parents, and to preserve his/her identity (entered into force in 1990). Japan ratified the UN Convention in 1994, however, donor anonymity continues to exist.

In some places in the world, information is available to DI offspring because anonymous donations are prohibited or access to information is available upon approval (Allan, 2017). Evidently, a decreasing number of people in Japan in recent years are holding onto staunch beliefs that donor-conceived individuals should not be given the right to donor information; however, a considerable number of people continue to hold negative opinions about the abolition of donor anonymity.

In 1998, a public attitude survey on donor conception was conducted in Japan. The results revealed that 36.4 per cent of the 2,568 respondents from the general public considered that children should know about their origins, whereas 33.2 per cent reported the opposite (Yanaihara, 1999). In another survey on public attitudes toward donor conception conducted in 2003, the results were surprisingly different. Approximately half of the respondents expressed that parents should decide whether to tell their children the truth; 23.3 per cent disagreed, and only 16.4 per cent thought that donor offspring should absolutely be told the truth about their conception (3,649 male and female respondents aged 20–69 years; Yamagata et al., 2003). In 2014, a survey on public opinion on third-party reproduction found that 46.3 per cent of respondents (2,500 male and female respondents aged 20–50 years) agreed that donor offspring have the right to access their donor information, whereas 20.4 per cent disagreed (Yamamoto et al., 2018).

The study infers that this shift in awareness is largely due to the increasing number of professionals, such as lawyers, doctors, researchers, social workers, and psychologists who respect the human right of donor-conceived individuals to know as an important one, such that they introduce the concept to the Japanese society. In recent years, certain donor-conceived individuals emphasized the importance of knowing their donor through lectures, book publications, and the media, which have all seemingly contributed to the change in the Japanese mindset.

13.4   Debates and Legislation on Gamete Donor Anonymity

The JSOG guidelines also state that sperm provision should be limited to legally married couples and prohibit *in vitro* fertilization (IVF) using donated sperm, eggs, or embryos. Therefore, IVF using donated sperm has not been performed in Japan.[2] In addition, JSOG guidelines prohibit egg and embryo donation and the provision of donated sperm to infertile couples on a commercial basis.

In the late 1990s, certain cases related to donor conception were reported in Japan. For example, Excellence, which is the first commercial sperm bank in Japan, was established in 1996. In 1998, an ob-gyn disclosed disobedience of JSOG guidelines and implemented IVF using donated eggs. In December of the same year, society paid attention to a ruling of a DI-related lawsuit. The wife underwent DI without the consent of the husband, who denied paternity of the child. The court ruled in favor of the husband (Semba, 2010). In response to these cases, a group of experts convened by the Japanese Government began the discussion of legislation related to donor conception in earnest and the issue of the right of donor offspring to obtain donor information. The following section provides information about the relevant groups and their discussions about donor anonymity.

13.4.1   The Assessment Subcommittee (1998–2000)

In 1998, the Ministry of Health and Welfare (currently the Ministry of Health, Labour, and Welfare) established the Assessment Subcommittee for Advanced Medical Technologies of the Health Science Council

---

[2] But some fertility clinics which I interviewed have broken JSOG guidelines and performed IVF using donated sperm.

(in Japanese: *Kōsei kagakushingikai sentan iryōgijutsu hyōkabukai seishoku hojoiryōgijutsu ni kansuru senmoniinkai*). This subcommittee pioneered the public discussion on the issue of providing donor information to donor-conceived individuals. In December 2000, the Assessment Subcommittee published a *Report on Ideal Reproductive Treatment Using Donor Sperm, Eggs and Embryos*,[3] which concluded as follows:

> – A donor-conceived person is able to obtain non-identifying information of donor within the range approved by the donor when he or she will reach adulthood.
> – The persons who donated sperm/egg/embryos are able to change the range of his/her information before the information gets disclosed.
> – A donor-conceived person is able to confirm if the person who he/she wishes to marry has a biological relationship with him/her.

In other words, the Assessment Subcommittee concluded that using donated sperm/eggs/embryos should be allowed and that the right of donor-conceived individuals to obtain donor information should be limited. One of the reasons for these decisions was that the majority of sperm donors were students recruited by physicians conducting the DI, who considered anonymity was required to protect the interests of donors (Ono et al., 2004). The results of a survey on male infertile patients who had a child via DI conducted in 2000 also seemingly contributed to the decision. The results demonstrated that 63 per cent of respondents answered they would never disclose the conception to their children; 18 per cent would not disclose if they could; 18 per cent were undecided; and only 1 per cent would disclose if they could (Kuji et al., 2000). Moreover, donor-conceived individuals were invisible in society at the time because they never spoke publicly. Thus, the subcommittee respected the interests of donors and wishes of parents rather than the right of donor offspring to know.

13.4.2   *The ART Subcommittee (2001–2003)*

Based on the Assessment Subcommittee's report, the Ministry of Health, Welfare, and Labour created the Subcommittee on ART, Health Science Council (*kōsei kagakushingikai seishoku hojoiryō bukai*; the ART Subcommittee) in June 2001 to advise on drafting a new bill regarding ART and donor conception. It held discussions on the legal framework until

---

[3] The Japanese title is "*Seishi/ranshi/hai no teikyō tōniyoru seishoku hojoiryō no arikata nitsuite no houkokusho*". www.mhlw.go.jp/www1/shingi/s0012/s1228-1_18.html#34 (last accessed November 10, 2021).

March 2003. The ART Subcommittee did not adopt the proposal of the Assessment Subcommittee that the right of donor-conceived individuals to obtain donor information should be limited. It arrived at a different conclusion in its *Report on the Development of an Assisted Reproductive Medicine System through the Provision of Sperm, Eggs and Embryos,*[4] published in April 2003.

> A person who is 15 years of age or older may request disclosure of information concerning a donor of sperm, egg, or embryo, including name, address, and so on, that can identify the donor, with regard to the information that they wish to have disclosed, if they are a child born through or suspect themselves to have been born through assisted reproductive technology with provided sperm, egg, or embryo.

The ART Subcommittee offered the following reasons for this change: (1) Confirming whether they were conceived using donated sperm eggs or embryos and having information about the gamete donor is important for donor-conceived individuals. (2) With regard to the welfare of donor-conceived individuals, allowing such important rights to be influenced by the donor's preferences or for the donor-conceived individual to be born for whom the donor can be identified and those for whom the donor cannot be identified is inappropriate. (3) Respecting the will of a donor-conceived individual is necessary; the donor makes the donation out of free will, and anyone who does not wish to be identified is free not to donate. (4) Reducing donations of sperm, egg, and embryos can be arguable if information that can identify the donor in the contents of disclosure is disclosed; nevertheless, even if that occurs, such an action is inevitable on the basis of the welfare of the donor-conceived individual.

The conclusion of the ART Subcommittee that the right of donor-conceived individuals to know should be fully guaranteed was seemingly influenced by a public opinion posted by a DI-conceived woman. She described her experience as follows:

> If I would be allowed to meet my donor, of course I would like to meet him. But even if only the donor's non-identifying information would be disclosed, I hope that not only the donor's external characteristic but also his internal information (personality, way of thinking, hobbies, etc.) will be disclosed to donor-conceived people.[5]

---

[4] The Japanese title is "*Seishi/ranshi/hai no teikyō tōniyoru seishoku hojoiryō seido no seibi ni kansuru houkokusho*". www.mhlw.go.jp/shingi/2003/04/s0428-5.html (last accessed November 10, 2021).

[5] Public Opinion, receipt number: 56. Reference materials No. 1 for the 24th Assisted Reproductive Technology Subcommittee of the Health Science Council held on February 27, 2003. www.mhlw.go .jp/shingi/2003/02/s0227-10i.html (last accessed November 10, 2021).

Within the extent of the current research on various materials, the above-mentioned woman may be the first donor-conceived individual in Japan to publicize her background, which may have prompted members of the ART Subcommittee to recognize the existence of donor-conceived individuals in Japanese society for the first time. Her opinion was presented at the 24th meeting of the Subcommittee in February 27, 2003. Prior to the meeting, the majority of committee members agreed with the proposal of the Assessment Subcommittee to limit the information on donors provided to donor offspring. However, during the 25th meeting on March 13, 2003, many members changed their stance, that is, the right of children to know should be respected as broadly as possible.[6] The proposed legislation presented at the 26th meeting was changed: the donor offspring should be given the identifying information of the donor if they required.[7]

13.4.3   The ART Review Committee

Despite the work of the ART Subcommittee, legislation failed to advance in the slightest after the presentation of their proposal. However, Japanese society paid attention to one case related to surrogacy in 2004. In Japan, despite the fact that the JSOG guidelines had prohibited surrogacy since April 2003, a Japanese celebrity couple conceived twins through gestational surrogacy using their eggs and sperm in the United States in 2004. The couple intended to register the twins as their birth children with a government office in Tokyo. However, the office refused to accept the application because it was known that the wife underwent a hysterectomy due to uterine cancer. Clearly, she had not become pregnant and given birth to twins. The couple then initiated a lawsuit asking for the issuance of a birth certificate that legally recognizes their parenthood of the twins. However, the Tokyo Supreme Court denied their claim because under Article 772 of the Civil Law, the mother of a child is defined as the woman who gave birth to a child. They processed the twins as adopted children and took custody despite the fact that the twins were their biological children. The media covered the lawsuit, and people became interested in the issue of surrogacy. The case triggered the opinion that legislation on donor conception was required.

---

[6] 25th Meeting minutes of the ART Subcommittee on March 13, 2003. www.mhlw.go.jp/content/shingi_2003_03_txt_s0313-1.txt (last accessed November 10, 2021).
[7] Legislation draft on donor offspring's right to know by the ART Subcommittee www.mhlw.go.jp/shingi/2003/03/dl/s0326-10b.pdf (last accessed November 10, 2021).

In 2006, the ART Review Committee of the Science Council of Japan (*Nihon gakujutsu kaigi seishoku hojoiryō no arikata kentōiinka*) was established to examine issues on donor conception. However, discussion was focused on surrogacy, and a new consideration was not given to the rights of donor-conceived individuals.

13.4.4   Liberal Democratic Party Project Team

After the ART Review Committee published its final report in 2008, various significant events related to donor conception occurred in Japan. In 2009, a surrogacy between a mother and a daughter was publicized. In Japan, JSOG guidelines prohibited surrogacy. However, Dr. Yahiro Nezu disclosed that he implemented 10 cases of surrogacy between mother and daughter by October 2009, and a total of seven children were born via surrogacy (Nezu & Sawami, 2009). The increase in reproductive tourism of individuals seeking egg donation also attracted attention from Japanese society. Scholars estimated that 300–400 people venture abroad to seek donated eggs annually, according to research conducted in 2012 (Anonymous, 2014). Moreover, public interest was aroused by the case of a child whose legitimacy was rejected in the family register despite the parents being legally married, because the husband was a transgender man. He was born as a woman but legally changed gender status to male. He and his wife conceived a baby via DI and registered the child. The Supreme Court decided that the child was their legitimate child in 2013 (Kokado, 2015). Under such circumstances, the need for specific legislation regarding donor conception was once again raised, such that at the end of 2013, a project team called the Liberal Democrat Party (LDP-PT: *Jimintō* PT) was established to create a legal framework for donor conception. In October 2014, the LDP-PT presented the final draft of a bill that laid out the right of donor-conceived individuals to obtain donor information as follows:

> The most controversial question is whether to give the offspring the right to learn of donor information in cases when gamete donation is permitted. In light of the welfare of the offspring, identifying his/her genetic parents is necessary when offspring want to know this information. However, such a right would portend difficult consequences between a donor and the offspring, such that the number of donors would decrease. As a realistic approach, non-identifiable information about the genetic parents has to be accessible as much as possible. More discussion is needed. (Kokado, 2015)

The bill, however, was never submitted because the LDP-PT failed to reach a consensus on the pros and cons of surrogacy and the extent to which donor information should be disclosed (Matsuo, 2014). Once again, the legislative movement was suspended.

13.4.5 *The Special ART Law of 2020*

In the fall of 2020, members of the House of Councilors (*Sangiin*) began a discussion on ART legislation and drafted a bill addressing ART regulation and the parentage of resultant children. The bill cleared the Committee on Judicial Affairs on November 19, 2020, and the House of Councilors on the following day. On December 2, it passed through the Committee on Judicial Affairs of the House of Representatives (*Shūgiin*) and the House of Representatives on December 4 (Nagamizu, 2021). The Special ART Law (in Japanese: *Seishoku hojoiryō no teikyō oyobi koreniyori shushō shita ko no oyakokankei ni kansuru minpō no tokurei ni kansuru houritsu*) was then enacted as an amendment to the Civil Code regarding the parent–child relationship for donor offspring on December 4. The law focuses only on the parent–child relationship in donor conception cases and does not consider the right of donor-conceived individuals to access donor information, apart from mandating in its supplementary provision that necessary measures will be considered within two years. However, as of June 2022, the amendment bill has not been submitted to the diet.

13.5 Movement to Abolish Donor Anonymity in Japan

13.5.1 *DI Conceived People*

As previously mentioned, approximately 15,000–20,000 DI offspring have been born since the first DI birth in Japan in 1949. Until 2003, however, no donor-conceived child publicly declared that he or she was conceived by DI. A woman posted her experience and requested the right to obtain donor information, as a donor-conceived individual, to the ART Subcommittee during its discussion on donor conception legislation in February 2003. In other words, the DI offspring had been invisible in Japanese society prior to that moment.

After the ART Subcommittee published its report in 2003, a Japanese research project team (*DI Kenkyū kai*) was organized and conducted research on all aspects of DI in Japan. The team established a website for recruiting research collaborators in general and for seeking donor offspring, sperm recipients, and donors in particular. In November 2003, the *Mainichi Shimbun* (one of Japan's largest newspapers) published a story about a

Japanese male DI-conceived adult (Motomura, 2003). In the article, the man shared that he was looking for his donor with the intention of telling him that he had been born by his (the donor's) sperm donation. The following month, many newspapers in Japan published a story about a Japanese female DI-conceived adult who was adamant about wanting to know her donor.[8] At the same time, *DI Kenkyū kai* invited a donor-conceived woman from Sydney, Australia, named Geraldine Hewitt and held a symposium in Tokyo regarding the right of donor-conceived individuals to know identifying information about their donors. Hewitt spoke about her experience and insisted that although her father is the man who raised her, she wanted to know her donor because she was interested in his character and needed to know his biological background for health reasons. In addition, she said that she was worried about the number of half-siblings she may have and the risk of accidentally marrying one. She advocated that intended parents should disclose to their children the facts of their conception (Anonymous, 2003). As Japanese DI offspring had never appeared and spoken publicly at that point, her story as a DI-conceived adult received widespread attention. The media focused on the stories of DI-conceived individuals and addressed the issue of their right to gain access to donor information.

Beyond the issues of health and the prevention of consanguineous marriages, gaining the opportunity to know a donor can be an important part of identity formation for donor-conceived individuals. In September 2004, the research project team invited another donor-conceived adult named Bill Cordley from the United States and held a second symposium in Tokyo on donor anonymity. Cordley insisted on the importance of identifying donor information for donor-conceived individuals in preventing identity crises (Anonymous, 2004). In 2005, a support group for DI-conceived people, the DI Offspring Group (DOG), was established in Japan and continued lobbying against secrecy and donor anonymity with the support of counselors, social workers, and researchers in the fields of law, sociology, and ethics. Circa 2014, two members of the DOG spoke out in the media under their real names about the identity crises from which they suffered due to the lack of access to donor information. In May 2014, the DOG published a book titled *Born by AID* (*AID de umareru to iukoto*) with researcher Satoko Nagaoki of Keio University. Six members of the DOG contributed to the book by sharing their experiences and feelings as donor offspring. They described the harmful effects of secrecy and

---

[8] The following newspapers, among others, followed her story: *Gifu Shimbun, Toyama Shimbun, Hokkoku Shimbun, Akita Sakigake Shimbun, Fukuyama Shimbun, To-o Nippo,* and *Fukui Shimbun.*

donor anonymity and the importance of the right of donor offspring to obtain identifiable information of donor. The book attracted the attention of a group of DI parents and intended parents considering DI. Moreover, a few fertility clinics performing DI also recommended patients read the book as important information about donor-conceived children.

For more than 15 years, the DOG has called for the abolition of donor anonymity and the right to donor information through various lobbying activities. However, their goals remain to be realized.

13.5.2   *Parents and Intended Parents of DI Children*

When donor-conceived adults began campaigning for the abolition of the secrecy of DI and the need-to-know donor information, many parents of DI-conceived children and intended parents expressed negative feelings about their claims. In general, the reasons for supporting donor anonymity in DI may include protecting the child from "insurmountable social and psychological problems" or "psychological and emotional trauma"; protecting parents from the stigma and embarrassment of male infertility; protecting donors from inheritance claims or invasions of privacy; and protecting the inherent confidentiality of the medical profession (Achilles, 1993). According to a survey on infertile women who decided to use DI in 2003 in Japan, approximately 80 per cent reported that they will never disclose the DI conception to their children, whereas 10 per cent said they would tell and 10 per cent said they would consider it (Shimizu et al., 2007). Those who responded that they will never disclose cited the risk of family collapse or that it may cause more distress to the children because it is impossible to know the donor even if the parents inform their children. Furthermore, numerous couples in the survey were advised by doctors to refrain from disclosing about their use of DI to anyone.

A systematic review conducted in the Netherlands by Indekeu et al. (2013) on factors that contribute to parental decision-making in disclosing donor conception presents similar reasons for nondisclosure. According to the review, disclosers primarily underlined "the child's right to know" and "the principle of honesty" as essential aspects in building a trusting parent–child relationship. Furthermore, they highlighted the "best interest of the child," as the lack of knowledge would be harmful by undermining the child's sense of self and would cultivate shame, including "the difficulties in maintaining the secret," "the stress attached to it," and, consequently, "wanting to avoid accidental disclosure" and "no reason not to tell." Alternatively, undecided couples and nondisclosers emphasized "'the best interest of the child' by protecting the offspring from possible damage consequences of disclosure on family relationships, from perceived stigma, 'right of privacy,' and 'no benefit that could be identified from disclosure'" (Indekeu et al., 2013).

In 2003, *Sumairu Oyano Kai*, a support group for parents of DI-conceived children and intended parents, was established in Japan. The objective of the group is to empower parents and intended parents by providing a space for sharing sorrows and concerns related to male infertility in a setting with other parents who underwent similar experiences. The group holds study meetings (*benkyō kai*) facilitated by group members twice a year, where more than 1,000 parents or intended parents have participated in a total of 44 meetings since the establishment of the group.[9] At the meetings, parents discuss their experiences and exchange thoughts on telling the truth to their children or raising children among participants through free talk sessions. Moreover, they invite ob-gyns, donor-conceived adults, adoptive parents, counselors, and other specialists to hold various talks.[10] The participants in these study meetings have commented that, "we realise that we are not the only ones," "the study meeting really triggered a discussion between us (wife and husband)," and "we could collect a lot of information" (Shimizu, 2020).

When the bill on the Use of Regulations of ART and on the Special Provision of the Civil Code regarding the Parentage of Resultant Children (the special ART bill) was considered, Sumairu Oyano Kai made an input in the hopes of establishing a system that can secure the "right of donor offspring to know donor information" as a necessary consideration for conceiving and raising donor offspring in good physical and mental health.[11] Kiyomi Shimizu, who supported the group since its establishment, mentioned that more than 70 per cent of the participants of study meetings expressed positive remarks about openness and honesty regarding donor identity and the use of ART (Shimizu, 2020). A few members of the group have published books as informative guides for parents and aids for talking to donor-conceived children.

13.6   Conclusions

The phenomenon of donor conception was invisible in Japanese society until the beginning of this century, only first attracting public attention after

[9] Sumairu Oyano Kai home page, "What are study meetings?" www.sumailoyanokai.com/cont3/main.html (last accessed November 10, 2021).

[10] Sumairu Oyano Kai home page, p. l.

[11] Sumairu Oyano Kai home page, "We stated our opinions about the special ART bill," www.sumailoyanokai.com/cont6/15.html (last accessed November 10, 2021).

a donor-conceived woman presented her views to the ART Subcommittee about donor anonymity in 2003. Since then, DOG was established as a self-support group for donor-conceived people in 2005 and has spoken about issues regarding donor anonymity and the rights of donor offspring to obtain donor information at various academic, medical, legal, and public conferences, meetings, seminars, and events. The majority of parents of DI-conceived children used to hold negative feelings about openness because they were advised by DI practitioners to refrain from disclosing information to their children or other people about their use of ART. However, many parents have changed their attitudes and are now willing to be open with their children about DI conception. This shift occurred as a result of information being shared about other families with donor-conceived children, peer support in support groups, and advice from psychological and medical experts and researchers. Currently, couples considering conceiving a child through donor conception better understand the importance of the right of donor offspring to know their origins and are more likely to approach the use of DI on the premise of openness. In recent years, scholars reported that more than half of the general public in Japan accept the right of donor offspring to gain access to identifying donor information.

Yet despite the personal and cultural shifts, progress in meaningful legislation regarding donor conception is lacking even after nearly 20 years of discussion at the legislative level. Although the Special ART Law was enacted in 2020, it does not address the abolition of donor anonymity or the provision of donor information to donor offspring as demanded by DI-conceived individuals and certain parents of DI children.

Thus, we must ask: "Why is progress on this issue so slow in Japan despite the social demand for adequate legislation regarding openness in donor conception?" According to media, many issues related to the disclosure of donor information to donor offspring remain unresolved. These issues include determining the type of gamete donor information to be disclosed and the age at which the donor offspring should be given access to donor information (Anonymous, 2020). However, this delay is also seemingly caused by the fact that many Japanese politicians lack an understanding of the reality of donor conception and display low levels of awareness of the issue of the human rights of donor offspring. Moreover, favoring legislative change in the area of donor conception does not typically lead to electoral votes. The absence of a sufficient legal framework can lead to serious problems. For example, a large increase is observed for risky online sperm donations without the involvement of medical professionals

(Nakata et al., 2021). Furthermore, a tragic case in fact occurred. A woman sued a sperm donor for fraud after the donor lied about his education and ethnicity, where the woman claimed that the lies caused physical and emotional distress and led her to give up her donor-conceived child for adoption (Fahey, 2022).

These issues have been pending in the Japanese political sphere for nearly 20 years. Regardless of the undeniable complications regarding the abolition of donor anonymity and the rights of donor offspring to donor information, the continued procrastination of the Japanese government on these issues is not ethically or socially justifiable. How many more years will donor-conceived individuals, recipients, donors, and the Japanese society have to wait for the implementation of adequate legislation regarding donor conception?

In Japan, the Medical Practitioners Law stipulates that medical records must be kept for five years. In other words, discarding medical records and donor information five years after the implementation of DI is possible for medical institutions. Currently, however, taking legal action is necessary to ensure that the medical information of the donor currently stored in the medical institution is retained until the issue is resolved.

The discussion of the legal framework for ART should also be expanded to include the concerns of same-sex couples and single women, intrafamilial gamete donation, and the use of commercial sperm banks. If same-sex couples and single parents were allowed to use donated sperm under Japanese law, then more donor offspring would become visible in society, and the situation surrounding donor conception may change. Reports by the Assessment Subcommittee, ART Subcommittee, ART Review Committee, and LDP-PT all propose gamete donation without compensation and the prohibition of intrafamilial gamete donation. However, sperm donor shortage has recently become a serious issue. Further discussion of these issues will be required to prevent black market activities in the arena of donor conception gaining momentum in Japan.

References

Achilles, R. (1993). Protection from what? The secret life of donor insemination. *Politics and the Life Sciences*, *12*(2), 171–172. https://doi.org/10.1017/S0730938400023996

Allan, S. (2017), *Donor Conception and the Search for Information from Secrecy and Anonymity to Openness*. Routledge.

Ando, K. (1949). Funinshō ni taisuru Shindan oyobi Chiryō no Shinpo (Advances in the Diagnosis and Treatment of Infertility). *Nihon Rinshō 7*(4), 217–221.

Ando, K. (1960). Jinkō jusei no jissi jotai (The present performance of artificial insemination), in R. Koike, M. Tanaka, & Y. Hitomi (Eds.), *Jinkō jusei no shomondai: Sono Jittai to Hōteki Sokumen* (pp. 9–24). Tokyo: Hōgaku Kenkyu-kai, Keio University.

Anonymous (2003, December 25). Teikōseishi de tanjyō no gō josei rainichi, omoi kataru (Australian donor-conceived woman speaks her thoughts in Japan), *Gifu Shimbun.*

Anonymous (2004, September 11). Seishi teikyōsha wo shiru kenri wo (We want the right to know sperm donors), *Mainichi Shimbun.*

Anonymous (2014, April 27). Life Score 3: Jinsei no gakufu 3: Ranshi teikyō, susumanu hōseibi, "Ranshi" motomete kaigai he wataru joseitachi (Life Score 3: Egg donation, lack of progress in legislation, women going overseas to seek "eggs"), *Nikkei West*, www.sankei.com/west/news/140427/wst1404270075-n1.html (last accessed May 31, 2022).

Anonymous (2020, December 7). Giron kaishi kara rippōka made 20nen. Seishoku hojoiryōhō seiritsu ha naze okuretaka (Why was the enactment of the Assisted Reproductive Technology Law delayed? Twenty years from the start of discussion to legislation), *Mainichi Shimbun*, https://mainichi.jp/articles/20201207/k00/00 m/040/256000c (last accessed June 1, 2022).

Asahi Home & Welfare Weekly (Katei Asahi) (1949, September 10). Jinkōjusei mondai no hihan (Criticism of artificial insemination), 10.1–2.

Castro-Vàzquez, G. (2017). *Intimacy and Reproductive in Contemporary Japan.* Routledge.

Ethics Committee of the American Society for Reproductive Medicine. (2013). Informing offspring of their conception by gamete or embryo donation: a committee opinion. *Fertility and Sterility, 100*(1), 45–49. https://doi.org/10.1016/j.fertnstert.2013.02.028

Fahey, R. (2022, January 13). A Tokyo-based mum is suing the sperm donor she had sex with to conceive her second child for fraud, *Mirror Online*, www.mirror.co.uk/news/world-news/woman-puts-baby-up-adoption-25938939 (last accessed June 1, 2022).

Hibino, Y. & Allan, S. (2020). Absence of laws regarding sperm and oocyte donation in Japan and the impacts on donors, parents, and the people born as a result. *Reproductive Medicine and Biology, 19*(3), 295–298. https://doi.org/10.1002/rmb2.12329

Higashi, K. (2017). Nihon ni okeru rezubian mazā (Lesbian mother in Japan). IGS Project Series No. 17 2016 nendo Seishoku iryō de keiseisareru tayōna kazoku to tōjisha no uerubi-ing wo kangaeru kenkyūkai houkokusho, Institute for Gender Studies, Ochanomizu University: 28–41. www2.igs.ocha.ac.jp/ips/ips-17/ (last accessed November 10, 2021).

Indekeu, A., Dierickx, K., Schotsmans, P., Daniels, K. R., Rober, P., & D'Hooghe, T. (2013). (2013) Factors contributing to parental decision-making in disclosing donor conception: a systematic review, *Human Reproduction, 19*(6), 714–733. https://doi.org/10.1093/humupd/dmt018

Kuji, N. et al. (2000). Teikyo seishi ni yori kodomowo eta nihonjin fufu no kokuchi ni taisuru iken ni kansuru kenkyū (Survey of attitudes of male infertile patients who have a child via DI). *Japanese Journal of Fertility and Sterility* 45(3): 219–225.

Kuji, N. et al. (2005). *Wagakuni ni okeru seishi teikyōsha no 'shutsuji wo shiru kenri' ni taisuru ishiki chosa (Survey of sperm donors' attitudes toward 'the right to know of donor offspring' in Japan).* Health and Labor Sciences Research Grant: http://admin7.aiiku.or.jp/~doc/houkoku/h16/62795070.pdf

Kokado, M. (2015). A new phase in the regulation of assisted reproductive technology in Japan. *Zeitschrift für Japanisches Recht, 20*(40), 211–232.

Kusaka, K., Shimizu, K., & Nagaoki, S. (2006). Hi haigūshakan jinkōjusei de umareta hito no shinri (The identification of children born through AID). *Language, Culture and Communication* 37, 93–101.

Mainichi Shimbun Online (2020, December 5). Seishoku iryōho seiritsu: Mazu ippo 'Kūhaku no 20 nen' kurikaesanai tameni (Reproductive Medicine Act passed: First step to avoid repeating blank 20 years), https://mainichi.jp/articles/20201205/k00/00m/040/062000c (last accessed June 1, 2022).

Matsuo, Y. (2014, November 6). Dairi shussan, jinkō jusei, IVF... Seishokuiryō no giron kara nigeruna (Do not run away from the debate on reproductive medicine), *Tokyo Express,* http://tokyoexpress.info/2014/11/06/%e4%bb%a3%e7%90%86%e5%87%ba%e7%94%a3%e3%80%81%e4%ba%ba%e5%b7%a5%e6%8e%88%e7%b2%be%e3%80%81%e4%bd%93%e5%a4%96%e5%8f%97%e7%b2%be%e3%80%82%e7%94%9f%e6%ae%96%e5%8c%bb%e7%99%82%e3%81%ae%e8%ad%bo/ (last accessed November 10, 2021).

Miyazima, A. (2017). *Seishokuiryō to datsu "shutuji" shakai (Assisted Reproductive Technology and an Escape from the Society of Respecting "Biological" Origin).* Tokyo: Health System Kenkyusho.

Motomura, Y. (2003, November 24). "Chichi" sagasu jinkō juseiji no ko (DI Offspring is looking for "biological father"), *Mainichi Shimbun.*

Nagamizu, Y. (2021). Arubeki seishoku hojoiryō hōsei wo megutte kentō subeki kadai (In search of an appropriate policy on regulating assisted reproductive technologies and ascertaining the parentage of children born as a result of ART). *Momoyama Gakuho, 35*(21). www.jstage.jst.go.jp/article/momoyamahougaku/35/0/35_1/_pdf (last accessed November 10, 2021).

Nezu, Y., & Sawami, R. (2009) Haha to musume no dairi shussan (Surrogacy between mother and daughter), *Haru shobō.*

Ninomiya, S. (2010). Kodomo no shiru kenri nitsuite (Donor children's right to know). *Gakujutsu no Dōkō,* 15(5), 40–45.

Nomura, M. (2018, October 30). Daisansha teikyo no jinkō jusei chūshi: Keio byōin kokunaino hansū jisshi (Keio University Hospital which had been performing half of DI in Japan discontinue DI), *Yomiuri Shimbun,* Morning edition, p. 32.

Ono, T., Kaneko, S., & Tanabe, K. (2004) Shutsuji wo shiru kenri – Hitoku to Kaiji (Right to know – Confidentiality and disclosure). *Sanfujinka no Sekai,* 56(2), 113–119.

Osaki, T. (2020, December 27). "DM if interested": Sperm donors in Japan operate in a gray zone, *The Japan Times*, www.japantimes.co.jp/news/2020/12/ 27/national/science-health/japan-sperm-donors/ (last accessed November 10, 2021).

Saimura, M. (2008). Kodomo no jinken shingai to sōsharu wāku (Human rights violation against donor children and social work). In M. Saimura ed., *Seishoku hojoiryō de umareta kodomo no shutsuji wo shiru kenri (Right to Know of Donor Children)*, 264–281 Tokyo: Fukumura Publisher.

Sakai, R., & Kasuga, M. (2004). *Tsukurareu inochi (Creation of Life)* Tokyo: NHK Book.

Semba, Y. et al. (2006). AID ni okeru "shutsuji wo shiru kenri: AID de umareta hitotachi ga motomeru teikyō jyōho toha (The "right to know" in AID: Donor information sought by AID offspring). *Seimei Rinri: Journal of Japan Association for Bioethics*, 17(1), 147–153.

Semba, Y., Chang, C., Hong, H., Kamisato, A., Kokado, M., & Muto, K. (2010). Surrogacy: donor conception regulation in Japan. *Bioethics*, 24(7), 348–357. https://doi.org/10.1111/j.1467-8519.2009.01780.x

Shimizu, K., Kusaka, K. & Nagaoki, S. (2007) The experiences of women who decided to use DI (Japanese: Hi haigushakan) *Journal of Japanese Society of Fertility Nursing*, 4(1), 16–25.

Shimizu, K. (2020). Kokuchi ni taisuru oya no omoi – Oya no kai no jissen kara (Parents' thoughts on telling truth – From the activities of parents' groups). In *Watashitachi ga taisetsu ni shitai mono: AID de kazoku ni natta hitotachi no kokuchi heno omoi to jissen kara (Parents' thoughts on telling: through the activities of self-support group of parents. Story of Our Family)*. Tokyo: JSPS, 145–153.

Wakabayshi, M., & Horioka, C. Y. (2006). Is the eldest son different? The residential choice of siblings in Japan. NBER Working Paper Series. www.nber.org/ system/files/working_papers/w12655/w12655.pdf (last accessed November 10, 2021).

Yamagata, N., Hoshi, K., Hirata, S., et al. (2003). *Seishoku hojoiryō nitsuiteno ishiki chōsa 2003 Shūkei kekka (The survey of public attitudes towards donor conception 2003)*. www.mhlw.go.jp/wp/kenkyu/db/tokubetu02/index.html (last accessed November 10, 2021).

Yamamoto, N., Hirata, T., Izumi, G., Nakazawa, A., Fukuda, S., Neriishi, K., Arakawa, T., Masashi Takamura, M., Harada, M., Hirota, Y. Koga, K., Wada-Hiraike, O., Fujii, T., Irahara, M. & Osuga, Y. (2018). A survey of public attitudes towards third-party reproduction in Japan in 2014. *PLOS ONE*. https://doi.org/ 10.1371/journal.pone.0198499

Yanaihara, T., & Yamagata, N. (1999). Survey on patient awareness of assisted reproductive technology: National survey (in Japanese, Seishoku hojoiryō ni taisuru kanja no ishiki ni kansuru kenkyū). *Report on 1999 Children and Home Comprehensive Research Project* (Grant-in-Aid from the Japan Society for the Promotion of Science (JSPS)) www.niph.go.jp/wadai/mhlw/1999/h1118028.pdf (last accessed November 10, 2021).

Yokota, A., & Watanabe, R. (2020, December 7). Giron kaishi kara rippōka made 20 nen: Seishoku Iryōhō ha naze okuretaka) (20 years from the start of discussions to legislation: Why did it take so long for Assisted Medicine Act to be passed?), *Mainichi Shimbun Online*, https://mainichi.jp/articles/20201207/k00/00m/040/256000c (last accessed June 1, 2022).

Yomiuri Shimbun Online (2021, April 16). SNS de seishi torihiki ga kyūzō: Funin fūfura riyō, kisei naku muhō jōtai (Sperm donation on SNS are increasing rapidly. Used by infertile couples, no legal regulations); www.yomiuri.co.jp/national/20210416-OYT1T50093/ (last accessed November 10, 2021).

Yui, H. (2011). Hi-haigushakan jinkō jusei niyotte shushō shitaka hito no raifu sutorī (A life story of a person conceived through artificial insemination by donor). *Ritsumekan Ningen Kagaku Kenkyū*, 24, 35–48.

Yui, H. (2012). Nihon hatsu no jinkō jusei seikōrei ni kansuru rekishiteki kentō: Ishi no gensetsu wo chūshin ni (A history study about first experience of successful artificial insemination in Japan: An analysis of doctors' statements), Core *Ethics*, 8, 423–432.

Yui, H. (2015). *Jinkō jusei no kindai (Modern History of Artificial Insemination)*, Tokyo: Seikyusha.

Yui, H. (2021). A history of Japanese follow-up surveys of children conceived through artificial insemination by donor: The evidence of "superior" children and positive eugenics. *EASTS, 16, 50–69*. www.ncbi.nlm.nih.gov/pmc/articles/PMC4498171/pdf/FVVinObGyn-7-137-143.pdf

CHAPTER 14

Donor Linking in the Digital Age
Where to Next?

Fiona Kelly, Deborah Dempsey, and Adrienne Byrt

Donor-linking in the digital age is shaped by evolving social and cultural norms across a diverse array of legal frameworks. This collection has interrogated notions of secrecy and openness within donor-conceived families, highlighting the ways in which do-it-yourself (DIY) methods of finding and linking with genetic relatives defy the constraints of regulation. The collection has also explored the diverse lived-experiences of donor-linked families. Bonds are formed in nuanced and cautious ways, while boundaries are established to ensure newfound and often difficult-to-name familial roles can be safely and ethically negotiated. Belonging conjures ambivalence for donor-conceived people, as they deal with shifting identity through (un)knowing their genetic links.

Amid the context of do-it-yourself conceiving, searching, and linking, the question of the role of law across all jurisdictions included in this collection is complicated by tension in the pace of the digital world and the slowness of legal processes. What this collection shows is that within discourses of the right to know one's genetic origins, the purported end of anonymity is not necessarily the end of the donor-conception debate. Donor-conceived families will continue to contend with secrecy, openness, and complex relationships within and beyond regulatory frameworks, highlighting the need for more nuanced understanding of these familial networks and how linking can be activated and supported.

14.1 Secrecy and Openness: Is This the End of Anonymity?

Curiosity and the 'right to know' one's genetic relatives mobilises donor-conceived people, donors, and parents to pursue unregulated methods for identifying donor relatives. The DIY approaches explored in this collection (e.g., online sperm donors, online sleuthing, and direct-to-consumer genetic testing (DTCGT)) are innovative and creative, yet do not supplant the need for those seeking to unearth genetic ties to proceed with caution.

At times, the ramifications of discovering – or not discovering – genetic information can lead to emotional turmoil. Legal and cultural barriers constrain access to information for donor-conceived people and recipient parents across jurisdictions. Evidently, in the digital age, institutionalised donor anonymity persists. Just as there are strong cultural impulses in play supporting legislative openness, as the chapter about donor conception in New Zealand exemplifies, there may also be very strong cultural barriers to ending anonymity at the level of policy and law, as the case study of Japan exemplifies.

Despite legal and cultural constraints, the ease with which donor-conceived relatives seek and find one another in the digital age gives rise to distinct challenges for promises of anonymity. The notion of the gate-keeping clinic or sperm bank is undeniably challenged by adept consumers using digital means to find, watch, and contact genetic relatives in the unregulated landscape of social media. In Part I of this collection, it is clear that for donor-conceived people, and sometimes donors, DIY methods embolden curiosity and enable access to donor relatives, with or without the knowledge of the subject of their search. Here, we return to our earlier question: does ending anonymity via digital means inevitably lead to openness, or at the very least, the end of secrecy? Adams and colleagues demonstrated how readily DCPs can connect to donor relatives through DTCGT, driving the consumer-led revolution towards openness, while minimising the authority of clinics and legislation to control the space. Zeghiche et al. showed how DNA testing unveils insemination fraud, often shocking participants, or at times, providing relief. Familial decisions about secrecy or openness lose relevance in the context of DTCGT. The information is held firmly in the hands of the person who pursued the DNA test on their own terms, with or without the knowledge or support of their parents who used a donor. As a result, decades-old secrecy might be challenged and confronted by this consumer-led discovery, though emotional turmoil often lingers.

Beyond the acquisition of genetic knowledge through DTCGT, the digital affordances of social media mobilise the search for donor relatives, providing more avenues to undermine anonymity. However, in the quest for perceived openness, donor-conceived people and donors do not necessarily make their actions known to the subjects of their search, as Byrt and Dempsey highlighted. Stealth becomes a mechanism of the search, as participants enact digital 'creeping' to satisfy curiosity, and hopefully to gain access to deeper meaning about the people to whom they are genetically linked. Kelly's chapter showed how recipient parents used social media sleuthing and DTCGT to connect with donors and their children's donor-siblings, whether they were legally entitled to or not. The desire to acquire knowledge of their child's genetic relatives and the potential to build relationships superseded any concerns about the legal implications of their actions. Yet, recipient parents still supported formal regulation of donor-linking systems.

The quest for openness also raises many relational issues concerned with knowing your place in a constellation of potential connections involving multiple family groupings of recipient parents, donors, and the donor conceived. The different families using the same donor may well have different ideas about how openness should be managed. Some of our contributors have explored how respecting the wishes of recipient parents may require both donors and donor-conceived adults who find genetic siblings to withhold information, generating new dilemmas about secrecy in families. Once knowledge about one's donor-conceived status is gained, whether overtly or by chance, some donor-conceived people and recipient parents embark on a relationship with their genetic relatives. Once linked, further complexities arise in the ongoing negotiation of these connections as the family constellation grows.

14.2   Belonging, Bonds, and Boundaries: Navigating Dis/Connection in Donor-Linked Families

Beyond the discovery of one's genetic relatives through donor-linking processes, whether DIY or statutory, newly formed links between donor-families must be navigated. Donor-linked families experience connections for which language rarely exists. The notion of the normative family is challenged by the diverse family forms presented throughout the collection. Donor-linked families create new family stories as they connect with genetic relatives, redefining normative roles and expectations within biological families. In Part II of this collection, these complexities were explored within differing cultural contexts. Riggs and colleagues argued that for men, trans/masculine, and non-binary gestational parents, openness is an act of rebellion and an opportunity to challenge and resist cis-genderism. Openness in trans-families can celebrate the joys of conception while also teaching their children through social scripts about their place in a cis-heteronormative world.

The value of genetic relatedness is keenly felt by donor-conceived people, in that the absence of knowledge of one's genetic relatives can lead to '(unbe) longing' or a sense of identity adrift, as Newton described. As such, donor sibling relationships may be entered into freely and were for many a source of connection and joy, while relationships with donors were approached with more cautious regard for boundaries and expectations. As Hertz pointed out, it is difficult to know if donor-sibling relationships will transform perceptions of the heteronormative family, but for donor-conceived relatives wishing to connect with genetic relatives, the donor-sibling connection is often one of grounding and solidarity. Importantly, Hertz highlighted that while the donor-sibling connection was meaningful, it required work and ongoing intimacy or sustained social relations between donor siblings were by no means assured.

Conversely, Indekeu and Maas showed how vast numbers of donor siblings complicated feelings of closeness and presented difficulty maintaining relationships. Gaining knowledge of large numbers of siblings and the challenges faced getting to know them may lead donor-conceived people to feel adrift, as if they don't belong amid an ever-expanding family of strangers. Evidently, for both linked and unlinked donor-conceived people, identity and belonging are shaped by connections and disconnections. In the absence in many jurisdictions of effective regulation of numbers of offspring who can be born using the same donor's sperm, numbers of offspring can be in the tens or even hundreds. This raises a practical issue of how to manage the sheer number of potential sibling relationships yet also the resulting loss of identity that may ensue. Although knowledge of genetic origins is for many implicated in having a firmer grip of one's sense of self, it can also lead to losing a sense of one's individuality and distinctiveness when there are exceptional numbers of donor-linked siblings. We are only just beginning to understand how donor-conceived people who learn of large networks of genetic siblings make sense of these connections, and how this knowledge of being one of many may threaten as well as strengthen a sense of identity.

For recipient parents and donors, bonds and boundaries are negotiated with care and caution. In New Zealand, in order to nurture their child's cultural identity and belonging, Māori parents of donor-conceived children upheld bonds with donor relatives, including the donor's relatives. Shaw showed that for Māori parents of donor-conceived people, knowledge of whakapapa to understand lines of genealogy is significant. Relationships with known donors and their whānau were often grounded in friendship and maintaining a whānau across households in an informal capacity to ensure children were linked to whakapapa and iwi. In the UK context, boundaries become salient as parents manage relationships between donors and donor offspring. Gilman and Nordqvist argued that discourses of openness among donor-conceived families have changed the meaning of a donor's role in a child's life. Donors are expected to remain both distant and close, traversing a tentative boundary between their own openness and availability to the child and knowing when to stay in their lane. Importantly, Gilman and Nordqvist highlighted that beyond the family of the donor-conceived child, the ripples of connection between a donor and the genetic child are felt in the donor's own family. Connections become 'messy, multiple, and networked', complicating a donor's role in an age of openness.

Across all contexts, the lived experiences of donor-linked families are complex, shaped by connection and '(unbe)longing'. Language and familial stories are evolving as donor-linked people contend with personal boundaries, limitations to access one another, and cope with emotional upheaval as they manage new and potentially ongoing relationships.

14.3   Relatedness and Regulation: Where to Next?

The complexities of managing donor-linked relationships in an increasingly consumer-led landscape of DIY linking highlight the pertinence of the question: Is there still a role for the law or the state in legislating for, and facilitating, openness in the digital age? This collection has highlighted the ease of DIY linking and the ingenuity of donor-conceived people to access information about their donor and donor siblings, just as recipient parents feel entitled to track down their child's donor and make contact outside of regulatory frameworks. As Cahn observed, in the USA, regulation remains limited given the suggestion that ending anonymity could lead to fewer donors. Semba suggested that in Japan, donor anonymity persists, as there is little political motivation for legislators to move towards openness as it is viewed as a niche issue. In these different cultural contexts, the law privileges donor anonymity and highlights ongoing institutional resistance to openness.

Kelly's finding that recipient parents still supported formal regulation of donor-linking systems, despite sleuthing outside of statutory frameworks, shows that there may still be a place for law in the Australian context. This finding suggests that linking behaviours have evolved faster than the legislative framework, highlighting the speed with which linking practices are becoming normative in the donor conception community. Beyond finding and linking with genetic relatives, the evidence suggests that mechanisms to manage and monitor the process of donor linking are useful. The pressure on governments to enact linking laws is strong in many jurisdictions, but the rapid emergence of DIY linking means that the law must co-exist with the affordances created by the digital age.

In closing, one of the most significant questions for legislatures in the years to come will be how and to what extent donor-sibling relationships should be honoured and facilitated. Most jurisdictions, with the notable exception of the Netherlands and Victoria through its voluntary register, do not support donor siblings who wish to know of each other's existence or share identifying information. The contributors to this volume have emphasised this considerable gap. Perhaps this silence or omission reflects the extent to which the law tends to respect conventional nuclearised notions of bounded family units. Our volume has emphasised the extent to which the children and adults born of donor insemination, and their parents, are curious about and open to connecting with those who are born of the same donor. This potentially outstrips interest in the donor him or herself. We encourage legislators in all jurisdictions to consider how this donor-sibling tie can be acknowledged as meaningful and a source of identity for those who seek it. Doing justice to this issue will also require that legislators give serious consideration to the ethics of permitting a single donor to produce tens or even hundreds of children.

Index